AN ESSAY ON THE LAW OF BAILMENTS

CYMDEITHAS HANES CYFRAITH CYMRU

THE WELSH LEGAL HISTORY SOCIETY

Cyfrol IV : Volume IV

AN ESSAY ON THE LAW OF BAILMENTS

By

Sir William Jones

Edited by

David J. Ibbetson, FBA
Regius Professor of Civil Law
University of Cambridge

BANGOR
CYMDEITHAS HANES CYFRAITH CYMRU
THE WELSH LEGAL HISTORY SOCIETY
2004

Cyhoeddwyd gan
CYMDEITHAS HANES CYFRAITH CYMRU

Published by
THE WELSH LEGAL HISTORY SOCIETY

British Library Cataloguing in Publication Data. A catalogue record for this book is available from the British Library

ISBN 0-9541637-3-7

Printed in Wales by Infographics, Ltd., Cowbridge

Distributed by

Cymdeithas Hanes Cyfraith Cymru
Ysgol y Gyfraith, Prifysgol Cymru, Bangor, LL57 2DG.

The Welsh Legal History Society
Bangor Law School, University of Wales, Bangor, LL57 2DG.

CONTENTS

PREFACE

Sir William Jones was one of the more extraordinary polymaths of the eighteenth century, and the *Essay on the Law of Bailments* one of the more extraordinary books of the Common law. First published in 1781, it went into three further editions in England, the last in 1833, and was several times reprinted in America. Though eclipsed as a legal text by Joseph Story's *Commentaries on the Law of Bailments* and later works, it has retained its place in the writings of legal historians and legal theorists as perhaps the best example of the late eighteenth-century 'scientific' approach to English law. That might in itself be sufficient to justify making the text more easily available to modern readers. More importantly, it is not easy for the scholar of the twenty-first century to penetrate beneath the arguments and to evaluate them in their late eighteenth-century context. Jones was not always good at referencing his sources, still less at explaining his own relation to them. I have attempted, so far as I was able, to identify these, and thereby to bring out both the very wide range of material which he called upon in order to elucidate English law and also the extent to which he was in fact heavily dependent on a relatively small proportion of these for much of his analysis. The argument in Jones's essay is substantially underpinned by his understanding of the history of the bailee's liability in the Common law. This is a topic which has been – with good reason – heavily neglected by English legal historians, but since it is difficult to evaluate Jones's treatment of the subject without some understanding of the way in which it might be understood today I have included by way of excursus a chapter attempting to tease out the history of the topic between the first stirrings of the Common law in the middle of the twelth century and the watershed decision in *Coggs* v. *Barnard* at the beginning of the eighteenth.

My interest in Jones as a lawyer was first stimulated by Peter Birks, and has been kept alive over a good number of years by Richard Youard and Thomas Watkin. To the last of these, too, are due thanks for his patience during the production of this edition. Jones himself was not reliable when it came to the timely completion of editions of classical English legal texts which he promised, so I may be allowed to plead his example in mitigation if not in justification.

Like practically everybody else who has worked on the polymathic Jones, in the preparation of this edition I have repeatedly come up against the limitations of my own abilities and range of partial expertise. Katherine Brown and Mitra Sharafi willingly shared their knowledge about Jones and India; Mara Kalnins and John Drew helped with advice about the orientalist component in eighteenth- and nineteenth-century literature; Jonathan Hills, Robin Osborne and James Warren helped with problems of Greek, Yazeed Said with mediaeval Turkish; Melanie Taylor provided me with useful references about some of the by-ways of eighteenth-cetury popular culture; Michael Prichard willingly shared his expertise on the Court of Admiralty; and David Feldman kept me on the straight and narrow on the subject of the American Constitution and the right to bear arms. Paul Brand, Mark Godfrey, Warren Swain and Ian Williams helped with the identification and verification of references. Debts of gratitude are owed to the librarians and staff of a host of libraries, but in particular to Patrick Zutshi, Keeper of Manuscripts in the Cambridge University Library, and David Wills, Librarian of the Squire Law Library. John Baker generously read the manuscript and gave advice on a number of points of English legal history; and Jean Meiring's close reading frequently led me to clarify my thinking. Above all, I should express my thanks to Stelios Tofaris, who read the whole text with a critical eye and led me to sharpen and deepen my argument at many points.

On behalf of the Society, too, I would like to thank Mr. Goronwy James Cleaver, Honorary Fellow of the University of Wales, Bangor, himself a native of Anglesey like William Jones Sr., whose generosity has allowed the publication of the volume; and the Selden Society, whose subvention has enabled the production of additional volumes to be circulated to its members. Finally, but by no means least, it is a pleasure to record with gratitude the work of Mr. Liam Sullivan and his colleagues at Infographics Ltd.; their advice and professionalism turned the production of what might have been a difficult text into a thankfully easy task.

David Ibbetson
Cambridge
April 2007

TABLE OF CASES

England

America

India

TABLE OF ABBREVIATIONS

A.F.	Ames Foundation
B. & M.	J. H. Baker and S. F. C. Milsom, *Sources of English Legal History*
Bas.	Basilica
B.L.	British Library
Blackstone, *Commentaries*	Sir William Blackstone, *Commentaries on the Law of England*
Bro. Abr.	Brooke's *Abridgment*
C.	Justinian's Codex
Cannon, *Life and Mind*	Garland Cannon, *The Life and Mind of Oriental Jones*
Co. Litt.	Sir Edward Coke, *Commentary on Littleton*
C.R.R.	Curia Regis Rolls
C.U.L.	Cambridge University Library
D.	Justinian's Digest
Fitz. Abr.	Fitzherbert's *Abridgment*
Inst.	Justinian's Institutes
Letters	Garland Cannon, ed., *The Letters of Sir William Jones*
L.I.	Lincoln's Inn
M.G.H.	Monumenta Germaniae Historica
Pothier, *Oeuvres*	*Oeuvres de R.-J. Pothier* (Brussels, 1831)
P.P.	Parliamentary Papers
P.R.O.	Public Record Office
PS.	Pauli Sententiae
Ro. Abr.	Rolle's *Abridgment*
S.S.	Selden Society
Stath. Abr.	Statham's *Abridgment*
Works	*The Works of Sir William Jones* (London, 1807)
YB	Year Book

SIR WILLIAM JONES, ORIENTALIST AND JURIST

Sir William Jones was born in Westminster in September 1746.[1] His father, also William, had been born into Anglesey farming stock; but in his youth he moved away from Wales, and after a short time teaching mathematics on a warship he became tutor to Philip Yorke, later Lord Chancellor Hardwicke, and subsequently to Thomas Parker, the future Lord Chancellor Macclesfield.[2] He was a mathematician of some ability, elected Fellow of the Royal Society in 1712, a friend of Edmund Halley and Isaac Newton and editor of some of the latter's works for the press. Jones senior died when William was only three years old, and he was brought up by his mother, Mary née Nix, an intellectual woman who taught William to read and write and fostered in him a wide-ranging curiosity which was his most obvious characteristic in later life. As a schoolboy at Harrow, which he attended from 1753 to 1764, his academic talents flourished. He proved a first-rate linguist, mastering Greek and Latin to a level that his headmaster, Robert Sumner, was to say that he knew more Greek than did his master. Alongside this he taught himself sufficient Hebrew to enable him properly to study religious texts, and began to study Arabic. The latter he continued when he went up to University College, Oxford in 1764 (taking with him his own Arabic tutor, Mirza, a native of Aleppo whom he had met in London), adding to it Persian, a language which opened up a rich literature as well as being of practical utility should he choose to travel out to Mughal India. He was elected into a fellowship at University College Oxford in

[1] For Jones's life, Garland Cannon, *The Life and Mind of Oriental Jones* (Cambridge, 1990) substantially supersedes all previous work; the following paragraphs are heavily indebted to it. See also S. N. Mukherjee, *Sir William Jones: A Study in Eighteenth-Century British Attitudes to India* (London, 1987), M. J. Franklin, *Sir William Jones* (Cardiff, 1995), and the article on Jones in the *Oxford Dictionary of National Biography* (Oxford, 2004) (by M. J. Franklin). I have before essayed some remarks on Jones from a legal standpoint in: 'Sir William Jones as a Comparative Lawyer', in A. Murray, ed., *Sir William Jones, 1746-94: A Commemoration* (Oxford, 1998), 19; 'Sir William Jones', in T. G. Watkin, ed., *Legal Wales: Its Past, Its Future* (Welsh Legal History Society, vol.1; Cardiff, 2001), 41; and 'Sir William Jones and the Nature of Law', in A. Burrows and Lord Rodger, eds., *Mapping the Law: Essays in Memory of Peter Birks* (Oxford, 2006), 619.

[2] For Jones senior, see the article in the *Oxford Dictionary of National Biography* (Oxford, 2004) (by R. Wallis).

1766, and alongside his studies took on the post of tutor to the seven year-old Viscount Althorp; together these provided him with sufficient income to enable him to continue with his studies into Oriental languages. His reputation was sufficiently widely spread that he was recommended to the King of Denmark as the best person to undertake a translation into French of the official biography of the Persian ruler Nadir Shah; this appeared in 1770 as the *Histoire de Nader Chah*, accompanied by Jones's own work in praise of Arabic and Persian poetry, *Un Traité sur la Poësie Orientale*. These were followed a year later by his *Dissertation sur la Littérature Orientale* and *A Grammar of the Persian Language*; in 1772 by his first substantial translations of Eastern poetry, *Poems, Consisting chiefly of Translations from the Asiatick Languages*; and in 1774 by his principal study, *Poeseos Asiaticae Commentariorum*. By the time that the last of these works appeared, Jones had been elected to a Fellowship of the Royal Society on the basis of his 'learning in polite literature and the Oriental languages'[3] and earned himself a reputation as a scholar of oriental languages and literature.[4]

Already as a schoolboy Jones may have dabbled in the writings of the great Common lawyer Sir Edward Coke,[5] and in a letter to the Hungarian scholar Charles Reviczky in 1768 he recommended Sir Thomas Smith's *De Republica Anglorum* and Sir John Fortescue's *De Laudibus Legum Angliae* as a source of information about English law and customs.[6] In September 1770, following urgings from his family and friends, he turned to the law as a profession and joined the Middle Temple. He did not immediately reject the world of letters,[7] though in the preface to his English *Introduction to the History of the Life of Nader Shah* (1772) he announced his resolve to leave aside the unlucrative profession of literature 'in pursuit of that branch of knowledge, in which it is my chief ambition to excel,'[8] and in 1774 he wrote that he had left idle at Oxford all his books and manuscripts not rele-

[3] Royal Society Archives, EC/1772/13.

[4] (1774) 44 *Gentleman's Magazine* 579.

[5] Cannon, *Life and Mind*, 8.

[6] *Letters*, 7 (trans. at 11). The '*leges nostrae et consuetudines*' of the letter is perhaps an echo of Bracton's *Tractatus de Legibus et Consuetudinibus Angliae*.

[7] *Letters*, 83 (trans. at 85).

[8] *Works*, 12.353.

vant to the law.[9] Not that the study of law was uncongenial to him: in a letter of January 1771 he had written of his having read most attentively the first two volumes of Blackstone's *Commentaries* and of being unable to understand why it was said that the study of law was 'dry and unpleasant';[10] and a few years later, while admitting the delights of fine literature, he asserted that there were other and greater arts bearing the sweetest of fruit, including notably the 'study of native and universal law'.[11] Law, too, became symbolically the centre of his universe. In a manuscript dating from the mid-1770s he sketched a wheel with Law as its hub, and other arts and sciences as spokes radiating from its centre: Logic, Metaphysics, Rhetoric, Declamation, Poetry, Exercises, Natural History, Anatomy, Chemistry, Languages, Ethics, Politics, Arts, Antiquities, History Ancient and Modern, Mathematics.[12]

Called to the Bar in January 1774,[13] Jones appeared in Westminster Hall and practised on the Oxford and the South Wales circuits. The 'highly declamatory' style of his delivery, considering himself 'as much a public orator as Cicero or Hortensius could have done', is described by Henry Hawkins,[14] though this does not seem to have held him back from earning a reasonable living as a barrister, especially through cases on the Welsh circuit. Right from the beginning, on the Lent circuits of 1775, he picked up a certain amount of work, though he recognised that it would not be for some years that he would be regarded as a 'leader' who might expect a good practice in his own right.[15] The Summer circuit of that year he described as a time of 'pleasure and profit', in which he had had his share of the business which had arisen.[16] That of 1776 was attended by (among other things)

[9] *Letters*, 163 (trans. at 166).
[10] *Letters*, 78.
[11] *Letters*, 163 (trans. at 167).
[12] B.L. MS Add. 8889 f.4. There is a similar sketch at f.2v, with a slightly different set of spokes. The date 1775 is given on f.5v, though a reference (scored out) at f.3 to Nathaniel Halhed's *Code of Gentoo Laws*, published in 1776, points to the notebook having been written over a period of time.
[13] J. Hutchinson, *A Catalogue of Notable Middle Templars* (London, 1902), 135.
[14] Laetitia-Matilda Hawkins, *Memoirs, Anecdotes, Facts and Opinions* (London, 1824), 1.244-5, quoted in Cannon, *Life and Mind*, 67; 'A Barrister's First Speech' (1837) 14 *Legal Observer* 456.
[15] *Letters*, 185.
[16] *Letters*, 196.

'speeches, gold, fame',[17] that of 1777 was 'pleasing and successful.'[18] Two letters of May 1778, when the prospect of a judicial position in India was first appearing on the horizon, show him more or less well-satisfied with the progress his career had made: he had a handsome income, and his gains from practice were ever-increasing.[19] In a retrospect of November 1782,[20] when the question of the Indian judgeship was still unsettled and Jones was seriously contemplating marriage, he calculated that the income from his practice at the bar had been about £400 per year for the previous five or six years, supplemented by around £100 per year from his fellowship in Oxford and £100 as a Commissioner in Bankruptcy, a legal-administrative position to which he had been appointed through the patronage of Lord Chancellor Bathurst in 1775 which involved the appointment and overseeing of assignees in bankruptcy.[21] Assuming these figures are fairly reliable – and the context suggests that they probably are – Jones's early income would have put him well on a par with those barristers who were destined for very successful careers.[22]

As with all young barristers, work did not come so quickly that he had no time for study; and for Jones study was inextricably married to scholarship. He prepared an edition and translation of Littleton's *Tenures*, based on Hoüard's edition of 1766, which he clearly envisaged for publication,[23] and his notebook points towards plans for the edition and publication of a series of ancient treatises of English law: Glanville, Bracton, Horne's *Mir*-

[17] *Letters*, 221.
[18] *Letters*, 241.
[19] *Letters*, 269, 271.
[20] *Letters*, 598.
[21] Blackstone, *Commentaries*, 2.480. S. Marriner, 'English Bankruptcy Records and Statistics before 1850' (1980) 33 *Economic History Review* 351, 361-365; S. C. Hicks and C. Ramsay, 'Law, Order and the Bankruptcy Commissions of Early Nineteenth Century England' (1987) 55 *Tijdschrift voor Rechtsgeschiedenis* 123, especially at 133-141.
[22] Daniel Duman, *The Judicial Bench in England 1727-1875* (London, 1982), 58-59, 104-110.
[23] D. Hoüard, *Anciennes Loix des François Conservées dans les Coutumes Angloises* (Rouen, 1766), B.L. 708.g.22-26. The first volume contains Jones's MS title-page, projecting publication at the Clarendon Press, Oxford, 1776. See below, 148.

ror of Justices, Britton, Fleta, Hengham, Littleton and Fortescue.[24] The notebook suggests too that he was equally interested in foreign legal systems, listing the sources from which they could be studied.[25] The two most important works from this period of his life, his edition and translation of *The Speeches of Isaeus* (1779) and *An Essay on the Law of Bailments* (1781), are replete with comparative illustrations.[26]

In 1777 the death of Stephen Caesar Lemaistre created a vacancy on the recently-established Supreme Court of Bengal.[27] Jones was already pressing his claims to appointment as Advocate General, a post whose vacancy was expected in the September of that year, but on news reaching him of Lemaistre's death he refocused his attention on the judicial position.[28] He had strong expectations of the support of Lord Chancellor Bathurst and hopes of the support of Lord Mansfield and Lord North, but would not be qualified for the appointment – it was only open to those who were of five years standing at the Bar – until the January of 1779.[29] His hopes of procuring a formal nomination before that date[30] proved fruitless, and by the time he was of appropriate standing his patron Lord Bathurst had resigned the Chancellorship. Bathurst's successor, Lord Thurlow, was no supporter of Jones, whose radical political leanings – visible in his repeated assertions of the need to impose and reinforce checks on the exercise of political power[31] – might be an irritant to those in whom political power was vested. His preference would have been for Francis Hargrave,

[24] B.L. MS Add 8889 f.5. At f.4v he had listed the whereabouts of some manuscripts of these works.
[25] B.L. MS Add 8889 f.3v. He lists the laws of the following: Jews, Athenians, Spartans, Persians, Romans, Chinese, Germans, Goths, Lombards, Saxons, Britons, Normans, Arabs, modern Persians, Indians (scored out), Turks, Italians, French, English, Spanish and Russians.
[26] See below, 55; and for the *Speeches of Isaeus*, Ibbetson, 'Sir William Jones as a Comparative Lawyer', in Murray, ed., *Sir William Jones*, 19, 34-37.
[27] A. C. Banerjee, *English Law in India* (New Delhi, 1984), 28-40. The Court had been set up in 1773 by Stat. 13 Geo. III c.63, s.14.
[28] *Letters*, 271; contrast *Letters*, 268-69, where his sights are still set on the Advocate Generalship.
[29] Though Jones himself believed he would be eligible in November 1778.
[30] *Letters*, 272.
[31] Ibbetson, 'Sir William Jones', in Watkin, ed., *Legal Wales*, 41, 47-51. See further below, 14, 18-21.

but in the event the post was to be left unfilled for five years. During this time Jones's practice at Westminster Hall stagnated; he attributed this directly to his uncertainty over the appointment to the judgeship in India, on the basis that he could not work towards that goal at the same time as attending Westminster Hall assiduously during the law terms.[32] His merits as both lawyer and linguist were obvious, and he was to underscore the value of his combination of skills by his translation from Arabic of *The Mahomedan Law of Succession to the Property of Intestates* in 1782: by this time it had been settled that the Supreme Court should determine questions of succession according to Hindu or Muslim law depending on the religion of the deceased, so Jones's work would have an immediate practical value in India.[33] Finally, in March 1783, through the intercessions of the Prime Minister, the Earl of Shelburne, Jones was appointed puisne judge of the Supreme Court of Bengal and knighted.

The move to India marked the third and final phase of Jones's life, in which he combined his judicial work with wide-ranging researches into all aspects of Indian history, flora and fauna, culture and language. He proved to be a sound and reliable judge: the political radicalism which he had shown in England was left behind; his enthusiastic defence of the British jury did not carry over into India; his earlier stance against Blackstone's positivism did not prevent him applying the law as he found it in the books; his belief that law was rooted in the customs of peoples did not stand in the way of his careful application of English law to native Indians. As a judge he was obliged to apply both Muslim and Hindu law in matters of succession and contracts, but for information on these he preferred not to be dependent on native maulvis and pandits, whom he regarded as untrustworthy and partial.[34] He could read the Arabic for himself and had already published *The Mahomedan Law of Succession to the Property of Intestates* before his appointment; but for Hindu law he was forced to rely on Halhed's unsatisfactory *Code of Gentoo Laws*,[35] a compilation of texts translated

[32] *Letters*, 520, 537, 569, 595, 598-99.

[33] Stat. 21 Geo. III c.70, s.17 (1781); as noted in (1782) 66 *Monthly Review* 442.

[34] Below, 15.

[35] Nathaniel Brassey Halhed, *A Code of Gentoo Laws* (London, 1776); Rosane Rocher, *Orientalism, Poetry, and the Millennium: The Checkered Life of Nathaniel Brassey Halhed, 1751-1830* (Delhi, 1983), 48-72. Jones's criticisms of Halhed are voiced in *Letters*, 699, 797.

from Sanskrit into Bengali into Persian into English, or more directly on Persian translations of Indian texts. Unsatisfied with this, he took it upon himself to learn Sanskrit so that he could read and interpret the texts in their original language, bringing this knowledge to bear in deciding cases which came before the court.[36] He translated into English one of the most important of these, the *Mānavadharmaśāstra*, publishing it as *The Institutes of Indian Law, or the Ordinances of Menu* in 1794, and put in train the more ambitious production of a collection and translation of legal extracts from other Sanskrit texts which would constitute a Digest on the model of Justinian's great compilation of Roman juristic writings.[37] Alongside the conscientious despatch of his judicial work, Jones stimulated the serious study of Indian – and, more generally, Asiatic – themes. Within weeks of his arrival he initiated the foundation of the Asiatic Society of Bengal to bring together European scholars interested in the study of Asian, especially Indian, civilisation and natural history, and in the ten years up to his death he was its most active member both in terms of attendance at its meetings and delivery of papers on a host of different subjects.[38]

Jones's intention had been to stay in India for only a few years, saving from his judicial salary enough money to enable him to return to England where he could be a gentleman-scholar at the same time as taking part in political life. He never did so. His wife Anna, whose health in India had never been good, returned to England at the end of 1793. Jones had himself intended to stay in India for another two years in order to see his Digest through to completion, but in the event brought forward his plans so as to rejoin her. He too, though, was in failing health; and before he could leave, in April 1794, he died of an inflammation of the liver.

[36] See for example *D.D. Munololl Baboo* v. *Gopee Dutt* (1786) Mort. Montr. 290, 294-5; *Kistnochurn Mullick* v. *Ramnarain Mullick* (1788) Mort. Montr. 297; *Doe d. Sree Oodoy Cower* v. *Mohun Lall Bussay* (1790-91) Mort. Montr. 311, 313; *Dialchundro Addie* v. *Kissorey Dossey* (1793-95) Mort. Montr. 371, 376.

[37] This was produced in Sanskrit under Jones's superintendence, translated by Henry Colebrooke, and published (with a dedication to the memory of Jones) as *A Digest of Hindu Law on Contracts and Successions, with a Commentary by Jagannát'ha Tercapanchanana* (Calcutta, 1797-8).

[38] O. P. Kejariwal, *The Asiatic Society of Bengal and the Discovery of India's Past* (New Delhi, 1988).

Oriental Jones

Jones's standing as an oriental scholar is beyond question. It was on this basis that he had been elected to the Royal Society, and the obituaries published on his death concentrated on his contribution to the study of the East. In the view of the *Gentleman's Magazine* he was 'the most eminent Oriental scholar in this or perhaps any other age',[39] while the *European Magazine* stressed his especial contribution to India: 'In Sir William Jones, India has lost her greatest ornament, the Commentator of her Poetry, the Investigator of her History, and the Elucidator of her Antiquities, her Laws, her Manners, and her Opinions.'[40] Neither made mention of his legal attainments, except in so far as they described him as a judge of the Supreme Court of Bengal. A note in the *Analytical Review* described him as an eminent lawyer and a profound scholar,[41] not so much marginalising as ignoring any profundity there might have been in his legal work. Significantly, the only epitaph concentrating on his contribution to the law was that composed by his close friend and fellow judge, Sir William Dunkin, who listed as his first virtue that he was learned in the law.[42]

In the (more or less) popular imagination Jones is associated primarily with the foundation of comparative Indo-European linguistics,[43] stemming from remarks on the relationship between Sanskrit, Greek and Latin made in his *Third Anniversary Discourse* to the Asiatic Society in 1786:

> The *Sanscrit* language, whatever be its antiquity, is of a wonderful structure; more perfect than the *Greek*, more copious than the *Latin*, and more exquisitely refined than either, yet bearing to both of them a stronger affinity, both in the roots of verbs and in the forms of grammar, than could possibly have been produced by accident; so strong indeed, that no philologer could examine them all three, without believing them to have sprung from a common source which, perhaps, no longer exists…[44]

[39] (1795) 65 *Gentleman's Magazine* 347.
[40] (1797) 31 *European Magazine* 40.
[41] (1795) 21 *Analytical Review* 246, note.
[42] (1795) 65 *Gentleman's Magazine* 347.
[43] For what follows, see R. H. Robins, 'The Life and Work of Sir William Jones' (1987) 85 *Transactions of the Philological Society* 1, and Anna Morpurgo Davies, *Nineteenth-Century Linguistics* (= G. Lepschy, ed., *History of Linguistics*, vol. IV) (London, 1998), 60-66.
[44] *Works*, 3.35.

Jones was by no means the first to notice the similarities between the three languages, though most of his predecessors had based their observations on the rather shaky evidence of vocabulary lists.[45] His fellow Harrovian and younger contemporary, Nathaniel Brassey Halhed, had commented on it in his *Grammar of the Bengal Language* in 1778, a work which Jones had studied carefully, and in a letter of 1779 which had very probably come to Jones's attention he had suggested that the grammatical similarities in the three languages might point in the direction of Greek and Latin having been derived from Sanskrit.[46] A few years before this, in 1768, a communication from the Frenchman Gaston Coeurdoux had been read to the Académie des Inscriptions et Belles-Letters in which it had been half-suggested – though the suggestion was rejected – that the three languages were derived from a lost predecessor; but this was not to be published until 1808,[47] and there is no evidence that Jones was aware of it. Jones's exact position in the history of Indo-European linguistics may be controversial;[48] his primary concerns in the *Third Anniversary Discourse* were ethnological, and while it is clear that in this passage he had no intention of fostering a new approach to the analysis of language, the idea that Sanskrit, Greek and Latin were sister-languages (rather than parent and children) is one to which he seems genu-

45 J.-C. Muller, 'Early Stages of Language Comparison from Sassetti to Sir William Jones (1786)' (1986) 31 *Kratylos* 1.

46 N. B. Halhed, *A Grammar of the Bengal Language* (Hoogly, 1778), iii; R. Rocher, 'Nathaniel Brassey Halhed, Sir William Jones and Comparative Indo-European Linguistics', in J. Bingen, A. Coupez and F. Mawet, eds., *Recherches de Linguistique: Hommages à Maurice Leroy* (Brussels, 1980), 173; the text of the letter can be found in Rocher, *Orientalism, Poetry, and the Millennium*, 293-309.

47 *Mémoires de Littérature, tirés des Registres de l'Académie Royale des Inscriptions et Belles-Lettres*, vol. 49 (Paris, 1808), 647-667, reprinted in M. Mayrhofer, 'Sanskrit und die Sprachen Alteuropas' (*Nachrichten von der Akademie der Wissenschaften in Göttingen, Philologisch-Historische Klasse*, Göttingen 1983, no. 5). For Coeurdoux, see S. Murr, *L'Inde Philosophique entre Bossuet et Voltaire*, vol. 2, *L'Indologie du Père Coeurdoux: Stratégies, Apologétique et Scientificité* (Publications de l'Ecole Française d'Extreme-Orient, vol. 146(2), Paris, 1987), especially at 26-33.

48 Davies, *Nineteenth-Century Linguistics*, 79 n.13; O. Szemerényi, 'About Unrewriting the History of Linguistics', in G. Brettschneider and C. Lehmann, eds., *Wege zur Universalienforschung* (Tübingen, 1980), 150, 150-160.

inely to have been committed.[49] Whatever the truth of this, the fact that his brief remarks published in the *Asiatick Researches* should have been taken as having launched the new philological science of the nineteenth century is a clear indication of his standing in the world of European scholarship.

For most contemporaries, though, Jones's primary significance was not as a linguist as such, but as the re-worker and translator of literature, especially poetry, from Arabic, Persian and Sanskrit.[50] He has been treated as the father of the serious study of Arabic poetry in Europe, not least because of his bringing to it his own sensitivity as an English poet.[51] In introducing the exuberantly rich imagery found in his Arabic and Persian originals into the English literary consciousness he aimed to bring life to what he regarded as the tired conventions of English poetic language; and he thereby fuelled the 'oriental' component of the early Romantic movement.[52] His later translations from the Sanskrit were no less significant. Once again he introduced English readers to wholly unfamiliar poetry, and as with his translations from Arabic his failure to give a literal rendition of the original was counterbalanced by his own poetical sensitivity.[53] Most important of all was his translation of the *Śakuntalā* of Kālidāsa, described by him as 'the Shakespeare of India',[54] which was first published in Calcutta and reprinted twice in London within three years and whose German translation of 1791 was to influence Goethe, Schlegel and Herder and through them nineteenth-century German romanticism.[55]

[49] Thomas R. Trautmann, *Aryans and British India* (Berkeley, 1997), 28-61. Compare *Letters*, 711, 727, 780.
[50] See, for example, the brief entry on Jones in the 'Biographical List of Living English Poets' (1792) 62 *Gentleman's Magazine* 505.
[51] Alan Jones, 'Sir William Jones as an Arabist', in Murray, *Sir William Jones*, 69.
[52] G. Cannon 'The Literary Place of Sir William Jones (1746-94)' (1960) 11 *Journal of the Asiatic Society* (4th series) 47, 54-60; J. Majeed, *Ungoverned Imaginings: James Mill's The History of British India and Orientalism* (Oxford, 1992), 11-46, 47, 57.
[53] L. S. R. Krishna Sastry, *Sir William Jones: Interpreter of India to the West* (Visakhapatnam, 1998), 22-70.
[54] *Sacontalá; or the Fatal Ring*, Preface, in *Works*, 9.369.
[55] Cannon, *Life and Mind*, 313-4; R. Schwab, *The Oriental Renaissance: Europe's Rediscovery of India and the East, 1680-1880* (trans. G. Patterson-Black and V. Reinking (New York, 1984)), 53-54, 57-61; J. J. Clarke, *Oriental Enlightenment*

On a broader front, in the ten years or so which he spent in Calcutta Jones initiated the serious study of Asia, and especially India. Edward Said describes his researches, and those which he fostered through his foundation of the Asiatic Society of Bengal, as one of the two major orientalist projects before Napoleon's invasion of Egypt, and accepts A. J. Arberry's assessment of him as the undisputed founder of Orientalism.[56] Jones's inaugural discourse as President of the Asiatic Society in 1784 and the ten anniversary discourses given between 1785 and 1794 set the tone for the Society's activities; and his papers at its meetings, given at the rate of almost three a year and published in the Society's Proceedings, ranged widely across Indology and beyond.[57] It has been said, without serious exaggeration, that Jones 'invaded almost every branch of learning'.[58] Some of his contributions were very sharply focused – his natural historical essays on the pangolin and the slow loris, for example – but others had more substantial ramifications. His work on Hindu chronology contributed significantly to the serious process of extracting Indian history from the mythology into which it had largely sunk; in his *Orthography of Asiatick Words* he drew attention to the misunderstandings which had grown out of the different ways of representing words from Asiatic languages in western scripts and introduced what was to become the basis of a standard form of transliteration into the Roman alphabet; and through both of these, and most clearly through his dissertation on *The Gods of Greece, Italy, and India*, he located Indian history and culture within the classical framework of Greece and Rome. Behind all of this lies the programme of research which Jones sketched out for himself on the sea-voyage from England to India in 1783, under the heading 'Objects of Enquiry during my residence in Asia':

1. The Laws of the Hindus and Mohammedans.
2. The History of the *Ancient* World.
3. Proofs and Illustrations of Scripture.
4. Traditions concerning the Deluge, etc.
5. Modern Politics and Geography of Hindustan.

(London, 1997), 61-67. For contemporary German responses to Jones, see J. D. Reuss, *Das Gelehrte England* (Berlin, 1804), 1.557 with the references there.

[56] Edward Said, *Orientalism* (London, 1995), 76, 78; A. J. Arberry, *Asiatic Jones* (London, 1946), 34.

[57] Kejariwal, *Asiatic Society of Bengal*, 29-75.

[58] Kejariwal, *Asiatic Society of Bengal*, 35.

6. Best Mode of governing Bengal.
7. Arithmetic and Geometry, and mixed Sciences of the Asiatics.
8. Medicine, Chemistry, Surgery, and Anatomy of the Indians.
9. Natural Productions of India.
10. Poetry, Rhetoric, and Morality of Asia.
11. Music of the Eastern Nations.
12. The Shi-King, or 300 Chinese Odes.
13. The best accounts of Tibet and Cashmir.
14. Trade, Manufactures, Agriculture, and Commerce of India.
15. Mogul Constitution, contained in the Defteri Alemghiri, and Ayein Acbari.
16. Mahratta Constitution.[59]

His orientalism was not simply the adventitious discovery of an intellectually curious man thrown by fate to serve as a judge in a little-known country; it was utterly purposeful.

Jones has been criticised for failing properly to treat Indian culture on its own terms. Edward Said, for example, alludes to his sanitised version of the East, in which he closed down the large vistas which were beginning to open up, through a process of codification, tabulation and comparison. There is undoubtedly some truth in this, though to a degree it amounts to little more than the criticism which could be made of any scholar trying to make sense of a complex subject matter.[60] More to the point is the observation that in his literary works he repeatedly refracted Indian culture through a western – commonly classical – lens. As one scholar has described it, he was 'lured by the pleasure of recognizing the familiar in the demand to

[59] Text from Lord Teignmouth's life of Jones, in *Works*, 2.3-4. See too Jones's 'Desiderata' printed by Teignmouth in *Works*, 3.xi-xii.

[60] Said, *Orientalism*, 77. For more favourable approaches to Jones, bringing out the acute tensions within his work, see John Drew, *India and the Romantic Imagination* (Delhi, 1987), 45-82, Rosane Rocher, 'British Orientalism in the Eighteenth Century: The Dialectics of Knowledge and Government', in C. A. Breckenridge and P. van der Veer, eds., *Orientalism and the Postcolonial Predicament* (Philadelphia, 1993), 215; R. K. Kaul, *Studies in William Jones: An Interpretation of Oriental Literature* (Shimla, 1995), 1-27, and Michael J. Franklin, 'Accessing India: Orientalism, Anti-'Indianism' and the Rhetoric of Jones and Burke', in T. Fulford and P. J. Kitson, eds., *Romanticism and Colonialism* (Cambridge, 1998), 48.

transform what was strange.'[61] His description of Kālidāsa as the Shakespeare of India[62] is as clear an act of literary annexation as can be imagined; so too his description of Firdausi as the Persian Homer or Háfiz the Persian Anacreon;[63] related to this is the syncretism implicit in his identification of Indian deities with their Greek or Roman equivalents. These characteristics did not only affect his literary works; as will be seen, they created serious problems for his legal writings too.[64]

Jones the Lawyer

The obituaries or brief biographies written in the years after Jones's death make bare reference to his legal work, either as advocate and judge or as legal writer. This side of his life was not ignored by Lord Teignmouth, but it does not occupy any substantial part of his memoir of Jones which first appeared in 1799 as an appendix to the first published collection of the works.[65] Except in America, where he was he was treated as the model of the lawyer-writer, with the lawyer predominating over the writer,[66] the first serious attempt to treat him as a lawyer did not occur until 1830, in Henry Roscoe's *Lives of Eminent British Lawyers*.[67] Remarking somewhat ingenuously that Jones's reputation as a lawyer had been rather eclipsed by his fame as a linguist and scholar in the decades after his death,[68] Roscoe

[61] Jenny Sharpe, 'The Violence of Light in the Land of Desire; Or, How William Jones Discovered India' (1993) 20 *boundary 2* 26, 35; Kate Teltscher, *India Inscribed: European and British Writing on India 1600-1800* (New Delhi, 1995), 192-228.
[62] Above, 10.
[63] Cannon, *Life and Mind*, 64.
[64] Below, 15-17.
[65] *Works*, vols. 1 and 2.
[66] Robert A. Ferguson, 'The Emulation of Sir William Jones in the Early Republic' (1979) 52 *New England Quarterly* 3. A good example of the American view of Jones, taken from a legal journal, is 'The Life and Writings of Sir William Jones' (1830) 2 *United States Law Intelligencer and Review* 1, 37, 77, 157; note in particular the judgement (at 159) that his great virtue lay in his combination of book-learning and practical common-sense.
[67] Henry Roscoe, *Lives of Eminent British Lawyers* (London, 1830), 306-328.
[68] By this time Jones had become a central figure in the dispute about the nature of British Orientalism, stemming from James Mill's attack on him in *The History of British India*: see Majeed, *Ungoverned Imaginings*, 138-140, 143-145.

focused his biographical sketch on Jones's life as a lawyer in England, saying little about his work as a judge in India and still less about his legal writings. More recently, those who have made reference to his legal work have concentrated on his published output. It was as a 'jurist' that he appeared in S.G. Vesey-Fitzgerald's treatment of 1946,[69] stressing that the regard due to him as a lawyer depended almost exclusively on the value of his published works. The brief entry on him in A.W.B. Simpson's *Biographical Dictionary of the Common Law* described him as an 'Orientalist and Legal Author';[70] and although the heading of the second edition of the Dictionary of National Biography is 'Sir William Jones, Orientalist and Judge', in the text more is made of his publications than his judicial work.[71] The most recent Indian biographical dictionaries either ignore him entirely or make no reference to his legal activities. In so far as his reputation as a lawyer is anything to go by, Jones's star seems to be very much in the descendent in the west and below the horizon in the east.

Though Jones was a capable barrister, so far as we can judge from his statements about his earnings, he was never sufficiently senior that his work as an advocate had any real historical importance. It might have been different. In 1777 he was approached by the City of London to argue against the government that the impressment of freement of the City was unlawful. This, Jones wrote to Althorp, would be his '*prima causa publica pro Libertate dicta*', his first public case in defence of liberty.[72] In the event, though, the case was not in fact heard, and Jones did not get the opportunity to speak. His work as a judge in India was, no doubt, more significant. A full assessment of it must await the detailed study of the early years of the Supreme Court in Calcutta, but two features stand out. First

[69] S. G. Vesey-Fitzgerald, 'Sir William Jones the Jurist' (1946) 11 *Bulletin of the School of Oriental and African Studies* 807.

[70] A. W. B. Simpson, *Biographical Dictionary of the Common Law* (London, 1984), 285.

[71] *Oxford Dictionary of National Biography* (Oxford, 2004), *sub nom.* (Michael J. Franklin). Compare the first edition (Oxford, 1891) where the heading has him simply as an oriental scholar, though H. M. Stephens' text describes him in passing as a 'great jurist'.

[72] *Letters*, 232; Cannon, *Life and Mind*, 78; J. A. Woods, 'The City of London and Impressment 1776-1777' (1956) 8 *Proceedings of the Leeds Philosophical and Literary Society* 111.

was his willingness to read Sanskrit texts for himself, rather than relying on the explanations and interpretations of the pandits, and then through his translations to provide a more authentic set of legal material for his anglophone fellow-judges than Halhed's *Code of Gentoo Laws*; though against this we must set his rather unappealing justification for doing so in the first place, that the native lawyers were unreliable and sometimes corrupt.[73] Secondly, as a judge he displayed a greater respect than many of his fellows for what modern lawyers would call civil liberties: as he had done in England, he stressed the centrality of the jury as a check on the exercise of power,[74] and in one notable case involving an alleged abuse of authority by a constable delivering a trenchant dissent from the views of the other judges, who had found in favour of the constable.[75]

Of greater interest are Jones's writings. These divide neatly into two groups: his translations of legal works from Greek, Arabic and Sanskrit, and his writings on English law. The former group consists of his edition of the *Speeches of Isaeus*, two Arabic works on succession, *The Mahomedan Law of Succession to the Property of Intestates* (1782) and *Al Sira'jiyyah: or the Mohammedan Law of Inheritance* (1792), and his translation from Sanskrit of the *Mānavadharmaśāstra*, published as *The Institutes of Indian Law, or the Ordinances of Menu* (1794).[76] The last three of these had a significant practical dimension. As Jones stated in the preface to the earliest of them, it was expressly provided in the Statute on which the jurisdiction of the Supreme Court in Bengal was grounded that matters of inheritance and contracts should be governed not by English law but by Hindu or Mohammedan law if appropriate to the parties,[77] with the consequence that English

[73] R. Rocher, 'Weaving Knowledge: Sir William Jones and Indian Pandits', in G. Cannon and K. R. Brine, eds., *Objects of Enquiry* (New York, 1995), 57. See in particular *Letters*, 684, 686, 720, 742, 762, 795; and Jones's advice to Burke, 'The Best Practicable System of Judicature', reproduced in *Letters*, 643. A similar trope is visible long before his move to Calcutta: *A Grammar of the Persian Language* (1771), Preface, in *Works*, 5.173.
[74] *Charge to the Grand Jury of Calcutta*, 1792 (*Works*, 7.67-70).
[75] *Tyler* v. *Deatker* (*cf.* Cannon, *Life and Mind*, 254; Ibbetson, 'Sir William Jones as a Comparative Lawyer', 24).
[76] *Works*, 9.1-362; 8.159-196; 8.199-321; 7.73-8.158. There is a good modern edition and translation of the *Mānavadharmaśāstra*: P. Olivelle, *Manu's Code of Law* (Oxford, 2005).
[77] Stat. 21 Geo. III c.70, s.17 (1781).

judges needed a sufficient knowledge of the relevant rules to be able to apply them. All were translations, so it is difficult to extract from them any real clues about Jones's conception of law; but we can usefully make four observations. First is that, following the assumptions lying behind Warren Hastings' plan and the Statute of 1781, he was guilty of transplanting into other systems western beliefs about the nature of law.[78] The Hindu *dharma*, a concept of great complexity, was considered as crudely equivalent to law.[79] Both Mohammedan law and Hindu law were treated as rule-based systems of exactly the same type as English law or Roman law, ignoring the role of variable local customs and the crucial interpretative role of learned maulvis and pandits; and there was no recognition of the different jurisprudential schools in either tradition.[80] Secondly, reflecting Jones's 'scientific' conception of law as brought out in the *Essay on the Law of Bailments*,[81] it was at heart something to be found in authoritative books – authoritative old books, for preference – rather than something rooted in social practice.[82] Thirdly, there is a hint of mapping Hindu literature onto a

[78] For the wider context of Jones's translations, see Tejaswini Niranjana, *Siting Translation: History, Post-Structuralism, and the Colonial Context* (Berkeley, 1992), 11-19, esp. at 16-18.

[79] On *dharma*, see R. Lingat, *The Classical Law of India* (trans. J. D. M. Derrett; Berkeley, 1973), 3-7; W. Halbfass, *India and Europe: An Essay in Understanding* (New York, 1988), 310-333; J. D. M. Derrett, *Religion, Law and the State in India* (Oxford, 1999), 75-96; R. W. Lariviere, 'Dharmaśāstra, Custom, 'Real Law' and 'Apocryphal' Smṛtis' (2004) 32 *Journal of Indian Philosophy* 611; A. Wezler, 'Dharma in the Veda and the Dharmaśāstras' (2004) 32 *Journal of Indian Philosophy* 629; P. Hacker, trans. D. Davis Jr., 'Dharma in Hinduism' (2006) 34 *Journal of Indian Philosophy* 479 (originally published 1965).

[80] M. R. Anderson, 'Islamic Law and the Colonial Encounter in British India', in D. Arnold and P. Robb, eds., *Institutions and Ideologies: A SOAS South Asia Reader* (London 1993), 165, especially at 174-175; and for the problematic nature of Hindu 'schools' of law, L. Rocher, 'Schools of Hindu Law', in J. Ensinck and P. Gaeffke, eds., *India Maior: Congratulatory Volume Presented to J. Gonda* (Leiden, 1972), 166.

[81] Below, 53-56.

[82] *Eleventh Anniversary Discourse*, in *Works*, 3.241-242. For the origins of this 'brahmanisation' of the law in Warren Hastings' plan for the governance of Bengal, based on a supposed 'ancient constitution' rather than the supposed arbitrary despotism of the Mughal state, see Bernard S. Cohn, 'Law and the Colonial State in India', in J. Starr and J. F. Collier, eds., *History and Power in the Study of Law*

Roman model in the designation of thc *Mānavadharmaśāstra* as 'Institutes' of Indian law, especially when coupled with the 'Digest' of Hindu law with which he was occupied at the time of his death.[83] Jones cannot fail to have been aware of the link, but it is perhaps significant that it was only in 1792, relatively late in the production of his translation of the *Mānavadharma-śāstra*, that he began to refer to it by the title 'Institutes';[84] and his projected 'Digest' was far more faithful to the native Indian tradition of digests, in which the compiler interwove his own comments with the collected texts, than to Justinian's collection of unglossed extracts.[85] Finally, within the translation of the *Mānavadharmaśāstra* it is possible to see him using technical terminology derived from English or Roman law to describe Indian institutions which are not quite equivalent;[86] and in his letter to Cornwallis on the desirability of producing an Indian Digest he wrote of the need for an exposition of the Indian law on the twelve nominate contracts of Ulpian, a clear borrowing from one of the texts discussed at length in the *Essay on the Law of Bailments*, D.50.17.23.[87] Despite his recognition and acceptance of the differences between Hindu law and English and Roman laws, he was never quite able to distance himself completely from the systems with which he was most familiar.[88]

The most important of Jones's writings on English law, undoubtedly, is the *Essay on the Law of Bailments*, dealt with at length in the next chapter. This was not, though, his first English legal work. A year before this he had published a pamphlet written in the wake of the Gordon Riots of June 1780, events in which he had himself been caught up, joining the volunteer

(Ithaca, 1989), 131, 137-147. Contrast with Jones the more modern approach in Donald R. Davis, Jr., 'A Realist View of Hindu Law' (2006) 19 *Ratio Juris* 287; and for an attempt to locate *dharma* alongside other sources of Indian law, Davis, 'Intermediate Realms of Law: Corporate Groups and Rulers in Medieval India' (2005) 48 *Journal of the Economic and Social History of the Orient* 92.

[83] Above, n.37.

[84] *Letters*, 908. There is perhaps an earlier reference in B.L. MS Add. 8885 f.18.

[85] On the Indian digests, see Lingat, *Classical Law of India*, 115-122; for an example, see L. Rocher, ed., *Jīmūtavāna's Dāyabhāga: the Hindu Law of Inheritance in Bengal* (Oxford, 2002).

[86] Ibbetson, 'Sir William Jones as a Comparative Lawyer', 32-33.

[87] *Letters*, 797.

[88] Ibbetson, 'Sir William Jones and the Nature of Law', in Burrows and Rodger, *Mapping the Law*, 619, 634-639.

force of lawyers defending the Inns of Court.[89] The *Inquiry into the Legal Mode of Suppressing Riots: with a Constitutional Plan for Future Defence* was not a polished work – according to the title-page of the second edition (1782) it had originally been published the month after the riots had taken place[90] – and no doubt as a result of its hurried production it is very revealing about both Jones's legal and political preconceptions and also his Common law methodology.

The starting point of the *Inquiry* was that there had been no necessity to use the military to put down the Gordon Riots; the system must be defective if the civil state had no power in itself to quell such uprisings without calling upon the soldiery, since at any time the militia might be called away to defend the shores against foreign invasion.[91] Jones proceeded to demonstrate that the old Common law did provide such a power, sheriffs and Justices of the Peace being able to call upon the *posse comitatus* – consisting of any and all citizens, armed – to aid them in carrying out their offices.[92] This was not an especially radical argument – it was put forward by Blackstone, Hale, and a host of other writers – but behind it there lurked a proposition altogether more alarming to the government, that citizens had a right to keep arms not only to protect the realm against insurrection but also to protect themselves against the excessive exercise of power by the executive.[93] This latter proposition was only lightly adumbrated in the *Inquiry*; it was to be stated more explicitly in Jones's political pamphlet *The Principles of Government, in a Dialogue between a Scholar and a Peasant*,[94] a *jeu d'esprit* resulting from a conversation with Charles de Vergennes and Benjamin Franklin in which he had asserted that it was possible to formulate the basic principles of political philosophy in a form sufficiently simple that they could be easily understood by the most uneducated reader, resulting in the trial for sedition of the pamphlet's publisher, Jones's brother-in-

[89] Cannon, *Life and Mind*, 127-130.

[90] Jones refers to it in a letter of 21st July 1780: *Letters*, 423.

[91] *Works*, 8.464.

[92] *Works*, 8.466-490.

[93] *Works*, 8.497.

[94] *Works*, 8.525-537. In the second edition (1797) the scholar had become a gentleman and the peasant a farmer.

law William Shipley, Dean of St. Asaph.[95] Similar arguments to those of Jones, and perhaps influenced by them, were put forward a year later by Granville Sharp;[96] and they fed into the American debates leading to the Constitution's Second Amendment.[97]

Several features of Jones's legal arguments in the *Inquiry into the Legal Mode of Suppressing Riots* were to recur in the *Essay on the Law of Bailments*. At a structural level, there is a tendency to begin by identifying the conclusion to be reached and then moving to demonstrate that it is in fact correct: the suggestion that the law would be defective if it did not allow for non-military methods of suppressing riots moves almost inevitably to the legal analysis showing that civil methods were available within the traditional boundaries of the Common law. His proof of this sometimes involved rather questionable steps of reasoning. Authorities might be twisted to support the conclusion which he was already committed to reaching. *Bedingfield's Case*,[98] for example, was treated as 'irresistibly strong authority' to show that a sheriff had an obligation to raise an armed posse to quell a tumult; but in truth it had held that a sheriff might – not must – lawfully raise an armed band (here three hundred men) in order to recover goods which had been improperly taken.[99] Sir Matthew Hale, though recognising the right of citizens in a posse to carry arms, had sug-

[95] Cannon, *Life and Mind*, 185-186, 194; J. Oldham, *The Mansfield Manuscripts* (Chapel Hill, 1992), 2.794-800. The whole event verges on the bizarre, both professionally and personally. It was, to say the least, decidedly odd for a man to be appointed to judicial office at the same time as a work which he had admittedly written was the subject of a trial for sedition, with only the future Chief Justice, Jones's friend Lloyd Kenyon, apparently of the view that it should perhaps be a disqualification (T. B. Howell, *A Complete Collection of State Trials* (London, 1814), 21.869); and his departure for India looks to have occurred with an unseemly haste (*Letters*, 615). No less curious is the apparent insouciance with which Jones wrote about the trial in the course of his voyage to India (*Letters*, 615-616).

[96] [Granville Sharp], *The Ancient Common Law Right of Associating with the Vicinage*, in *Tracts, Concerning the Ancient and Only True Means of National Defence by a Free Militia* (London, 1781). For Jones's close and friendly relationship with Sharp, see his letter in Gloucestershire County Record Office, D3549, 13/1/J7.

[97] L. W. Levy, *Origins of the Bill of Rights* (New Haven, 1999), 136-141.

[98] YB H. 3 Hen. VII f.1 pl.1; YB T. 3 Hen. VII f.10 pl.4; Bro. Abr., *Office et Officer*, 23; Bro. Abr., *Riots*, 2 (1488).

[99] *Works*, 8.475-479.

gested that marching in an armed band might in some circumstances constitute the levying of war;[100] Jones countered this with a statement of Bracton,[101] taken out of context and over-interpreted, to the effect that an act could not be wrongful if the intent with which it was done was good.[102] More generally, from the rules which he had identified relating to the summoning of the posse he articulated a number of corollaries which he claimed followed necessarily as a matter of reason, but which, clearly, did not. The obligation of the sheriff to call a posse and the obligation of citizens to respond to the call, coupled with the 'principle of natural justice' that none should be required to do anything impossible nor denied the means of performing their duty (a principle which was simply asserted without any additional justification), led to the conclusion that all those liable to be called to join the posse should continually be ready to do so, that they should be competent in the use of the musket and the bayonet since these were the most effective weapons, and that in order best to use them as a body they should regularly train as platoons.[103] The conclusions which he had reached, he said, were nothing more than 'the conclusions of natural reason from the simplest and surest premises',[104] thereby prefiguring the Natural-law reasoning which was to lie at the base of the *Essay on the Law of Bailments*. Linked to this, in a more purely English context, was his repeated praise for Common law over statutes, on the basis that it was in general the 'perfection of human wisdom'.[105] Moreover, as a matter of observation, the statutes which he had discussed had done nothing to undermine

[100] M. Hale, *Historia Placitorum Coronae* (London, 1736), 1.131; *cf.* 1.495.
[101] Bracton, *De Legibus et Consuetudinibus Anglie* (London, 1569), f.133 (= G. Woodbine, ed., and S E Thorne, trans., *Bracton, On the Laws and Customs of England* (Cambridge, Mass., 1968), 2.375): *voluntas et propositum distinguunt maleficia* (also at f.2b (ed. Thorne, 2.23), f.101 (ed. Thorne, 2.289), f.136b (ed. Thorne, 2.384).
[102] *Works*, 8.487-489.
[103] *Works*, 8.473-474.
[104] *Works*, 8.486.
[105] *Works*, 8.489. *Cf. Works,* 8.492, stressing its rooting in the 'wisdom of ages'. For further remarks about the benefits of the Common law over statute, see *Letters*, 553-554.

the effect of the leading cases, nor had the current Riot Act of 1714[106] in any way derogated from the Common law.[107]

This conception of the Common law as something derived from reason was made explicit in some remarks appearing in an oration which Jones had planned to give at the Encaenia in Oxford in 1773, but which was not in the event to be delivered, and which was only published in 1782.[108] Praising Blackstone for the way in which he had formulated the principles of the Common law which had formerly been 'dispersed at random in an infinite number of volumes', he remarked on the zeal which the *Commentaries* must inspire for laws

> which flow, as from an abundant fountain, from the clear deductions of reason, wisdom, justice, and humanity, and in which the most intricate cases are generally reducible to a few transcendent truths, which no perverseness can deny, no folly contradict, no tyranny subvert.[109]

It was this vision of the law which was to lie at the root of the *Essay on the Law of Bailments*.

[106] Stat. 1 Geo. I Stat. 2 c.5.
[107] *Works*, 8.489-490.
[108] *An Oration Intended to have been Spoken in the Theatre at Oxford IX July MDCCLXXIII*, printed with *An Inquiry into the Legal Mode of Suppressing Riots* (2nd edn., London, 1782), 61-75 (not in *Works*). For the context, see Cannon, *Life and Mind*, 60-62.
[109] *Oration Intended to have been Spoken in the Theatre at Oxford*, 69.

NATURAL LAW, ROMAN LAW AND ENGLISH LAW IN THE ESSAY ON THE LAW OF BAILMENTS

It is impossible not to be impressed by the *Essay on the Law of Bailments*. It stands alone in the literature of eighteenth-century English law for its attempt to synthesise English and foreign legal materials, particularly the texts of Roman law, and for its apparent depth of analysis in doing so. The number of other legal systems to which Jones makes reference is little less than astonishing, all the more so because of the linguistic range they reveal. Strongly influenced by Blackstone's reduction of the Common law to scientific principles, he gave to this branch of the Common law a sound abstract framework and provided a model which might have been used for short treatises on other areas of law. So easy is it to be dazzled by Jones's virtuoso display that the work's eighteenth-century context can be forgotten and the details of its argument glossed over. The following pages aim to go behind the surface of the *Essay*, looking in turn at the Natural law context and Jones's use of Natural law arguments, at his analysis of Roman law, and finally at his interpretation of the English Common law.

Before embarking on this, one fundamental observation needs to be made. From the English lawyer's standpoint, the bailment relationship, *i.e.* where one person holds property (typically moveable property) belonging to another, raises a number of complex legal questions. Jones's *Essay* looks at one of these, and one only: the level of care required to be taken by the bailee. Other questions, such as the extent to which the bailee can claim to be owner of the goods as against third parties or the legal consequences of the bailor not being the owner of the goods in the first place, are completely ignored. Though there is no acknowledgment of the fact, underpinning the whole of Jones's conception of the law of bailments was the Roman assumption that it was concerned with the contents of the contractual relationship between the bailor and bailee: in Roman law, with a small number of minor exceptions, the borrower acquired no proprietary or possessory rights, so the proprietary issues with which English law was concerned simply did not arise. It is for this reason, no doubt, that the *Essay* begins by speaking of the 'contract' of bailment, and for this reason that the legal focus of the work is so narrow.

Natural Law

In 1665, when Samuel Rachel was appointed Professor of the Law of Nature and Nations in the University of Keil, he became the first professor of Natural law in Europe.[1] His appointment marked the elevation to academic respectability of the subject, whose modern form could be traced back a generation to the appearance of Hugo Grotius's *De Jure Belli ac Pacis* in 1625.[2] For the following century or more its influence spread right across Europe, playing its part in the systematisation of national laws and injecting into them moral values which were thought to be rationally discoverable and (according to some versions of Natural law theory) to have a measure of objective validity independent of the positive law of any particular state.[3] It underpinned the thought of Gershom Carmichael and other members of the Scottish Enlightenment;[4] and, both through translations of Grotius and Pufendorf and through the writings of such men as Thomas

[1] C. Rodenberg and V. Pauls, *Die Anfänge der Christian-Albrechts Universität Keil* (Neumünster, 1955), 278. Pufendorf was to claim the distinction on the basis of his appointment at Heidelberg in 1660, but here he was only *professor extraordinarius* of the law of nations, not the law of nature: L Krieger, *The Politics of Discretion* (Chicago, 1965), 19-22. He was appointed Professor of the Law of Nature and Nations in Lund in 1667.

[2] For the seventeenth-century development of Natural law, see Knud Haakonssen, 'Divine/Natural Law Theories in Ethics', in Daniel Garber and Michael Ayers, eds., *The Cambridge History of Seventeenth-Century Philosophy* (Cambridge, 1998), 1317 (also in his *Natural Law and Moral Philosophy* (Cambridge, 1996), chap. 1). As Haakonssen points out, Grotius was building on a very long tradition of Natural law theorising; but he was seen by moral philosophers of the seventeenth and eighteenth centuries as representing a major watershed, and it is this that justifies the modern treatment of him as the progenitor of a new tradition. There is a useful collection of important essays on seventeenth- and eighteenth-century Natural law thought in Knud Haakonssen, ed., *Grotius, Pufendorf and Modern Natural Law* (Aldershot, 1999).

[3] H. Thieme, *Das Naturrecht und die Europäische Privatrechtsgeschichte* (Basel, 1954); J. M. Kelly, *A Short History of Western Legal Theory* (Oxford, 1992), 258-262; F. Wieacker, *A History of Private Law in Europe* (trans. T Weir, Oxford, 1995), 213-221, esp. at 217-218.

[4] J. Moore and M. Silverthorne, 'Gershom Carmichael and the Natural Jurisprudence Tradition in Eighteenth-Century Scotland', in I. Hont and M. Ignatieff, eds., *Wealth and Virtue: The Shaping of Political Economy in the Scottish Enlightenment* (Cambridge, 1983), 73; Haakonssen, *Natural Law and Moral Philosophy.*

Rutherforth and William Paley,[5] it moulded ethical theory in England.[6] English legal writers of the eighteenth century commonly rooted their conceptions of the law in the law of nature.[7] Towards the end of the seventeenth century Grotius, and more especially Pufendorf, were recommended by John Locke for their general educational value;[8] a century later the same authors were lauded by James Mackintosh in Lincoln's Inn.[9] In the universities, where the study of the Civil law was moribund and the study of the Common law only just starting in the 1750s, practically all exposure to le-

[5] Thomas Rutherforth, *Institutes of Natural Law* (London, 1754-6); William Paley, *Principles of Moral and Political Philosophy* (London, 1785).

[6] A. Dufour, 'Pufendorfs Ausstrahlung im französischen und im anglo-amerikanischen Kulturraum', in K. Å. Modéer, ed., *Samuel von Pufendorf 1632-1982* (Stockholm, 1986), 96; N. E. Simmonds, *The Decline of Juridical Reason*, (Manchester, 1984), 48-67. Grotius's *De Iure Belli ac Pacis* was first translated into English in 1654, with subsequent translations and editions in 1655, 1682, 1715, 1738 and 1749. Pufendorf's magnum opus, *De Jure Naturae et Gentium*, was translated by Basil Kennet as *The Law of Nature and Nations* in 1703, and had four further editions (1710, 1717, 1729, 1749); his more compendious work, *De Officio Hominis et Civis*, first appeared in translation (by Andrew Tooke) under the title *The Whole Duty of Man According to the Law of Nature* in 1691 (further editions in 1698, 1705, 1716 and 1735). The last two editions of *The Law of War and Peace* and the second and subsequent editions of *The Law of Nature and Nations* were accompanied by the notes of Jean Barbeyrac. For the central importance of Barbeyrac as translator and commentator, see David Saunders, 'The Natural Jurisprudence of Jean Barbeyrac: Translation as an Art of Political Adjustment' (2003) 36 *Eighteenth Century Studies* 473.

[7] M. Lobban, 'Custom, Nature, and Authority: the Roots of English Legal Positivism', in D. Lemmings, ed., *The British and their Laws in the Eighteenth Century* (Woodbridge, 2005), 27, 29-32.

[8] John W. Yolton and Jean S. Yolton, eds., John Locke, *Some Thoughts Concerning Education* (1693) (Oxford, 1989), 239; E. S. de Beer, ed., *The Correspondence of John Locke*, vol. II (Oxford, 1976), 780 (1686). Locke described Pufendorf's *De Jure Naturae et Gentium* as 'the best book of that kind': 'Some Thoughts Concerning Reading and Study for a Gentleman', in *A Collection of Several Pieces by Mr John Locke* (London, 1720), 237.

[9] James Mackintosh, *Discourse on the Study of the Law of Nature and Nations* (Dublin, 1799), 14, 18, 26.

gal thought was refracted through the lens of Natural law.[10] Thomas Bever, lecturing in Oxford at the same time as Jones was a student, saw as the great virtue of Roman law that it contained 'the most compleat collection, now extant, of the *natural* rules of justice and reason' and described Grotius and Pufendorf as 'the founders of modern jurisprudence'.[11] William Blackstone, the first Vinerian professor, who was also teaching at Oxford in the 1760s and whose lectures Jones might have attended, incorporated arguments from Natural law into his *Commentaries* and more generally carried many of the Natural lawyers' presuppositions about the nature of law into his 'general map of the law'; so too did his successor Robert Chambers and Chambers' successor Richard Wooddesson.[12] Arguments from Natural law are found in English cases, sometimes succeeding in overturning pre-existing Common law rules; and, most importantly of all, Natural lawyers' analyses can be demonstrated to have infiltrated into the Common law (both through judicial reasoning and through the work of treatise writers and commentators) and to have provided a rational structure for English legal rules which had formerly been locked into a shape which was largely governed by the mediaeval forms of action.[13]

[10] J. L. Barton, 'Legal Studies', in L. S. Sutherland and L. G. Mitchell, eds., *The History of the University of Oxford, Volume V, The Eighteenth Century* (Oxford, 1986), 593-607; Victor Morgan, *A History of the University of Cambridge, Volume II, 1546-1750* (Cambridge, 2004), 438-440; Peter Searby, *A History of the University of Cambridge, Volume III, 1750-1870* (Cambridge, 1997), 187-188.

[11] Thomas Bever, *A Discourse on the Study of Jurisprudence and the Civil Law* (Oxford, 1766), 23, 35 (emphasis added); Henry J. Bourguignon, *Sir William Scott, Lord Stowell* (Cambridge, 1987), 35-36, quoting All Souls College, Oxford MS 109c; Sutherland and Mitchell, *History of the University of Oxford, Volume V, The Eighteenth Century*, 474, 598, 601.

[12] Blackstone, *Commentaries* (Oxford, 1765), 1.35, 39-43; David Lieberman, *The Province of Legislation Determined* (Cambridge, 1989), 35-40; M. Lobban, *The Common Law and English Jurisprudence, 1760-1850* (Oxford, 1991), 17-46; N. E. Simmonds, 'Reason, History and Privilege: Blackstone's Debt to Natural Law' (1988) 105 *Zeitschrift der Savigny Stiftung für Rechtsgeschichte (Germanistische Abteilung)* 200.

[13] D. J. Ibbetson, 'Natural Law and Common Law' (2001) 5 *Edinburgh Law Review* 4.

The *Essay on the Law of Bailments* fits comfortably into this late eighteenth-century mould.[14] Its rooting in the Natural law tradition is visible in three ways: in its explicit commitment to law as a scientific discipline susceptible to rational analysis; in the structure of its argument, from Natural law through the positive law of different states to a synthesis of general principles; and, most clearly, in the observations on Natural law appearing at the start of the work.

Lawyers from the fifteenth century and before had been arguing whether law was a science or an art, balancing its description in Justinian's Institutes as the science of the just and the unjust, *iusti atque iniusti scientia*, with that of Ulpian that it was the art of the good and the fair, *ars boni et aequi*.[15] Seventeenth- and eighteenth-century Natural lawyers had no doubts that it was a science. The parallel between natural science and moral science, between mathematics and ethics, had often been drawn.[16] Grotius had likened his mode of analysis to that of the mathematician,[17] and Leibniz had moved almost seamlessly from the one to the other.[18] Pufendorf's teacher, Erhard Weigel, Professor of Mathematics at Jena, had made the connection fundamental to his work, unmistakeably so in the title of his *Arithmetical Description of Moral Wisdom*.[19] Pufendorf's first work on Natural law, his *Elements of Universal Jurisprudence*, was written firmly under this influence, proceeding from axioms and definitions to conclusions;[20] and although this rigid structure was wholly absent in his *Law of*

[14] Lieberman, *Province of Legislation Determined*, 34; J. M. Finnis, 'Blackstone's Theoretical Intentions' (1967) 12 *Natural Law Forum* 163, 182.

[15] Inst. 1.1.1.1, D.1.1.1; I. Maclean, *Interpretation and Meaning in the Renaissance* (Cambridge, 1992), 21-27.

[16] W. Röd, *Geometrischer Geist und Naturrecht* (*Bayerische Akademie der Wissenschaften, Phil.-Hist. Klasse Abhandlungen*, N.F. 70) (Munich, 1970); Peter Stein, 'Systematisation of Private Law in the Sixteenth and Seventeenth Centuries', in J. Schröder, ed., *Entwicklung der Methodenlehre in Rechtswissenschaft und Philosophie vom 16. bis zum 18. Jahrhundert* (Stuttgart, 1998), 117, 124-126.

[17] *De Jure Belli ac Pacis*, Prologue § 58.

[18] G. Leibniz, *Nova Methodus Discendae Docendaeque Iurisprudentiae* (Leipzig, 1748).

[19] E. Weigel, *Arithmetische Beschreibung der Moralweisheit* (Jena, 1674); *Synopsis Jurisprudentiae Mnemoneutica* (Jena, 1669).

[20] *Elementorum Jurisprudentiae Universalis Libri Duo* (The Hague, 1660) (reprint, with translation by W. A. Oldfather, Oxford, 1931).

Nature and Nations the work was none the less dependent on a process of apparently deductive reasoning.[21] A generation or so before Jones, Christian Wolff had placed scientific analysis right at the heart of his treatment of the subject in his eight-volume analysis of the Law of Nature,[22] and the *Essay on the Law of Bailments* fitted firmly into this tradition. For Jones it was important that law was a science and not merely a set of unconnected rules, and as a science it must be reducible to a set of identifiable principles whose validity could be determined both by reason and by observation:

> [I]f law be a science, and really deserve so sublime a name, it must be founded on principle, and claim an exalted rank in the empire of reason; but, if it be merely an unconnected series of decrees and ordinances, its use may remain, though its dignity be lessened, and He will become the greatest lawyer, who has the strongest habitual, or artificial, memory.[23]

This was to colour Jones's whole approach to legal analysis: if law was indeed deducible by reason there was little independent scope for authority, and he only grudgingly recognised that there was any role for it at all, as something which could give clear guidance when lawyers proceeding by reason alone might disagree on the true answer to some legal question.[24] Exactly what he meant by 'reason' is not wholly clear, but we may take it as being a high degree of principled coherence, ensuring that the different rules of the system were substantially both consistent with each other and, probably, consonant with some picture of what was demanded by justice.[25]

The belief that law could be analysed scientifically lay at the root of Jones's argument. It was framed according to a tripartite model traceable back to the German jurist Johann Gottlieb Heineccius, whose work was influential in University College, Oxford, where Jones was by then a fel-

[21] T. Hochstrasser, *Natural Law Theories in the Early Enlightenment* (Cambridge, 2000), 40-71.

[22] C. Wolff, *Jus Naturae Methodo Scientifica Pertractatum* (Frankfurt, 1740-48).

[23] *Bailments*, [202]; *cf.* [155], and note also [2], describing Blackstone's *Commentaries* as 'the most correct and beautiful outline, that ever was exhibited of any human science'. See too his *Oration Intended to have been Spoken in the Theatre at Oxford*, 69, quoted above, 21.

[24] *Bailments*, [87]. See below, 54-55.

[25] For the link between science and ethics in Jones's developed thought about law, see *Eleventh Anniversary Discourse*, in *Works*, 3.241-242, 245.

low.[26] First came an analytical part, in which the subject was sketched out according to the first principles of natural reason; this was followed by an historical, or empirical, part, in which it was shown how the rules of developed legal systems conformed to this natural model; finally there was a relatively brief synthetic part, formulating a set of rules based on his conclusions in the first two parts.[27] The closeness of this approach to that recommended by George Turnbull, the translator of Heineccius, is immediately apparent:

> And it would not certainly be an improper way of studying our laws first to get well acquainted with the laws of nature (large commentaries upon which are generally at the same time commentaries upon the Roman laws, the examples being commonly taken from thence), and then to go over the same laws of nature again in order, and to enquire into our laws under each head, and try them by the laws of nature, as the Roman laws are commonly canvassed by the maxims of natural equity, in treatises upon universal law.[28]

Given this ordering of the analytical and historical parts of the argument, it is hardly surprising that Jones's interpretations of positive law were strongly coloured by his views of what natural law prescribed.

Equally, though, his view of Natural law was coloured by positive law, particularly Roman law. This is transparent in the initial, analytical, part of the work, which opens with a definition of bailment as a contract incorporating an obligation on the part of the borrower to return the property to the lender in due time, from which he deduced three conclusions:

(a) the bailee must keep the property, and be responsible to the bailor should it be lost or damaged;

[26] J. G. Heineccius, *Elementa Iuris Civilis Secundum Ordinis Institutionum*, Praefatio, in *Opera Omnia* (Geneva, 1747), 5.iii-xi; R. Eden, *Jurisprudentia Philologica* (Oxford, 1744), vi. For the dependence of Eden, a Fellow of University College, on Heineccius, see Barton, 'Legal Studies', in Sutherland and Mitchell, eds., *The History of the University of Oxford, V: The Eighteenth Century*, 599.
[27] *Bailments*, [4]. For this tripartite approach, see Haakonssen, *Natural Law and Moral Philosophy*, 85-90.
[28] G. Turnbull, 'A Supplement concerning the Duties of Subjects and Magistrates', in J. G. Heineccius, *A Methodical System of Universal Law: or, the Laws of Nature and Nations deduced from Certain Principles, and applied to Proper Cases* (trans. G. Turnbull, London, 1763), 2.230-231, quoted in Hochstrasser, *Natural Law Theories in the Early Enlightenment*, 16-17.

(b) his responsibility only arose if the loss or damage was due to his fault through not exercising a proper degree of care;

(c) the measure of care required of the bailee depended on the type of bailment.[29]

Each of these statements represented a basic principle of Roman law, but none followed from the definition which he had given, however plausible each might seem in its own right. It might be admitted that the obligation to return the property entailed an obligation to look after it, but it could not be taken for granted that the failure to do so necessarily obliged the bailee to compensate. The second conclusion was based on the assumption that 'the bounds of justice would in most cases be transgressed, if he were made answerable for the loss of it without his fault'. Most (though not all) Natural lawyers would have agreed with the conclusion that liability depended on fault,[30] but that did not mean that the argument was well-founded as a matter of logic. Furthermore, if it was the case that the bailment had arisen out of a contract (as Jones assumed it always would be), there was a clash between the principle of liability for fault and the orthodox Natural law view that the incidence of liability should depend on what it was that the parties had agreed.[31] If contract was indeed based on the intention of the parties, there had to be some reason for embedding within the contract of bailment a particular default rule imposing liability for fault, at the level appropriate to the relationship in question. Jones recognised this, but attempted to slip the noose by supposing that it was a 'fair presumption' that the parties had intended to incorporate the fault principle into their contract and allowing that they could depart from the normal rules by express agreement.[32] This achieved the necessary result, but rather too obviously begged the question. Nicolaus Gundling, Professor of the Law of Nature and Nations at the University of Halle, had earlier argued that it was impossible to deduce from the simple agreement to look after another's property that one would take

[29] *Bailments*, [4].

[30] Grotius, *De Jure Belli ac Pacis* 2.17.1; Pufendorf, *De Jure Naturae et Gentium* 3.1.6. But *cp*. C. Thomasius, *Larva Legis Aquiliae* (Halle, 1703), esp. at s 2 (ed. M. Hewett and R. Zimmermann (Oxford, 2000), 6).

[31] Pufendorf, *On the Duty of Man and Citizen*, 1.9. On the role of will and agreement generally, see J. Gordley, *The Philosophical Origins of Modern Contract Doctrine* (Oxford, 1991).

[32] *Bailments*, [16].

any particular measure of care of it.[33] Jean Barbeyrac had disagreed with this: in the version of his notes published with the fifth edition of the English translation of Pufendorf's *Law of Nature and Nations* (1749), he reasserted the principle that contract was based on the intention of the parties, though qualified this with the proviso that one might look behind the words in order to find that intention.[34] From this position, which Gundling would presumably have accepted as an abstract proposition, Barbeyrac made the unjustifiable leap to suggesting that it was obviously to be supposed that a depositee would exercise the care that he normally took about his own affairs or, if this was not known, that he would take reasonable care. Jones may well not have known of this interchange;[35] in any event it does not seem to have impacted upon his own thinking. As well, he was writing just a few years too early to be aware of William Paley's solution to the difficulty, the move away from an analysis rigidly framed in terms of the intentions of the parties to one in which the important thing was the identification of the expectations which had been aroused in a promisee by the words and conduct of the promisor.[36] Nor, as a matter of logic, was there any justification for Jones's third conclusion, that the standard of care to be demanded depended on the type of bailment; though, once more, it was something which was generally stated to be the case by Natural law writers.

It is in his discussion of the degrees of care that Jones revealed most transparently the extent to which his version of Natural law was in fact derived from Roman law. He began by explicitly distancing himself from Roman law, denying the utility of superlatives such as 'all possible dili-

[33] N. Gundling, *Ius Naturae et Gentium* (3rd edn., Halle, 1736), c.23 §83. Gundling had further cited Thomasius as holding the view that it was impossible to have a general rule determining the level of care required.

[34] *De Jure Naturae et Gentium* (London, 1749), 5.4.3 (485 note 8, at 486) (not in earlier editions). 'In all Conventions and Contracts we must, without Dispute, have regard to the Intention of the Party chiefly concern'd; an Intention deduc'd from the Nature of the Affair itself, even tho' it should not be formally express'd.'

[35] He was familiar with the *De Jure Naturae et Gentium* in an edition with Barbeyrac's notes, which he cites at *Bailments*, [95]; but he might have used an edition earlier than that containing the discussion of Gundling.

[36] *The Principles of Moral and Political Philosophy* (London, 1785), 107-108. Paley's principle of objective interpretation was of central importance in facilitating the adoption of the Will Theory of contract into English law: D. J. Ibbetson, *A Historical Introduction to the Law of Obligations* (Oxford, 1999), 221.

gence' which he claimed had marred the law of ancient Rome.[37] Rather, he said, there was a continuum of standards, with ordinary care – the care which every prudent man takes of his own property – occupying the central position. To the one side of this there was more than ordinary care, to the other side less than ordinary care.[38] In stressing the continuum of standards of care, Jones explicitly drew the parallel with the infinite convergent series in mathematics, gradually tending towards a limit without ever reaching it;[39] mathematical analogies had been made before in Natural law contexts,[40] though it may be that Jones's use of it owed more to his father's work as a mathematician, especially his edition of Sir Isaac Newton's treatise on the subject, than from any study of the works of Leibniz, Weigel or Pufendorf.[41] He might perhaps have been satisfied to stop at that point, but instead concretised what more than and less than ordinary care meant: the care 'which a man remarkably exact and thoughtful gives to the securing of his personal property' and the care 'which every man of common sense, though absent and inattentive, applies to his property'.[42] By defining his terms so precisely Jones undermined any serious argument that there was a continuum; rather there was a trichotomy of standards of care, equivalent to the Roman trichotomy of standards of liability for *culpa lata*, *culpa levis*, and *culpa levissima*.[43] Nowhere, it should be remarked, does he consider alternative tests which had been proposed by other writers as constituting

[37] *Bailments*, [7]; *cf.* [5], [8]. Compare Kennet's translation of Pufendorf, *De Jure Naturae et Gentium*, 5.4.3 ('utmost diligence').
[38] *Bailments*, [8].
[39] He had used the same metaphor in a different context in the Preface of his *Introduction to the History and the Life of Nader Shah*: '[I]n every art and science there are certain ideas of perfection, to which the works of human genius are continually tending, though, like the Logarithmick Spiral, they will never meet the point to which they are infinitely approaching.' (*Works*, 12.323).
[40] Above, 26-27.
[41] *Analysis Per Quantitatum Series, Fluxiones, ac Differentias* (London, 1711). Jones had studied mathematics in order to edit his father's works, and may have had a hand in the preparation of two of his previously unpublished works in the Philosophical Transactions of the Royal Society: ('Of Logarithms' (1771) 61 *Phil. Trans*. 455; 'Properties of the Conic Sections; deduced by a Compendious Method' (1773) 63 *Phil. Trans*. 340): Cannon, *Life and Mind*, 56-57.
[42] *Bailments*, [5].
[43] *Bailments*, [9]. See below, 38-39.

Natural law. In his notes to Pufendorf, Jean Barbeyrac had referred to these differences of opinion when considering the liability of a mandatee, where some writers agreed with Pufendorf that he should be required to take the utmost care and others argued that he should only be required to show the same care as he habitually showed in the conduct of his own business; Barbeyrac himself took a middle line, saying that he should be required to take the utmost care of which he was himself capable.[44] Since Jones referred elsewhere to Barbeyrac's notes we may be sure that he had read them, and we might have expected him to be aware that these differences existed even if he had not dug deeply into the literature; but his understanding of Natural law was so strongly influenced by his understanding of Roman law[45] that there was no room for consideration of such unorthodox opinions.

Jones then proceeded to relate these standards of care to the different types of bailment, applying the standard of ordinary care to contracts which are beneficial to both parties, less than ordinary care to a bailee in a contract which is of benefit only to the bailor (such as a deposit for safe-keeping), and more than ordinary care to a bailee in a contract of benefit to him alone.[46] Exactly the same approach could be found in the works of Grotius and Pufendorf,[47] and it was said by Jones to follow as a matter of Natural law; but no explanation was given of why this should be so. The principle involved was, in fact, drawn straight from Roman law;[48] though, as Grotius had been at pains to emphasise, the fact that the Natural law rules were the same as Roman law did not necessarily entail that they had been derived from it.[49]

Jones did not follow Grotius's or Pufendorf's orthodoxy absolutely slavishly, but did give his own spin to the principles. This did not always constitute an improvement. Alongside the degrees of fault he brought into play the standards of good faith and honesty, for example. This was not problematic when he suggested that a very great fault was almost equiva-

[44] Note to *De Jure Naturae et Gentium*, 5.4.3.
[45] Itself a very conservative understanding: below, 38-39.
[46] *Bailments*, [13]-[15].
[47] *De Jure Belli ac Pacis*, 2.12 13; *De Jure Naturae et Gentium*, 5.4.3, 5.4.6, 5.4.7.
[48] Below, 38-39.
[49] *De Jure Belli ac Pacis*, 2.12.13.2, quoted by Jones at *Bailments*, [114]. Grotius pointed out that the same principles were found in Jewish law: M. Maimonides, *Doctor Perplexorum*, 3.42 (trans. Johannes Buxtorfius, Basle, 1629), 469.

lent to a breach of common honesty – the same idea had been found in Roman law, and it had been incorporated into the standard analysis of the seventeenth and eighteenth centuries[50] – but Jones went further than this, linking the failure to take care with the violation of good faith by interposing a supposition that the honest bailee was by nature ordinarily prudent.[51] This made sense in a purely Roman context, where liability in the *actio commodati*, *actio depositi* and *actio pigneratitia* was formally related to good faith, but when transplanted into the Natural law context it served merely to obfuscate the treatment of standards of care.

Nor was Jones's Natural law unalloyed; he was sensitive to what modern lawyers would call the policy dimension, though normally not to such an extent that pragmatic criteria would take precedence over moral conclusions. Hence the adoption of the relatively low standard of care of the gratuitous depositee, where the bailment benefited the bailor alone, was additionally justified by saying that few people would be willing to accept goods on the terms that they should be liable for anything more than gross neglect, to the general detriment of social existence.[52] So too in the reverse case, few people would be willing to lend their property to others for no reward unless the borrower was required to be more than ordinarily careful.[53] Sometimes, though, pragmatic considerations did come to the fore, as where Jones justified the strict liability imposed on common carriers on the grounds that they might otherwise be tempted to enter into conspiracies with vagabonds at the expense of their clients.[54]

Roman Law

By the middle of the eighteenth century the serious study of Roman law in England, in so far as it had ever existed, had largely died out. Perhaps the only work of any scholarly pretensions, John Ayliffe's *New Pan-*

[50] D.11.6.1.1 (Ulpian), D.16.3.32 (Celsus); Vinnius, *In Quatuor Libros Institutionum Imperialium Commentarius*, Inst 3.15, *de Commodato* (at p.548 in the Amsterdam 1703 edition).
[51] *Bailments*, [10]. A similar linkage had been made by Holt C.J. in *Coggs* v. *Barnard* (1703) 2 Lord Raym. 909, 919.
[52] *Bailments*, [14].
[53] *Bailments*, [15].
[54] *Bailments*, [137]-[138].

dect of the Roman Civil Law,[55] was substantially a failure, bringing to an uninterested and largely non-existent readership a knowledge of the Bartolist tradition of Roman law. Beyond this, there was little of greater intellectual depth than Thomas Wood's *New Institute of the Civil Law,*[56] or the dully competent works of Robert Eden and Samuel Hallifax,[57] neither of which added significantly to what could be read in Justinian's Institutes, the Commentary of Vinnius, or the various works of Johann Gottlieb Heineccius. Neither in Oxford nor in Cambridge were the Regius Professors remotely active in the study or teaching of law;[58] Jones's 'much-esteemed friend', Thomas Francis Wenman, Regius Professor at Oxford from 1789 to 1796, was more interested in natural history, meeting his death by drowning when in search of water-plants in the Cherwell.[59] A typical approach to Roman law was that of Thomas Bever, whose *Discourse on the Study of Jurisprudence and the Civil Law* had been derived from lectures given in Oxford in substitution for those which should have been given by the Regius Professor, Robert Jenner:[60]

> I shall point out to your observation those fundamental rules of natural justice and equity, which have been generally deemed the most essential to the well-being of man, in his social and civil capacity. As the chief of these are to be found in the writings of the ancient Roman lawyers, from whence they have been copied, with large improvements, by the most eminent civilians of subsequent ages, we usually call this branch of learning the civil law; though, in a general sense, it may more properly be named jurisprudence.[61]

[55] J. Ayliffe, *A New Pandect of the Roman Civil Law* (London, 1734); D. Coquillette, *The Civilian Writers of Doctors' Commons, London* (Berlin, 1988), 209-214.
[56] Thomas Wood, *New Institute of the Imperial or Civil Law* (London, 1704); R. B. Robinson, 'The Two Institutes of Thomas Wood: A Study in Eighteenth Century Legal Scholarship' (1991) 35 *American Journal of Legal History* 432.
[57] R. Eden, *Philologica Juridica* (Oxford, 1744); S. Hallifax, *An Analysis of the Roman Civil Law* (London, 1774). J. Taylor, *Elements of the Civil Law* (Cambridge, 1755), was less pedestrian, but was more a work of history than of law.
[58] Barton, 'Legal Studies', in Sutherland and Mitchell, eds., *History of the University of Oxford, Vol. 5*, 593-600; Searby, *History of the University of Cambridge, Vol. 3*, 187-189.
[59] *Oxford Dictionary of National Biography, sub. nom.* (W. P. Courtney, rev. M. J. Mercer); Jones, *Letters*, 362.
[60] Thomas Bever, *A Discourse on the Study of Jurisprudence and the Civil Law* (Oxford 1766); Barton, 'Legal Studies', 598.
[61] *Discourse on the Study of Jurisprudence and the Civil Law*, 2.

Against this background, Jones's *Essay on the Law of Bailments* stands out in two ways: the range of literature (all, almost inevitably, continental) which it cites; and its willingness to engage with both the Roman legal texts themselves and with the opinions of later civilian writers.

Jones's range of citations is impressive. Leaving aside the primary texts of Roman law, he makes reference to some twenty-five different commentators; by contrast, in his broadly comparable *Law of Pledges* the civilian John Ayliffe had in passing touched on no more than three.[62] We cannot, of course, assume from mere citation that Jones had actually read the texts to which he had referred. His list of writers who had discussed D.50.17.23, for example, was copied straight from Jacques Godefroy: Bocer, Campanus, D'Avezan, Del Rio, Le Conte, Rittershusius and Giphanius, to which Jones added Godefroy himself.[63] None the less, Jones does state that he had perused 'most of these', and evidence from elsewhere in the *Essay* points to his having used at least the works of Bocer, Campanus, D'Avezan, Del Rio, and Le Conte, as well as Godefroy himself.[64] These were all writers of the sixteenth or early seventeenth century, but there is substantial discussion of some more recent material: of the *Essai sur la Prestation des Fautes* of the French writer Denis Le Brun,[65] and more importantly of various works of Robert-Joseph Pothier, whom Jones introduced to the English legal audience.[66] Equally to the point is the sentiment underlying the *Advertisement* printed at the end of the Essay, making reference to the *De Usu Practico Doctrinae Difficillimae Juris Romani de Culparum Praestatione in Contractibus* of Christian Thomasius.[67] Jones had been informed of the existence of this work after he had completed the *Es*-

[62] John Ayliffe, *The Law of Pledges, or Pawns, as it was in Use among the Romans, and as it is now practiced in most Foreign Nations* (London, 1732). I have excluded Ayliffe's references to contemporary continental practice.
[63] *Bailments*, [25]; J. Godefroy (Gothofredus), *In Titulum Pandectarum De Diversis Regulis Iuris Antiqui Commentarius* (Geneva, 1652), 99.
[64] *Bailments*, [25], [27], [28], [29], [45], [101], [157].
[65] D. Le Brun, *Essai sur la Prestation des Fautes* (Paris, 1764).
[66] *Bailments*, [47]. Jones refers explicitly to the *Traité du Contrat de Mandat*, the *Traité du Contrat de Louage*, the *Traité du Prêt à Usage et du Précaire*, the *Traité du Contrat de Dépôt* and the *Traité du Contrat de Nantissement*. See below, 38-39, 52-53.
[67] *Bailments*, [129].

say,[68] but he had been unable to find a copy in Oxford, Cambridge or London, and a last-minute appeal to his friend Francis Hargrave had met with equally little success.[69] The slant of the work meant that it would have been, in all probability, of little value to Jones; but his scholarly concern to take into account views attributable to a highly respected continental writer is in marked contrast to the pedestrian approach of his contemporaries in England.

Most writers on Roman law in England had been willing simply to work with the texts as they stood; Jones went further. The first part of his discussion of Roman law involved the critical analysis of a text of Ulpian, D.50.17.23.[70] This was one of two main texts dealing generally with the standard of care demanded of a person holding property in a contractual or quasi-contractual relationship (the other, D.13.6.5.2, he discussed later). It listed two contracts, or more accurately relationships, in which the holder of the property was responsible only for *dolus*, deliberate wrongdoing. This was followed by a list of eight relationships in which liability was imposed for *dolus* and *culpa*, broadly translatable as 'blameworthy behaviour'. In its traditional form the text continued with the clause '*in his quidam et diligentiam*', but the Florentine manuscript, probably dating from the sixth century, gave a slightly different reading: '*in his quidem et diligentiam*'. The change of one letter, from *quidam* to *quidem*, was potentially important. The former would suggest that *diligentia* (taken by Jones to mean more than ordinary care[71]) was required in some of the preceding eight relationships, whereas the latter might mean that it was required in all eight of them. Jones gave a number of reasons for preferring the traditional reading of *quidam*, allowing a degree of flexibility in the determination of when the higher standard of care was demanded. Although his arguments are not wholly convincing,[72] and he did not consider the hint of Godefroy

[68] Jones should perhaps have known of the work earlier: above, 36.

[69] *Letters*, 475. The appeal was very last-minute: twelve days later he sent a newly printed copy of the work to Hargrave: *ibid.* There are now four copies of the work in the Bodleian Library, but they were not bought until the middle of the nineteenth century.

[70] *Bailments*, [23], [25]–[29].

[71] See below, 39.

[72] His linguistic argument (*Bailments*, [29]) that '*in his [contractibus]*' must mean 'among these [contracts]' is sound if the accusative *diligentiam* stands, since the

that the text might have been corrupted by the compilers,[73] his conclusion was orthodox if old-fashioned.[74] Whether he was right or wrong is not as important as the fact that he was willing to discuss the question at all. A similar willingness to look behind the wording of texts is seen in his discussion of the treatment of the liability of the *conductor* under a contract of *locatio conductio* in Justinian's Institutes 3.25(24).5, where the text refers to the care of a *diligentissimus*, or very diligent, *paterfamilias*, as opposed to that of a person of ordinary diligence as should be required according to the test propounded in D.13.6.5.2. Jones points out that the only jurist to make reference to the care of a *diligentissimus* person in this context was Gaius, and, supposing that Gaius was prone to use superlatives for emphasis rather than as a matter of substance, surmises that Justinian's text was derived from Gaius and should accordingly be interpreted as demanding no more than the ordinary standard of behaviour.[75] The conclusion that Gaius had a tendency to use extreme language was not original,[76] but, again, what is important is that the argument was made at all. A third example of the same critical stance can be seen in his analysis of D.13.7.13.1, where Ul-

verb *recipiunt* is demanded, and the only subject of this can be *contractus*. But if the reading is the nominative *diligentia*, which Jones says has some manuscript support, the point collapses. That the scholiast on the fourteenth-century *Hexabiblos* of Harmenopulus interpreted the text in the sense that only some of the preceding relationships demanded *diligentia* is of no real value; but the point (*Bailments*, [27]) that the compilers of the Greek *Basilica* seem to have used a text containing *quidem* is a telling point in the opposite direction. In substance, Jones's only real point is that D.50.17.23 is ambiguous and should be given an interpretation consistent with D.13.6.5.2; but this rather begs the question.

[73] Godefroy, *In Titulum Pandectarum De Diversis Regulis Iuris Antiqui Commentarius*, 141, addressing the apparent inconsistency between D.50.17.23 and D.13.6.5.2. See further V. Arangio-Ruiz, *Responsabilità Contrattuale in Diritto Romano* (Naples, 1933), 94-95.

[74] Godefroy, *In Titulum Pandectarum De Diversis Regulis Iuris Antiqui Commentarius*, 125-126 (though Godefroy himself would have disagreed).

[75] *Bailments*, [118], citing Gaius in D.19.2.25.7. But note that Jones raises no objection to D.13.6.18.pr, the only text in the Digest in which Gaius refers expressly to the standard of a *diligentissimus paterfamilias* (here in the context of *commodatum*, where Jones approved of the higher standard of care (*Bailments*, [93])).

[76] Godefroy, *In Titulum Pandectarum De Diversis Regulis Iuris Antiqui Commentarius*, 115-116; Le Brun, *Essai sur la Prestations des Fautes*, 93.

pian had appeared to say that the liability rule in pledge was the same as that in *commodatum*. Jones, following Pothier, rejected a conjectural emendation of Noodt, preferring to leave the text as it stood but to give it an interpretation – perhaps a plausible one – consistent with his theoretical approach.[77]

As well as looking behind the Roman texts themselves, Jones was willing to engage with the arguments of those who had written about them. He discussed and criticised, for example, Godefroy's departure from the so-called principle of utility of D.13.6.5.2;[78] he rejected the analysis of Donellus, who had denied the independent status of very slight negligence, *culpa levissima*;[79] and throughout the *Essay* he excoriated the views of the French scholar Denis Le Brun,[80] preferring to adopt the more orthodox views of Pothier. The balance of arguments, once more, was probably against Jones,[81] but it was his willingness to consider them at all which set him apart from his contemporaries in England.

Despite his openness to critical analysis, Jones's Roman law was highly orthodox. More precisely, it was heavily based on the self-consciously conservative approach taken by Pothier in his *Traité des Obligations* and reiterated in his *Observation Générale sur le Précédent Traité et les Suivans*, originally published as an appendix to his *Traité du Contrat de Mariage*[82] but thereafter associated with the *Traité des Obligations*.[83] His starting point, like Pothier's, was what has come to be known as the principle of utility, based on D.13.6.5.2-3.[84] Where one person's thing was

[77] *Bailments*, [108]; Pothier, *Traité du Contrat de Nantissement*, s.34.
[78] *Bailments*, [39]-[41].
[79] *Bailments*, [42].
[80] *Bailments*, [45]-[46]; and *passim*.
[81] There was a good deal of contemporary opposition to the independent standard of *culpa levissima*, for example: H.-J. Hoffmann, *Die Abstufung der Fahrlässigkeit in der Rechtsgeschichte* (Berlin, 1968), 123-129.
[82] Pothier, *Traité du Contrat de Mariage* (Orléans, 1768), Appendix to vol. 2.
[83] Reference hereafter is made to *Oeuvres de R.-J. Pothier* (Brussels, 1831).
[84] *Bailments*, [24]; Pothier, *Traité des Obligations*, s.142. Whether D.13.6.5.2-3, and the whole theory of utility, is classical has been doubted by some scholars (D. Nörr, 'Die Entwicklung des Utilitätsgedankens im Römischen Haftungsrecht' (1956) 73 *Zeitschrift der Savigny Stiftung für Rechtsgeschichte (Romanistische Abteilung)* 68, 73, 103-106, with further references), but this was not something which concerned Jones.

held under a contract which was for the sole benefit of the person handing over the property, as was the case in the contract of deposit, then the holder was liable only for *dolus*, deliberate wrongdoing (glossed elsewhere to include *culpa lata*, grave fault). Where the contract was for the benefit of both parties, the holder was liable for *dolus* and *culpa*; and when the contract was for the sole benefit of the holder that person was responsible also for *diligentia*, which could be interpreted as any slight fault (elsewhere referred to as *culpa levissima*) and which was translated by Jones as 'the omission of more than ordinary diligence'. Such a threefold division of standards of responsibility, and their mapping onto three different classes of contract, was utterly orthodox; so too were the equation of *culpa lata* to *dolus* and its definition as the omission of that care which even inattentive and thoughtless men never fail to take of their own property, the explanation of the ordinary standard of *culpa* in terms of the care which the generality of people take in their own affairs, and the framing of the lowest level of neglect, *culpa levissima*, as the failure to take the care that very attentive and vigilant people take of their own goods.[85] All of this was to be found in Pothier; Jones's treatment, in fact, is an almost word-for-word translation of Pothier's restatement of his position in the *Observation Générale*.[86] Nonetheless, however traditional this basis was, it raised difficulties both of textual interpretation and of analysis.

So far as textual problems were concerned, most of these were resolved by ignoring or side-stepping them. In Jones's scheme, for example, a person holding property under a contract of partnership should be liable for ordinary negligence. This was supported by Roman texts.[87] One text, though, suggested that it was not the care of an ordinary person that mattered, but the care that the individual was accustomed to take in his own concerns; in essence, that there was a subjective rather than an objective standard.[88] Partnership was not the only contract in which there were hints

[85] *Bailments*, [31], [32], [33].

[86] Pothier, *Observation Générale* (*Oeuvres*, 1.280). For Jones's close reliance on Pothier, see further below, 52-53. His echoing of Bynkershoek, that he 'had leisure sometimes to write, but never to copy' (*Bailments*, [155]), is rather piquant in the circumstances.

[87] D.17.2.36, 52.2, PS. 2.16.1; as well as Jones's principal texts, D.13.6.5.2 and D.50.17.23.

[88] D.17.2.72.

of such a subjective standard: it was referred to in deposit too, as well as in guardianship, dowry and joint ownership.[89] Jones passed over all of these. He did, it is true, touch on the possible relevance of the holder of the property being habitually either more or less careful than the norm,[90] but redefined the issue in terms of either the lender's knowledge or the holder's deceit[91] rather than facing squarely up to the tension between objective and subjective standards in the texts. Equally problematic was the supposition that *diligentia*, in D.13.6.5.2 and D.50.17.23, necessarily connoted the taking of more than ordinary care.[92] Although this was the orthodox understanding in the eighteenth century, it is not the natural reading of either text: *diligentia*, standing alone, might refer to the taking of care, but it requires further analysis to focus it onto any specific standard.[93] Jones's interpretation again reveals his uncritical adoption of the commonly held position, glossing over any textual difficulties arising out of it.

Analytically, it is in the friction between *culpa* and *custodia* that Jones's lack of sure-footedness is most clearly visible. In some of the Roman texts dealing with contracts in which liability should arise only for ordinary blameworthiness it was said that the holder should be liable for the seemingly stricter standard of *custodia*, i.e. that he should be liable if the property was stolen, though not if it was taken by robbers or lost through some other situation of *vis maior*.[94] This form of apparently strict liability created a clear potential for conflict with the fault-based principle of utility in D.13.6.5.2, but Jones ignored it. When he did refer to texts pointing to

[89] D.16.3.32, D.27.3.1.pr, D.23.3.17.pr, D.10.2.25.16. On the problematic nature of the texts imposing a subjective standard, see H. Hausmaninger, '*Diligentia Quam in Suis*: A Standard of Contractual Liability from Ancient Roman to Modern Soviet Law' (1985) 18 *Cornell International Law Journal* 179, 183-188; R. Zimmermann, *The Law of Obligation: Roman Foundations of the Civilian Tradition* (Cape Town, 1990), 210-212, 462-464, with further references.
[90] *Bailments*, [66] (deposit), [112] (pledge).
[91] The same connection between deceit and failing to look after the other's property as one's own is found in D.16.3.32, but the implications are not worked out.
[92] Above, 39.
[93] P. Voci, ''Diligentia', 'Custodia', 'Culpa'. I Dati Fondamentali' (1990) 56 *Studia et Documenta Historiae et Iuris* 29, 33-40.
[94] Zimmermann, *Obligations*, 193-195, with further references. For a careful analysis of the theories, see G. MacCormack, 'Custodia and Culpa' (1972) 89 *Zeitschrift der Savigny-Stiftung für Rechtsgeschichte (Romanistische Abteilung)* 149.

custodia liability, he seems simply to have assumed – following the orthodoxy of the time – that they were consistent with his principles since in allowing that the holder should be exonerated if the property had been taken or destroyed by robbery or other superior force they were implicitly applying the rule that a person who was not at fault should not be liable.[95] But the equivalence of the two approaches was by no means obvious: a holder might take the care of a reasonable person but still be the victim of theft.[96]

English Law

For all its demonstration of erudition in Roman law and other legal systems, the *Essay on the Law of Bailments* was meant to be a work of English law. Its purpose was, according to Jones himself, to fill a gap left by Blackstone, whose *Commentaries* had dealt with the topic in too cursory a manner;[97] and when he was subsequently to sketch out the plan of his life's work – whiling away his time on the long voyage to India in 1783 – one of the elements of this was a series of monographs on aspects of the law of England modelled on the *Law of Bailments*.[98] It is not surprising, then, that the section on English law forms the most substantial part of the book.

Underpinning the whole discussion is the supposition that, in its fundamentals, the English law on the subject was the same as the Roman. In a letter written seven years after the *Essay* he hinted that the similarities between the two systems stemmed from the fact that much of the Common law was derived from the law of Justinian, though English lawyers were in general too timid to acknowledge it,[99] but such a historical interpretation was very much a product of Jones's experience in India.[100] So far as the

[95] *Cf. Bailments*, [111]. For English law, see the discussion beginning immediately below.

[96] See in particular D.47.2.14.12, which seems to envisage situations in which the theft might have occurred without the fault of the borrower. J. Story, *Commentaries on the Law of Bailments* (London, 1839), 27-28, points out the weakness of Jones's assumption.

[97] *Bailments*, [2]; Blackstone, *Commentaries*, 2.452, 453, 454.

[98] 'Objects of Enquiry during my residence in Asia', in *Works*, 2.3-4 at 4.

[99] *Letters*, 796.

[100] D. J. Ibbetson, 'Sir William Jones and the Nature of Law', in A. Burrows and Lord Rodger, eds., *Mapping the Law: Essays in Memory of Peter Birks* (Oxford, 2006), 619.

Essay was concerned the reason for their (supposed) similarity was that both were substantially congruent with the Law of Nature. This is the basis of the structure of the work, moving from Natural law in the opening 'analytical' section to the laws of 'nations most eminent for legal wisdom'[101] in the 'historical' section.[102] It followed too, as Jones put it, that although Roman law had no formal authority in Westminster Hall, when 'rational law' was in issue resort might be had to the wisdom of ancient jurists: 'What is good sense, in one age, must be good sense, all circumstances remaining, in another; and pure unsophisticated reason is the same in Italy and in England, in the mind of a Papinian and of a Blackstone.'[103] Furthermore, at several places this assumption was incorporated into his reasoning on specific rules of Common law: some conclusion must be true, for otherwise English law would not be in harmony with the rational system which he had formulated or with the consent of nations.[104]

On a straightforward reading of the Common law of the late eighteenth century, many of the concrete rules which Jones identified might be thought to have been uncontroversially correct. The level of care required of different classes of bailee had been elucidated by Holt C.J. in the leading case of *Coggs* v. *Barnard*;[105] and since Holt's reasoning was substantially rooted in Roman law, taken directly from Justinian's Institutes or indirectly through Bracton, his rules were more or less in tune with the Romanised 'rational' principles which Jones had already identified in the *Essay*. Jones himself said that his work might be seen as a commentary on *Coggs* v. *Barnard*,[106] and it would have been very easy for him simply to have used this case as the source of the rules of English law. It is significant that he did not do so. Central to his conception of the Common law was that it rep-

[101] *Bailments*, [17], [60], [146].
[102] Above, 27-28.
[103] *Bailments*, [20].
[104] See for example *Bailments*, [109], [117], [146].
[105] (1703) 2 Lord Raym. 909, 3 Lord Raym. 163, 1 Com. 133, 1 Salk. 26, 2 Salk. 735, 3 Salk. 11, 3 Salk. 268, Holt K.B. 13, Holt K.B. 131, Holt 528. The main report, the one explicitly cited by Jones, is 2 Lord Raym. 909. See further below, 95-103.
[106] *Bailments*, [86]. The judgment in *Coggs* v. *Barnard* was to be printed as an appendix to the second and subsequent editions of the *Law of Bailments*.

resented the accrued wisdom of the ages,[107] and just as he had downplayed the role of statutes in the *Inquiry into the Legal Mode of Suppressing Riots* so in the *Essay* he would stress the essential continuity of the Common law rather than the authority of any recent decision. Paradoxically, in harking back to the law of Bracton and the Year Books he was displaying a fundamentally unhistorical approach to the Common law, in so far as he was effectively denying that it might have changed over time.

Jones's approach to the subject was to sub-divide bailment into different forms, and then to examine the rules applicable to each form. In this he followed Holt C.J. in *Coggs* v. *Barnard*, though his sub-divisions were not identical to Holt's: Deposit, or *Depositum*; Commission, or *Mandatum*; Loan for Use, or *Commodatum*; Pledge, or *Pignori Acceptum*; and Hire, *Locatum* (further sub-divided into *locatio rei* (hire of a thing), *locatio operis faciendi* (handing over a thing for work to be done on it), and *locatio operis mercium vehendarum* (carriage of goods)).[108] Transparently, Roman law was his starting point, emphasised by his insistence on giving the Latin names as well as the English. It was not, however, absolutely pure Roman law, nor even Roman law as it had been interpreted by the mediaeval and post-mediaeval commentators and as it had crystallised in the works of Pothier: they had not, for example, drawn any distinction between the carriage of goods and other forms of *locatio*. It is revealing that Jones chose to introduce this distinction, visible but substantially played down in *Coggs* v. *Barnard*, for as a matter of English law it was contracts of carriage which had generated the most difficulty, and it was not at all obvious that the rules applied to it were the same as the rules applied more generally to bailments for work to be done.[109]

However rational it might have been to sub-divide the subject in this way, it is not something that had been done as a matter of formal law before *Coggs* v. *Barnard*; nor had the English case-law been framed around different standards of care.[110] In so far as discussions along these lines did exist, they were to be found in discursive works drawing on the Roman law

[107] Above, 20-21.

[108] *Bailments*, [56]. Holt C.J. had treated *locatio rei* and *locatio operis* as different types rather than sub-forms of the same contract, and had not distinguished carriage from *locatio operis*.

[109] Below, 92-94.

[110] Below, 79-85, 87-94.

tradition, in particular Bracton and Christopher St. German's *Doctor and Student*.[111] Jones made full use of these to structure his treatment of the Common law, preferring them over the more purely English writings of Edward Coke or Henry Finch.[112] As a result he tended to misrepresent the historical dimension of the Common law, moving it in a direction more in harmony with the rules of Roman law which he had already elucidated. Moreover, in squeezing the cases into this framework, which cannot but have been alien to them, he repeatedly had to re-interpret the substance of their arguments.

Jones's approach to English material is well illustrated by his treatment of the first type of bailment with which he dealt, the contract of deposit, *i.e.* a gratuitous bailment for safe-keeping.[113] His starting-point was *Bowdon* v. *Pelleter*, *Bonion's Case*, as reported in the Vulgate Year Book and in Fitzherbert's *Abridgment*, a case in which goods allegedly bailed to the defendant in a locked box had been stolen.[114] The plaintiff denied that the box had been locked, and issue was joined. It was not obvious why it mattered whether the box was locked or not, but it had been explained away in Coke's report of *Southcote's Case* on the basis that a depositor who had locked the box and taken away the key (if this was the case) would have demonstrated thereby that he did not trust the depositee with the goods.[115] Holt C.J. had taken a more robust view, saying simply that the fact that it was in a box should not have made any difference.[116] Jones's approach to the problem of the case was to refer to a dispute between the Roman jurists Trebatius and Labeo.[117] Trebatius had said that where goods were deposited in a sealed chest the depositor might only bring an *actio depositi* for the chest and its contents, whereas Labeo had argued that an *actio depositi* might be brought claiming the contents alone. As Jones realised, this dispute related purely to the formal question of how the Roman

[111] Below, 76-79, 85-87.
[112] Co. Litt. 89; H. Finch, *Law, or a Discourse Thereof* (London, 1627), 2.18.
[113] *Bailments*, [57]-[77]. For what follows I draw heavily on my 'Sir William Jones and the Nature of Law', in Burrows and Rodger, eds., *Mapping the Law*, 619, 626-631.
[114] YB P. 8 Edw. II f 275; Fitz. Abr., *Detinue*, 59 (1315). Below, 80.
[115] *Southcote* v. *Bennet* (1601) 4 Co Rep 83b, 84.
[116] *Coggs* v. *Barnard* (1703) 2 Lord Raym. 909, 914.
[117] D.16.3.1.41.

actio depositi ought to be framed and had absolutely nothing to do with the circumstances in which the depositee ought to be liable for the loss;[118] but, he said, it might make a difference to the standard of care demanded of the depositee if the chest was sealed and he did not know what it contained, for a person who knew that he had a box of valuable jewels might be required to exercise greater care in their custody, so that he might be found guilty of gross negligence where one who thought he had only relatively worthless items would not be. According to Jones, this was the interpretation put on the text by Jean Domat in the late seventeenth century,[119] though it is impossible to see how such a meaning could be wrung out of Domat's text. The authority of *Bonion's Case* was thus weakened, so much so that it could be dismissed as incomprehensible. The rule of reason was that where there was a gratuitous deposit the bailee should be liable only for *culpa lata*, gross neglect. Since the goods had been taken by burglars it could not be said – in Jones's view – that the depositee had been guilty of this, and hence she should not have been liable.

That gross negligence was necessary, it was said, had been decided in the next significant case, a Year Book case of 1355.[120] In truth, though, neither the Year Book nor Brooke's *Abridgment* had made any mention at all of gross neglect, saying simply that a bailee should not be liable if the bailed goods were stolen if his own goods had been stolen at the same time. The version of the report in Fitzherbert's *Abridgment*,[121] it was said, showed the defendant being driven to the issue whether the goods had been taken by robbery (rather, that is, than by simple theft); but there is not the slightest warrant for this in Fitzherbert's text, which is to all intents and purposes identical to that of the Year Book and Brooke.

Jones then turned to the form of the rule in Coke's *Commentary on Littleton*, reflecting the decision of the Court of King's Bench in *Southcote*

[118] *Bailments*, [58]. The issue would have arisen where some single item had been taken from the chest. *Cf.* D.47.2.21.pr-21.8, referring at 21.pr to a similar approach of Trebatius.

[119] J. Domat, *Les Loix Civiles dans leur Ordre Naturel* (Paris, 1689), 1.7.1.17. Jones appears to have used a French edition rather than the English translation published in 1722.

[120] YB 29 Lib. Ass. f.163 pl. 28; Bro. Abr., *Bailment*, 7.

[121] Fitz. Abr., *Barre*, 304.

v. *Bennet* as reported by Coke.[122] For him, the depositee was liable if the goods were stolen unless he had received them explicitly to look after as he looked after his own goods. This, said Jones, was wrong for three reasons: it was repugnant to natural reason and the laws of other nations; it was based upon chance remarks in the Year Books, 'broken cases' and 'mere conversations on the bench'; and *Southcote's Case* did not itself justify the rule which Coke had derived from it.[123] Neither the second nor the third reason has much substance to it. As a matter of history, probably, Coke's interpretation of the case was correct, and at the very least it was plausible;[124] and the dismissal of the Year Book evidence as 'mere conversations on the bench' was rather too obviously a glib means to get round inconvenient case-law. The only real justification for the rejection of Coke's version of the rule was the first one, that it was contrary to natural reason and the law elsewhere. But since the whole point of Jones's argument was to show that the Common law was like other developed legal systems and consistent with reason, the rejection of Coke's position simply on the grounds that it was contrary to reason was quite perfectly circular. Transparently, the demonstration that as a matter of English law the liability of the depositee was limited to cases of gross negligence was very flimsy, grounded on little more than an assertion that this was what natural reason demanded. Case-law to the contrary, even principles associated with an authority as high as Sir Edward Coke, were padded away with a veneer of learning but with almost nothing at all which could pass muster as a serious argument.

No less circular was the continuation of his argument, that the general rule of liability for gross negligence was qualified by a number of exceptions.[125] The parties might agree that some other standard should apply; the bailee might have thrust himself forward in such a way that he had prevented the owner entrusting the goods to someone more careful; the bailee,

[122] 4 Co. Rep. 83b; Co. Litt. 89. See below, 89-92.
[123] *Bailments*, [60]-[64]. Holt C.J. had made a similar criticism of *Southcote* v. *Bennet*: (1703) 2 Lord Raym. 909, 913. But for him the case represented a 'great authority against me', which had to be avoided; once *Coggs* v. *Barnard* had been decided the authority of *Southcote* v. *Bennet* was enormously weakened, and there was no necessity for Jones to make the similar argument.
[124] Below, 90-91.
[125] *Bailments*, [67]-[74].

although commonly called a depositee, might have received something for his pains and so not be a depositee in the eyes of the law; and the bailment might have been made on the basis that the property would be used by the bailee if some appropriate occasion arose.[126] Only the first of these was demonstrably correct as a matter of English law, though it is noteworthy that the primary support for it was found in the Digest, and the English reference was *Doctor and Student* rather than any of the many cases found in the books. The second was once more derived from the Digest, and however plausible it was within the framework which Jones had adopted it could not be shown to represent the law of England. The third and fourth could be justified as a matter of logic; provided, that is, that one accepted the sub-divisions of bailments used by him.

Only at one point in the discussion did Jones address the dominant strand in the English case-law, the suggestion that the bailee should be required to take the same care as he did in looking after his own property.[127] Without referring to any of the English material, the test was dismissed as a general principle: the fact that the depositee might have been habitually careful would be no reason to make him liable for anything more than gross neglect. The converse, though, did not hold. In a concession towards this subjective standard, it was said, quoting Bracton and Justinian, that if the bailee was normally very neglectful of his own concerns, the bailor could not complain if the same care was taken of the bailed goods too.

If the section on deposit was heavily Romanised, that on *commodatum*, the loan for use, was even more so.[128] Jones prefaced his remarks with the statement that English law and Roman law were 'perfectly coincident' on the subject, imposing liability for the slightest negligence, but he gave no demonstration of this equivalence beyond referring to Bracton and *Doctor and Student*, as quoted in *Coggs* v. *Barnard*. The working out of the theme involved a reassertion of the rule, dismissing the opinions of those

[126] One can only marvel at the example given of the last of these (*Bailments*, [73]), George's going into the country and depositing with Charles a dress and jewellery, to be worn by Charles should there be a masked ball before George returned to town. For the context, see (from rather different standpoints) P. Ackroyd, *Dressing Up* (London, 1979), 57-60, and A. Ribeiro, *Dress in Eighteenth-Century Europe* (New Haven, 2002), 245-282.
[127] *Bailments*, [66]. See below, 80, 84-85.
[128] *Bailments*, [93]-[105].

continental writers who had argued for something different. Pufendorf, and following him Barbeyrac, had been guilty of 'much idle reasoning, which I am not idle enough to transcribe' in suggesting that the bailee might be liable without fault if the bailed goods were destroyed while the bailee's own property was left unscathed; Pothier, it was said, had shown the good sense of the orthodox analysis.[129] The bailee would not normally be liable if robbed of the goods, though in *Doctor and Student* Christopher St. German had made the point that even in this case liability would arise if the borrower had been foolish enough to leave the high road and pass through a dark thicket; this was plausible, but St. German's example had been (as Jones recognised) drawn from the Canonist *Summa Rosella* and was therefore hardly an independent testimony to the rule of English law.[130]

The same dependence on Roman law is found in his discussions of pledge and hire, *locatio conductio rei.*[131] 'Natural reason' and 'the wisdom of nations' dictated that a pledgee should be liable for the failure to take reasonable care; such was the rule found in Bracton,[132] and although this was copied straight out of Justinian's Institutes 3.14.4 it was said that it must be taken as representing English law, for it was Bracton's practice only to reproduce Roman law when English law was in conformity with it.[133] No basis is given for this supposition, in its nature incapable of proof since Jones's picture of the law of the thirteenth century was derived exclusively from Bracton itself. His approach to hire was similarly dependent on Roman law, beginning with the question-begging statement that 'the harmonious consent of nations will be interrupted, and one object of this essay defeated, if the laws of England shall be found, on a fair inquiry, to demand of the hirer a more than ordinary degree of diligence.'[134] This was not, though, the commonly held view of English law. Holt C.J., in *Coggs* v. *Barnard*, and Francis Buller, in his *Introduction to the Law of Trials at Nisi Prius*, had stated the rule as being that the hirer should take the greatest possible care, the same standard as was required of a gratuitous borrower. This was the form of the rule found in Bracton, whose requirement of the

[129] *Bailments*, [95].
[130] *Bailments*, [96].
[131] *Bailments*, [106]-[115], [117]-[121].
[132] *Bracton* f 99b (ed. Thorne, 2.284).
[133] *Bailments*, [107].
[134] *Bailments*, [117]-[119].

standard of care of a *diligentissimus paterfamilias* was derived directly from Justinian's Institutes and through them traceable back to Gaius, who was, it was said, prone to the use of unnecessary superlatives.[135] Better, according to Jones, was the version of the text found in Theophilus's Paraphrase of the Institutes,[136] where only ordinary diligence was required. So interpreted, English and Roman law were in harmony with the book of Exodus, where a clear distinction was drawn between hiring and borrowing.[137]

Jones's approach to English case-law was as fragile in these sections as in his treatment of deposit. In the context of pledge, a Year Book case of 1355 seemed to have adopted a different liability rule than that which was dictated by 'natural reason', treating a pledgee as not liable if his own goods were taken as well as those of the pledgor.[138] Had this been right, Jones said, it would have destroyed the harmony of his system. Therefore he asserted that it was wrong, citing statements from Bracton, *Doctor and Student*, and a dictum of Holt C.J. in *Coggs* v. *Barnard* – all of them, it should be noted, sources which were heavily dependent on the rules of Roman law out of which he had fashioned his analytical conclusions. In any event, he said, the 1355 case was not a simple case of theft at all, but a case of violent robbery, as was 'confirmed beyond any doubt' by the side-note in Brooke's abridgment of the case, 'Who shall bear the loss when the goods are robbed'.[139] But no reason is given why weight should be placed on Brooke, writing some two centuries after the case had been decided, rather than on the words of the Year Book report itself. The sparseness of his argument in dealing with the case contrasts markedly with Jones's robust defence of his position against Coke's explanation of the subjective test of liability.[140] Coke had justified it on the basis that the pledgee had 'a property' in the goods;[141] but, as Jones pointed out, every bailee had a

[135] Above, 37.
[136] Theophilus, *Paraphrasis*, 3.24.5 (ed. E. C. Ferrini, Berlin, 1897, 359).
[137] *Bailments*, [118]. Jones's squeezing of both English and Roman law into his preconceived framework was early criticised: 'Law School at Cambridge' (1833) 36 (59) *North American Review* 395, 408-411.
[138] YB 29 Lib. Ass. 28; *Bailments*, [109].
[139] Bro. Abr., *Bailment* 7.
[140] *Bailments*, [111]-[112].
[141] Co. Litt. 89a.

qualified property, so there was no basis for treating the pledgee in any way differently from the norm.

In stark contrast to the strongly Romanised orientation of these, Jones's other sections are rather more sharply focused on English law. These concern the carriage of goods or the doing of work on them either for payment (primarily identified with *locatio conductio operis*) or gratuitously (mandate, or commission),[142] and it can hardly be coincidental that these were the two situations with which the English case-law had been most occupied.[143]

Jones's section on *locatio conductio operis* is substantially based on English case-law. None the less, it has a strong Roman flavour, reflecting the way in which the English cases had gradually been realigned into a framework which was substantially consistent with Roman law. On the face of it, the rules of the two systems were very different. Roman law had made the *conductor* liable for failing to take ordinary (or perhaps extraordinary) care of the goods, whereas the English cases had imposed on him strict liability subject to defences of act of God, act of the bailor, and the act of third parties against whom the bailee could have no remedy.[144] In practice these invariably led to the same results except where the goods had been taken by robbers: Roman law exonerated the bailee in such a case, English law did not. Jones massaged the two systems more into line with each other by effectively limiting the English rule of liability for robbery to cases where the defendant was an innkeeper or common carrier (following the distinction which had been drawn by Holt C.J. in *Coggs* v. *Barnard*),[145] and only referring in passing to the earlier English cases which had made all bailees for reward liable if the goods were lost to robbers.[146] Jones recognised that this meant there were situations where English law imposed a harsher rule than did Roman law, but he attributed this to considerations of public policy, on the basis that there was a risk that professional carriers

[142] *Bailments*, [122]-[146], [78]-[92].
[143] Below, 79-85, 87-94.
[144] Above, 37; below, 81-85.
[145] 2 Lord Raym. 909, 918.
[146] *Bailments*, [138]. English law had begun with the general rule applicable to bailees for reward, which rule had been extended to common carriers on the assumption that they were not acting gratuitously: below, 92-93.

and inn-keepers might otherwise be tempted to enter into confederacies with malefactors.[147]

The most difficult form of bailment for Jones was the gratuitous commission, the Romans' mandate, for it was here that the English and Roman rules were most discordant. In line with the general principle of utility, the Romans had made the mandatary liable only for deliberate wrongdoing or gross negligence, *dolus* or *culpa lata*, on the basis that the contract was not for his benefit but for that of the mandator.[148] English law had taken a different approach: from the 1360s, cases of this type would have fallen straightforwardly within trespass on the case, and so liability would have been imposed for fault.[149] Following a hint in Lord Raymond's report of *Coggs* v. *Barnard*,[150] and a more explicit statement from Pothier which had been picked up earlier in the *Essay*,[151] Jones argued rather tortuously that an undertaking to do some task committed the undertaker to do all that he could to achieve the goal, so that the failure to take the care appropriate to it constituted a breach of good faith, *dolus*.[152] This was sufficient to bring *Coggs* v. *Barnard* itself, together with the earlier examples of actions on the case, into line with the abstract Romanised framework imposed by Jones. But in places, as with *locatio conductio operis*, the fit with English law was not quite perfect. The logic of his argument allowed no distinction to be drawn between cases of non-performance and cases of misperformance, leading him to adopt a tendentious reading of Year Book cases where such a distinction had been taken[153] – once again failing to take a historicist line that the law had simply changed since these cases were decided – and to ignore the theoretical problems of drawing the line between 'tortious' and 'contractual' claims in assumpsit which underlay the argu-

[147] *Bailments*, [137].
[148] Above, 38-39.
[149] Below, 82.
[150] Below, 101.
[151] *Bailments*, [35]; Pothier, *Observation Générale* (*Oeuvres*, 1.280); *Traité du Contrat de Dépôt*, s.71; *Traité du Contrat de Mandat*, s.46.
[152] *Bailments*, [78]. Pothier, by contrast, had treated this as an exception to the general principle: *Traité du Contrat de Mandat*, s.46.
[153] *Bailments*, [80]-[82], discussing YB M. 11 Hen. IV f.33 pl. 60 and YB H. 3 Hen. VI f.36 pl.33.

ments in *Coggs* v. *Barnard*.[154] Moreover, since all depended on the requirement of taking care appropriate to the commission, it followed that not all cases would require the mandatary to take care: gratuitous bailments to carry, it was said, would fall under the general rule that the bailee would not be liable for less than gross neglect.[155]

Behind all of the discussion of English law, and especially the Romanised sections, there looms the work of Pothier, whom Jones claimed proudly – and probably rightly – to have brought to the attention of English lawyers. The greatest part of what he had written, it was said, was as much law at Westminster as it was in Orleans;[156] and the sections of the *Essay* dealing with the English rules of *commodatum*, deposit and mandate were very heavily dependent on the way in which Pothier had dealt with those subjects in his treatises. This is most clear in the pages dealing with *commodatum*, which might almost be seen as a précis of the part of Pothier's *Traité du Prêt à Usage* concerned with the liability of the borrower. It is, perhaps, worth examining the parallels in some detail in order to see exactly how far Jones's borrowing went.

Jones's treatment begins at paragraph [93]. After a brief introduction, it is said that the principle of D.13.6.5.2 requires that there should be liability for *culpa levissima*; and while it is no defence that it was impossible for the bailee personally to reach such a standard, the fact that the bailee was, to the knowledge of the bailor, of such an age and quality that the highest level of care could not be expected of him would be taken into account in determining what the appropriate level of care was. Exactly the same points are made, in exactly the same order, in sections 48 and 49 of the *Traité du Prêt à Usage*. Moreover, Jones's citation of Charles Dumoulin's *De eo quod Interest* is precisely the same as that of Pothier. Paragraph [94] is based on Pothier's sections 53 and 54, the blind citation of D.13.6.20 being taken out of the middle of s.53. Paragraph [95] is little more than an abbreviation of Pothier's long s.55, Jones being 'not idle enough to transcribe' the reasoning of Pufendorf which is given by Pothier *in extenso*. Paragraph [96] begins with a clause taken from slightly earlier in Pothier's s.55, before moving off in a different direction with a discussion drawn from the *Summa Rosella*. Paragraph [97] returns to Pothier, continuing where he had

[154] Below, 95-96.
[155] *Bailments*, [90].
[156] *Bailments*, [47].

left off before the digression into the *Summa Rosella*. Paragraph [98] parallels Pothier's s.56, with a brief introductory clause taken from s.61. Paragraph [99] is taken directly from s.59, paragraph [100] from s.60, paragraph [101] from ss.62 and 63, the end of Pothier's discussion of the subject. Jones, though, continues, moving back to an earlier point in Pothier's *Traité*, with paragraphs [102] and [103] deriving from sections 50, 51, and 52. Ignoring Jones's final two paragraphs, containing references to Mosaic and Greek law, the whole of his analysis of *commodatum* in English law, apart from a few introductory lines and the half-paragraph based on the *Summa Rosella*, is effectively lifted from Pothier's pages.

Commodatum is, admittedly, an extreme example of Jones's reliance on Pothier, though clearly the sections on deposit and mandate too are strongly influenced by him. Pothier's discussion of the basic liability of the depositee in his *Traité du Contrat de Dépôt* is substantially condensed into one paragraph by Jones;[157] and Pothier's four exceptions to this general principle are then reproduced with only a minimal intertwining of English law.[158] The section on mandate begins with a substantially derivative paragraph,[159] but after this it is almost wholly focused on English materials. The later sections, on pledge and *locatio conductio* are even less dependent on Pothier, with only occasional bits being carried across into Jones's text.[160] None the less, even in these sections the influence of Pothier is very substantial, in so far as he provided the channel through which Jones's almost unquestioning adoption of the Roman principle of utility was obtained.[161]

Legal Science in the Essay on the Law of Bailments

> [I]f law be a science, and really deserve so sublime a name, it must be founded on principle, and claim an exalted rank in the empire of reason; but, if it be merely an unconnected series of decrees and ordinances, its use may remain, though its dignity be lessened, and He will become the greatest lawyer, who has the strongest habitual, or artificial, memory.[162]

[157] *Bailments*, [66]; *Traité du Contrat de Dépôt*, ss.23-29.
[158] *Bailments*, [68]-[73]; *Traité du Contrat de Dépôt*, ss.30-32.
[159] *Bailments*, [78]; *Traité du Contrat de Mandat*, ss.46-49.
[160] *Bailments*, [108], [111]; *Traité du Contrat de Nantissement*, ss.34, 35. *Bailments*, [120], [121]; *Traité du Contrat de Louage*, ss.190, 193.
[161] Above, 38-39.
[162] *Bailments*, [202].

At the very least, Jones's notion that the law was scientific meant that it had a substantial measure of principled coherence. Such a view of law would have been common in the late eighteenth century, and it is almost inevitably held by any writer committed to the exegesis of legal doctrine.[163] Classical Roman law had got fairly close to satisfying this scientific ideal, in as much as the juristic writers up to the early third century AD had worked largely by a process of analysis of a fixed set of legal forms found in the Praetors' Edict or by deduction from a small set of more or less uncontroversial norms. English law, though, was less susceptible to such scientific analysis, given the volume of legislation and other authoritative sources which were incorporated within it. Unless, by some happy chance, these determinate legal facts were consistent with the assumed normative framework, internal contradictions within the system were unavoidable.

In his *Commentaries*, Blackstone had faced up to the problem of the tension between reason and authority half a generation before Jones. Although paying lip-service to reason, in practice it was authority which won out: despite the fact that his work was underpinned by Natural law theory and was constructed around an analytical framework grounded in Natural law, when it came to describing the rules of the Common law his approach was almost wholly empirical.[164] With Jones the balance was reversed. He was well aware of this tension and explicitly recognised the importance of giving weight to authority and not simply relying on reason as the source of legal rules, going out of his way to criticise the dictum of Powell J. in *Coggs* v. *Barnard* that 'Nothing is law that is not reason'.[165] Though recognising its theoretical excellence, he was less convinced of its worth as a practical maxim. General rules had to be subject to exceptions (though we might counter that the exceptions themselves might be generated by the same exercise of reason as had created the rules in the first place). Moreover, different people had different ideas of what reason demanded, so to the extent that law was to be identified purely by reason it would be inherently

[163] Simmonds, *Decline of Juridical Reason*, esp. 1-36.
[164] J. M. Finnis, 'Blackstone's Theoretical Intentions' (1967) 12 *Natural Law Forum* 163; M. Lobban, *The Common Law and English Jurisprudence, 1760-1850* (Oxford, 1991), 17-46; N. E. Simmonds, 'Reason, History and Privilege: Blackstone's Debt to Natural Law (1988) 105 *Zeitschrift der Savigny Stiftung für Rechtsgeschichte (Germanistische Abteilung)* 200.
[165] 2 Lord Raym 909, 911; *Bailments*, [87].

uncertain. It followed therefore that fixed points were essential, that there needed to be authorities by which the courts were bound.[166] It is easy to take this at face value and treat Jones's scientific legal reasoning as primarily deductive, beginning with the legal rules and moving from there to articulate the doctrinal framework immanent within them.[167] But, for all that he said to the contrary, the argument in the *Essay on the Law of Bailments* is completely at odds with this. The structure of the work, as has been noticed before, put Natural law to the fore, albeit a Natural law whose contents were substantially based on Roman law.[168] His treatment of English law was very heavily coloured by this starting-point. The citation of Roman jurists was justified by saying that the 'pure unsophisticated reason' of Papinian and Blackstone were of equal weight,[169] and the extent to which he felt able to draw so heavily on Pothier can only be explained by having recourse to some similar explanation.[170] Jones had practically no legislation about bailment which required to be considered, but when faced with conflicts between the case-law and his principles of reason, it was almost always reason which won out: unless the authorities could be made to fit with these, he admitted, his whole enterprise would have failed.[171]

The intermittent citation of material from a range of other legal systems – Gothic, Greek, Hebrew, Turkish, Visigothic, Bavarian, Frankish, Welsh, Hindu[172] – reflects the same inversion. The express justification for referring to them was that they contain traces of 'sound reasoning and solid judgement',[173] giving supporting weight to his argument that positive laws reflected the principles deduced by reason. But he ventured no proper study of any of these systems, simply cherry-picking provisions which could be fitted into his pre-shaped framework; as result they provided little more than an ornamental gloss to the *Essay*, adding nothing of real value to the argument.

166 *Bailments*, [87].
167 Lobban, *Common Law and English Jurisprudence*, 45.
168 Above, 26-33.
169 *Bailments*, [20]; above, 42.
170 *Cf. Bailments*, [47]; above, 52-53.
171 Above, 48.
172 *Bailments*, [66], [76], [77], [104], [105], [115], [148], [149], [150].
173 *Bailments*, [147].

Exacerbating this tension within Jones's work was the lack of historical perspective in his treatment of the Common law. If part of the value of the Common law was to be found in the fact that it represented the accrued wisdom of the ages, it was almost inevitable that he should suppose that old authorities were of as much value as new ones. There was no great difficulty with the discursive writers on whom Jones relied heavily, Bracton and St. German, since their own theoretical framework was essentially identical to his own; but so far as the cases were concerned, given all the uncertainties associated with the history of the law of bailment[174] the earlier he went, the harder it was to interpret them in a way which was consistent with the theoretical framework. There was therefore something of a paradox in his treatment of the material: on the one hand, the old cases were treated as authorities as much as the new; on the other hand, and as a consequence of this, the degree of authority vested in them was minimal.

[174] Below, 74-103.

THE ESSAY ON THE LAW OF BAILMENTS AND ITS INFLUENCE

Whatever its weaknesses, the *Essay on the Law of Bailments* was a remarkable book. It was the first English work on the subject; and, it has been said, in treatise-writing as in mountaineering credit is rightly given to those who achieve firsts.[1] It was unique in the way in which it wove the historically derived rules of English law into a Roman fabric; and, more than any other legal treatise of the period, it embodied the post-Blackstonian fashion for organising legal materials according to a 'scientific' method.[2] In both of these aspects it looked forward to the text-book tradition of the nineteenth century, though few later works were as thorough-going in their intermeshing of English and foreign materials and none leaned as far in the extent of its reliance on speculative reason at the expense of orthodox legal rules discovered by the painstaking analysis of cases and statutes. In part, no doubt, Jones was committed to such an abstract model of law, though we may suspect that the fact that the book was apparently written in some haste might also have contributed to its being skewed towards a few general principles rather than a multiplicity of specific rules. Taken at face value, the *Essay* looked in the direction of a new Common-law world, a world less dependent on the authority of case-law than on the moral coherence of fundamental principles and on the logical deduction from them to rules applicable to concrete situations. In the event English legal literature, and with it English legal reasoning, was to pull back towards giving greater weight to precedent and authority, albeit with a more robust skeletal framework of abstract principles than would have been the norm before Blackstone.

This chapter looks briefly at the production of the *Essay*, and then examines its influence on the Common law.

[1] A. W. B. Simpson, 'The Rise and Fall of the Legal Treatise: Legal Principles and the Forms of Legal Literature' (1981) 49 *University of Chicago Law Review* 626, 652.

[2] S. F. C. Milsom, 'The Nature of Blackstone's Achievement' (2001) 1 *Oxford Journal of Legal Studies* 1, 8-12.

Jones and the Writing of the Essay on the Law of Bailments

The *Essay on the Law of Bailments* left the press of the printer, John Nichols, on 29th June 1781. On that day copies were sent to Jones's former tutee Viscount Althorp and to his friend Francis Hargrave, and on the following day to Edward Gibbon.[3] Even recognising his prodigious energy and rate of work, it is not easy to see how he could have had time to write it. Given the centrality of Pothier's treatises to his arguments, it is most unlikely that he had started on it before he had come across Pothier's works, something which occurred on his visit to Paris in the autumn of 1780. Newly returned from there, on 22nd October he wrote to Althorp that he had brought with him 'the works of a most learned lawyer, whose name and merit I shall have the honour of making known to our countrymen'.[4] Whether he had yet made the decision to use them in a treatise on bailments we cannot know, but there is no suggestion of it in his surviving letters. In the opening sentence of the *Essay* Jones refers to his having 'lately' had occasion to examine the subject of bailment,[5] presumably in the course of his legal work, and we might surmise this to have been at the earliest sometime in the latter part of 1780.[6] The main focus of his writing at this time was his translation of seven Arabic poems, the *Mu'allaqāt*, which was to appear in print shortly after the *Essay on the Law of Bailments*.[7] He had hoped to finish this, together with a commentary, in the long vacation of 1780, but had failed to do so.[8] The translation was not in fact completed until his winter holiday of 1780/81, spent in Cambridge, from where he wrote that he had no time to do anything else.[9] He was still working on the notes for these (in the event never to be completed or published) at the end of May 1781.[10] Meanwhile, alongside this and all his work as a rising law-

[3] *Letters*, 475, 478, 480.
[4] *Letters*, 442.
[5] *Bailments*, [1].
[6] *Cf. Letters*, 452, dated 23rd November 1780, where he refers to having spent two and a half hours in Westminster Hall arguing a knotty point of law.
[7] *The Moallakat, or Seven Arabian Poems which were Suspended on the Temple at Mecca* (*Works*, 10.1-193).
[8] *Letters*, 428.
[9] *Letters*, 453, 470-471.
[10] *Letters*, 473.

yer,[11] he managed to write the *Essay*. On 10th June he wrote from Oxford to the printer John Nichols that he hoped to complete the tract on the following day,[12] and a week later he was still trying to find a copy of Thomasius's *De Usu Practico Doctrinae Difficillimae Juris Romani de Culparum Praestatione in Contractibus*,[13] unsuccessfully, referring to his failure to do so in the *Advertisement* at the end of the *Essay*.[14] The *Essay* was not a work flowing from prolonged reflection on the subject.

Reactions to the Essay on the Law of Bailments

Despite the relative haste of production, the *Essay* was greeted favourably in the *Monthly Review*.[15] Jones, it was said, had shown 'the skill of a master':

> He has treated the subject with all the perspicuity and grace of which it is susceptible; and the luminous method he has pursued … is the justest model of a Law-tract that we recollect any where to have met with. We assert this with the greatest pleasure, as the Public has reason to expect, from the pen of this able Writer, some further attempts to digest and methodize the laws of his country.[16]

Though the tenor of this review was undoubtedly favourable, its focus was very much on the *Essay* as a literary production, and unsurprisingly no attempt was made to engage with it as a legal text in its own right. The same is true of the review in the *New Annual Register*; but here the reviewer, while disclaiming any ability to evaluate its technical merits, did claim to pass on at second hand the views of those who were in a better position to assess it: 'Those who are the best judges of the matter speak of it, as might be expected, in high terms.'[17]

The popularity of the work, as testified to by these reviews, is reflected in its reprintings and re-editions. The 1781 edition was reprinted in Dublin

[11] For this period see Cannon, *Life and Mind*, 141-153.
[12] *Letters*, 474. *Cp*. Cannon, *Life and Mind*, 150, interpreting this as a reference to the completion of the correction of proofs rather than the completion of the work.
[13] *Letters*, 475.
[14] Below, 197.
[15] (1782) 66(1) *Monthly Review* 298 (John Touchet). For bibliographical references see G. Cannon, *Sir William Jones: a Bibliography of Primary and Secondary Sources* (Amsterdam, 1979).
[16] *Ibid*., at 299.
[17] (1781) *New Annual Register* 216.

in 1790, and then again in Boston, Massachussetts in 1796. A second London edition appeared in 1798, with an Advertisement and Introduction by John Balmanno of Lincoln's Inn. Balmanno also provided notes which updated Jones's references to case-law and in places expanded on some of Jones's points; and as an appendix to the *Essay* he gave the text of Lord Raymond's report of *Coggs* v. *Barnard.* This edition, with Balmanno's additions, was reprinted four times in the United States: in Philadelphia in 1804, in Albany in 1806, and in Brattleboro, Vermont in 1807 and 1813. A third edition came out in London in 1823, with extensive notes by William Nichols of Lincoln's Inn, reprinted in New York in 1828 with Nichols' notes and further American references by William Halsted. By this time the character of the work was changing. Particularly in the section on English law the notes were beginning to swamp Jones's original text: the most extreme example was the section on carriage of goods, whose nine duodecimo pages in the 1781 edition had swollen to eighty-eight octavo pages in that of 1828. Counterpoised against Jones's principled discussion is the detailed, and occasionally dreary, recitation and analysis of case-law typical of practioners' texts of the early part of the nineteenth century. The fourth and final edition, by William Theobald, was published in 1833. This was based on the third edition, retaining some of Nichols' notes (though moving the long note on carriers to an appendix and abbreviating it considerably). By this time there had appeared in the United States a new work on bailment, by Joseph Story,[18] and Theobald added a substantial number of notes derived from there, sometimes expanding on Jones's points, sometimes noting where Story had said that Jones was wrong. As with the previous editions, the London printing was followed by an American one, this time printed in Philadelphia in 1836. Although the American edition claimed to have been taken from the 1833 London edition, there were considerable differences between the two books. The notes from Story are frequently worded very differently; there are references to American cases (sometimes identical to the form in which they had appeared in the notes to the American versions of the third edition), and also to the *Commentaries* of Chancellor Kent. Nichols' notes are sometimes retained where they had been dropped from the London edition, and the appendix on the law of carriers is both longer and closer to Nichols' original than is the London text.

[18] J. Story, *Commentaries on the Law of Bailments* (Cambridge, Mass., 1832).

The Essay on the Law of Bailments and the Common Law

Within a few years the *Essay* was being cited in the English courts for its interpretation of *Coggs* v. *Barnard*, though because the conventions of legal argument (or of law reporting) privileged references to case-law and statutes over doctrinal writings it is impossible to know how common citations actually were. In *Shiells* v. *Blackburne*[19] both Serjeant Adair (for the plaintiffs) and Serjeant Lawrence (for the defendant) based their arguments on different portions of the Jones's work, and Lord Loughborough based his judgment on the section which had been relied on on the part of the defendant. That the work was quarried for support by both parties testifies to the extent to which it was being treated as a source of authority. References to Jones in doctrinal literature are more revealing. Three years before *Shiells* v. *Blackburne*, William Cruise had quoted Jones in the preface to his *Essay on the Nature and Operation of Fines and Recoveries*, though only for his remarks on the scientific nature of law.[20] It was not until the 1790s that the substance of the *Essay* was coming to be regularly noted in legal writings. Edward Christian relied on it strongly in his notes to the twelfth edition of Blackstone's *Commentaries* (1794),[21] and it was one of only a handful of works to which he referred in the syllabus of his Cambridge lectures of 1797.[22] Capel Lofft praised it in his edition of Sir Geoffrey Gilbert's *Law of Evidence* in 1795;[23] so too, in the same year, did John Fonblanque in his *Treatise of Equity*,[24] though the substance of his description of the bailee's liability was in fact drawn directly from the judgment of Holt C.J. in *Coggs* v. *Barnard*. From the early years of the nineteenth cen-

[19] (1789) 1 Hy. Bl. 158.

[20] W. Cruise, *Essay on the Nature and Operation of Fines and Recoveries* (London, 1786), A2v. Remarks of the same tenor, though without the reference to Jones, are found in the preface to his *Essay on the Nature and Operation of Fines* (London, 1783), A2v.

[21] Blackstone, *Commentaries* (12th edn., London, 1794), 2.453. See too W. Curry, *The Commentaries of Sir William Blackstone ... Carefully Abridged* (London, 1796), 273.

[22] E. Christian, *A Syllabus; or, the Heads of Lectures Publicly Delivered in the University of Cambridge* (London, 1797), 49.

[23] *The Law of Evidence, by Lord Chief Baron Gilbert, Enlarged by Capel Lofft* (Dublin, 1795), 1.419, 439. Only the second of these references, a passing one, is present in the 1791 London edition.

[24] J. Fonblanque, *Treatise of Equity* (Dublin, 1795), 2.182-183.

tury editors of law reports too began to include references to the *Essay* in their footnotes and side-notes to decisions.[25]

The *Essay* was not only influential in England: the frequency of American reprints points to its transatlantic popularity, and the high status granted to Jones as the archetypal literary lawyer can only have enhanced this.[26] Even before the first American printing it was being cited in New Jersey as the source of principles applicable to the law of bailment,[27] and citations thereafter were very common indeed. In so far as we can base a judgement on the published volumes of reports, it was relied on in America far more frequently than in England. Laudatory remarks about the *Essay* abound. Typical are those of Parker C.J. in the Supreme Court of Massachussetts in *Foster* v. *Essex Bank*:

> ... the profound and brilliant treatise of Sir William Jones, in which, with a wonderful mixture of learned research and classical illustration, he has analyzed the complicated contract of bailment; and applied the principles of moral philosophy, the doctrines of the civil law, and the usages of all nations, ancient and modern, to the different branches of this diversified subject, so as to leave little room for speculation, except as to the application of his rules to particular cases, as they arise.[28]

In the early years of the nineteenth century the *Essay* was described as 'a work remarkable for the correctness and precision of its language',[29] 'a classical treatise',[30] and a 'beautiful, lucid and satisfactory essay'.[31] Jones was 'the great oracle of the law of bailments'.[32] The work was cited as authority many dozens of times in the half century or so after it appeared in

[25] *Leck* v. *Maestaer* (1807) 1 Camp. 138, 139n (published 1818); *Balchen* v. *Scott* (1795) 2 Ves. Jun. 678, 679n (published 1827); *Clark* v. *Earnshaw* (1818) Gow 30, 31n (published 1828); *Barclay* v. *Gana* (1783) 3 Doug. 389, 390n (published 1831).

[26] Above, 13.

[27] *Mott* v. *Pettit* (1795) 1 N.J.L. 344 (New Jersey Supreme Court).

[28] *Foster* v. *President, Directors and Company of the Essex Bank* (1821) 17 Mass. 479, 499.

[29] *Hodgson* v. *Dexter* (1803) 5 U.S. 345 (Supreme Court).

[30] *Camden and Amboy Railroad and Transportation Co.* v. *Burke* (1835) 13 Wend. 611, 625 (New York Supreme Court).

[31] *Reeves* v. *The Constitution* (1835) F. Cas. 461, 463 (Pennsylvania District Court).

[32] *Hurd* v. *West* (1827) 7 Cow. 752, 758 (New York Supreme Court).

America, and in a good number of cases Jones's doctrine was discussed. Even where there was disagreement with it, this was commonly accompanied by praise for the work itself. In *Hough* v. *Young*, for example, counsel argued against the law as it had been stated by Jones:

> [A]dmirable as is the arrangement, and systematic as is the reasoning of this treatise, it must be received, not as an adjudged case, but as the reasoning of an able lawyer. The author's great respect for the civil law sometimes leads him into mistake with regard to the common law.[33]

Even those opposed to Jones's mode of analysis might still be complimentary. In *Commonwealth* v. *Colquhouns*, a case relating to the inspection of tobacco, the Attorney-General of Virginia argued that more enlightenment was to be gained from an examination of the statutory framework than from 'any treatise on bailments, even that for which the world is indebted to the perspicuous mind and eloquent pen of Sir William Jones',[34] going on to take issue with the whole scientific premise on which Jones's work had been built:

> The application of general theories or principles, under all circumstances, and to all subjects, is a fruitful source of error in politics, philosophy, and law.[35]

But this sort of qualified negativity is unusual: the *Essay* was in general very well received in America.

The canonical but unauthoritative status of the *Essay* in America in the early nineteenth century is very well brought out in *Thorne* v. *Deas*, a New York decision of 1809.[36] The defendant had agreed, gratuitously, that he would arrange a policy of assurance on the plaintiffs' ship. He failed to do so, and when the ship was lost an action on the case was brought against him. Though this was not a case of bailment, Jones's discussion of the contract of mandate[37] was heavily relied upon by counsel for the plaintiffs in arguing that where loss was caused by the failure to do what one had said that one would do an action for damages would lie even in the absence of consideration. The fact that Jones, in his 'excellent essay', had asserted this lay at the base of the argument; but counsel proceeded to analyse the cases which Jones had cited, thereby formally grounding his reasoning in the

[33] (1824) 1 Ohio 504.
[34] (1808) 2 Hen. & M. 213, 216 (Supreme Court of Virginia).
[35] *Ibid.*, at 219.
[36] (1809) 4 Johns. 84 (New York Supreme Court).
[37] *Bailments*, [78]-[92].

case-law itself. Counsel for the defendant took issue with this, pointing out that this line of argument had been rejected in an English case post-dating the publication of the *Essay*, *Elsee* v. *Gatward*:[38]

> On this decision of the precise point, now before the court, we might safely rely, but the authority of Sir *William Jones* has been confidently urged against the defendant; it therefore becomes necessary to examine the foundation of his opinion. Though justly respectable for his great genius and learning, that opinion, we trust, will, on examination, be found erroneous. His 'Essay' was published before the decision in *Elsee* v. *Gatward*, and no notice of his doctrine is taken by the court, in that case. He must be considered as reasoning speculatively, and from the doctrine of the civil law, against what he considered as the *dicta* of respectable judges in the *English* courts, in the early stages of their jurisprudence.[39]

He too then went through the cases to show that – properly interpreted – they supported the conclusion that there should be no liability in this situation. Kent C.J. agreed with the defendant's argument, but in doing so he was careful to pay appropriate respect to Jones:

> Sir *William Jones*, in his '*Essay on the Law of Bailments*,' considers this species of undertaking to be as extensively binding in the *English* law as the contract of *mandatum* in the Roman law; and that an action will lie for damage occasioned by the non-performance of a promise to become a *mandatary*, though the promise be purely gratuitous. This treatise stands high with the profession, as a learned and classical performance, and I regret, that, on this point, I find so much reason to question its accuracy. I have carefully examined all the authorities to which he refers. He has not produced a single adjudged case; but only some *dicta* (and those equivocal) from the *Year Books*, in support of his opinion; and was it not for the weight which the authority of so respectable a name imposes, I should have supposed the question too well settled to admit of an argument.[40]
>
> The doctrine on this subject, in the *Essay on Bailments*, is true, in reference to the *civil law*, but is totally unfounded in reference to the *English* law; and to those who have attentively examined the head of *Mandates*, in that *Essay*, I hazard nothing in asserting, that that part of the treatise appears to be hastily

[38] (1793) 5 T.R. 143.
[39] 4 Johns. 84, 89-90.
[40] 4 Johns. 84, 96-97.

> and loosely written. It does not discriminate well between the cases; it is not very profound in research, and is destitute of true legal precision.[41]

This was not to be his final sally.

The first substantial discussion of the law of bailment after Jones's *Essay* was the chapter on the subject in Kent's *Commentaries on American Law*, first published in 1826-30.[42] Jones's influence on this is very marked. Its structure, sub-dividing bailments into five species, is explicitly taken from his analysis,[43] Kent's unquestioning adoption of the Roman principle of utility, muted by considerations of public policy, is identical to that of Jones, and the sections on *depositum* and *locatio conductio* are very clearly based on the way in which they had been treated in the *Essay*.[44] Kent, though, had not failed to notice Jones's dependence on Pothier:

> While on the examination of this contract of gratuitous bailment, and which Lord Holt calls a *depositum*, I have been struck with the learning and sagacity of Sir William Jones. But after studying Lord Holt's masterly view of the doctrine, and especially the copious treatise of Pothier, the admiration which was excited by the perusal of the English treatise has ceased to be exclusive. Pothier's essay on that particular species of bailment is undoubtedly superior in the extent, precision and perspicuity of its details, and in the aptitude of the examples by which he explains and enforces his distinctions.[45]

His discussion of *commodatum*, the topic on which Jones himself had been least original,[46] is derived more or less directly from Pothier, largely unmediated by the *Essay*;[47] and that of *pignus* is taken largely from Pothier, relying on Jones's 'great acuteness and learning' only for his criticisms of Coke's statements about English law.[48] The fifth species, *mandatum*, was the one in the context of which Kent, as Chief Justice, had spoken most

[41] 4 Johns. 84, 100. In later cases where the issue arose it was the decision in *Thorne* v. *Deas* which took precedence over Jones's argument: *Leverick* v. *Meigs and Reid* (1824) 1 Cow. 645 (New York Supreme Court); *Hough* v. *Young* (1824) 1 Ohio 504 (Ohio Supreme Court). *Thorne* v. *Deas* was in addition frequently cited and followed without any reference to Jones's contrary view.

[42] James Kent, *Commentaries on American Law* (New York, 1826-30 (this volume 1827)), 437-475, Lecture 40.

[43] *Commentaries on American Law*, 437.

[44] *Commentaries on American Law*, 437-443, 456-475.

[45] *Commentaries on American Law*, 442.

[46] Above, 47-48.

[47] *Commentaries on American Law*, 446-449.

[48] *Commentaries on American Law*, 449-456, esp. at 451.

critically of Jones in *Thorne* v. *Deas*.[49] These criticisms were repeated in the *Commentaries*: though the Civil law, explained by Pothier and adopted by Jones, had imposed a stringent duty of care on the mandatary, this was emphatically not the effect of the English cases.[50]

The discussion in Kent's *Commentaries* was followed five years later by the very substantial *Commentaries on the Law of Bailments* by the Harvard professor, Joseph Story.[51] Although making copious reference to Jones's work, Story's treatise marked a new departure in the study of the subject: he aimed to provide 'a systematical view of the whole of the common law in relation to Bailments' by contrast with the 'mere outline', 'very imperfect in details, and occasionally quite erroneous in its principles',[52] as Jones's *Essay* was described. Most obviously, the *Commentaries* was very much bigger than the *Essay*, and it was less encumbered by what might have been regarded as antiquarian learning. Story, it is true, cited heavily from the Digest and from Civilian writers, especially (though by no means exclusively) Pothier, but he was perfectly willing to say that the Common law on the subject was different from the Civil law if that was where the analysis of the case-law led him.[53] Not being committed to Jones's 'scientific' assumption that the rules of the Common law should be deducible from first principles, nor to the syncretic and ahistoric suppositions that the Common law should have been always the same and always congruent with Roman law, Story was able to take a more nuanced view of the case-law than Jones. Instead of the elegant essay accompanied by a heavy apparatus of notes, which is what Jones's work had become by this time, the cases were reintegrated into the substance of the text, making for a study which

[49] Above, 64-65.

[50] *Commentaries on American Law*, 443-446.

[51] Joseph Story, *Commentaries on the Law of Bailments; with Illustrations form the Civil and the Foreign Law* (Cambridge, Mass., 1832). I have used the English reprint of this edition (London, 1839). As Circuit Justice, Story had followed Jones in *Buffum* v. *Merry* (1824) 4 F. Cas. 604 (Rhode Island Circuit Court).

[52] *Commentaries on the Law of Bailments*, Preface, xxiii. See too the review of Story's *Commentaries* in (1832) 7 *American Jurist* 128, 137, where Jones's work is described as 'much overrated', and he is rather unfairly excoriated for his lack of sound method; and *cf.* J. B. Wallace, 'Remarks upon the Law of Bailment' (1837) 16 *American Jurist and Law Magazine* 253, 254.

[53] *E.g.* §§ 21, 39, 66, 82, 166, 173-177, 377, 406, 434 (all situations where Jones had suggested that Civil law and Common law were identical).

was both more readable and analytically more accurate than the *Essay*. Unsurprisingly, therefore, within a short time Jones's work was coming to be seen as obsolete, and references to it in the American case-law began to be swamped by references to Story.[54]

Exactly the same phenomenon occurred in England, where Story's *Commentaries on the Law of Bailments* was reprinted in 1839 from a copy which had been in the possession of the Admiralty judge Lord Stowell, perhaps a gift from Story himself.[55] In his introduction to the work its editor, Richard Charnock, expressed surprise and astonishment that there was not already any systematic treatise on the law of bailments, given the commercial importance of the subject. It was not that he had forgotten Jones; but the earlier work was, he wrote, no more than 'an essay on the principle of the law of bailments', and not at all a proper treatment of the subject based on a full examination of the authorities.[56] The same point was made when the work was reviewed in the *Law Magazine* a year later, contrasting Story's 'valuable compendium' with the 'meagre dimensions' of Jones's work.[57] The *Monthly Law Magazine* published a laudatory review of Story almost as soon as it had appeared, and followed this up with a series of substantial articles discussing it.[58] William Theobald, editor of the fourth edi-

[54] Though it still continues to be referred to today, in a variety of contexts: J. Oldham, 'The Survival of Sir William Jones in American Jurisprudence', in G. Cannon and K. R. Brine, eds., *Objects of Enquiry* (New York, 1995), 92, 95-99. Note the description in John Marvin's *Legal Bibliography* (Philadelphia, 1847), 429 (quoted in part by Oldham at 93): 'It possesses very great merits as a literary production, but moderate value as a legal work for the present day. The definitions are often faulty, and, after all, the Essay is but a collection of some of the leading rules of the Law of Bailments, a first attempt to give form and symmetry to a subject, at that time not thoroughly rooted in the Common Law. Compared with Story on Bailments, it is a very slender performance in every respect, and furnishes scarcely a tithe of the information that the practitioner needs at the present day.'

[55] *Commentaries on the Law of Bailments*, Editor's Preface, ix; W. W. Story, *Life and Letters of Joseph Story* (London, 1851), 1.557 (promising Stowell that he would send American materials from time to time).

[56] *Commentaries on the Law of Bailments*, Editor's Preface, vi-vii.

[57] (1840) 23 *Law Magazine, or Quarterly Review of Jurisprudence*, 250, 251-252.

[58] (1839) 4 *Monthly Law Magazine* 84, further developed in (1839) 4 *Monthly Law Magazine* 208 (comparing Story favourably to Jones at 211-212 and 216), 288 (critical of Jones in the note at 292-294, praising him at 294), (1840) 7 *Monthly*

tion of Jones's *Essay* (1833) made substantial use of Story's work, published only one year earlier; and, tellingly, after Story had been published in England there were no further editions of Jones.[59] Almost immediately, counsel began to cite Story in argument, and judges began to incorporate his analysis into their judgments.[60] At the same time, citations of Jones all but disappeared; where we do find the *Essay* referred to it is almost always either in conjunction with Story, or in the context of an earlier case which had mentioned it directly.[61] Such authority as Jones had was further weakened by the appearance of John William Smith's *Leading Cases* in 1837, containing an authoritative and regularly updated commentary on the decision in *Coggs* v. *Barnard*, based on Story's classificatory framework.[62] Although in no sense an analysis rivalling Jones's treatment of the subject, it did provide guidance for practitioners who needed to find their way through the increasing mass of case-law, and the structure given to his judgment by Holt C.J. ensured that the commentary was not simply an indigestible mass of authorities.

Given Jones's importance in the history of Indian law, we should not ignore his influence there. Although this came about primarily through his

Law Magazine 267 (preferring Story to Jones at 275 and 278), (1840) 8 *Monthly Law Magazine* 69 (preferring Story to Jones at 73), 151, 229, (1840) 9 *Monthly Law Magazine* 61, 134, 195, (1841) 10 *Monthly Law Magazine* 193, 282 (critical of Jones at 287 and 288).

[59] Though there were no specifically English editions of Story, the subsequent American editions (there were nine in all) were sufficiently frequently cited that we may be sure that these were available to English lawyers.

[60] *Muddle* v. *Stride* (1840) 9 C. & P. 380; *Cairns* v. *Robins* (1841) 8 M. & W. 258; *Wyld* v. *Pickford* (1841) 8 M. & W. 443; *Pickford* v. *Grand Junction Railway Co.* (1841) 8 M. & W. 372; *Harris* v. *Birch* (1842) 9 M. & W. 591; *Hinton* v. *Dibbin* (1842) 2 Q.B. 646; *Franklin* v. *Neate* (1844) 13 M. & W. 481; *Cooper* v. *Willomatt* (1845) 1 C.B. 672; *King* v. *Simmonds* (1845) 7 Q.B. 289; *Tobin* v. *Murison* (1845) 5 Moore 110. Many dozens of cases from the following decades could be cited.

[61] For rare examples of Jones being cited on its own, see *Donald* v. *Suckling* (1866) L.R. 1 Q.B. 585; *Giblin* v. *McMullen* (1868) L.R. 2 P.C. 317; *South Australian Insurance Co.* v. *Randell* (1869) L.R. 3 P.C. 101; *Pandorf* v. *Hamilton* (1886) 17 Q.B.D. 670; *Sutcliffe* v. *Great Western Railway Co.* [1910] 1 K.B. 478; *Thompson* v. *Nixon* [1966] 1 Q.B. 103.

[62] J. W. Smith, *A Selection of Leading Cases on Various Branches of the Law* (London, 1837), 1.82

translation of *Manu*, the *Essay* played its part too. Since, at least as a matter of theory, Indian contractual disputes heard in the Supreme Courts would not normally be judged by English law but by the law of the parties, there was on the face of it little scope for Jones's work to be brought into the equation; but his underlying argument that the laws of all civilised nations on the point were at heart the same meant that Hindu law could be treated as being structured along the same lines as that of Rome and England. Sir Thomas Strange, in his *Elements of Hindu Law*, dealt with the law of bailments in precisely this way, making repeated reference to Jones's treatment as a source of rules of Hindu law, which of course he had touched on only in passing.[63] A similar approach can be found in the case-law: in *Sibnarain Ghose* v. *Russick Chinder Neoghy*[64] it was argued that the question whether a Bengali mortgage could take effect without the passing of possession could be answered by looking at the rules of Roman law and of other non-feudalised nations, following Jones's supposition that through these the law of 'pure unbiassed reason' could be discerned.[65] More generally, though, the trajectory of Jones's influence followed the same lines as in England and America, falling off after the works by Story and others had gained a foothold.[66]

The Essay on the Law of Bailments and the Fabric of the Common Law

Although eclipsed after fifty years, Jones's *Essay* indubitably left its mark on the law of bailments. It had fed into the case-law in England, though it is sometimes difficult to be certain how great its influence was given the close similarity between Jones's rules and those of Holt C.J. in *Coggs* v. *Barnard*. Sometimes, though, when Jones and Holt diverged, it was Jones who prevailed. A very good example of this is in the contract of

[63] Sir Thomas Strange, *Elements of Hindu Law, Referable to British Judicature in India* (London, 1825), 278-294. Jones's framework had probably also influenced the translations of Sanskrit texts which had appeared in Colebrooke's Digest.
[64] (1842) Fulton 36.
[65] *Ibid.*, at 40-44, *per* Grant J.
[66] See for example *Whateley* v. *Pálanji Pestanji* (1866) 3 Bombay High Court Reports (Original Civil Jurisdiction) 137; *Rádhábái* v. *Shámá* (1867) 4 Bombay High Court Reports (Appellate Civil Jurisdiction) 155; *Hongkong and Shanghai Banking Corporation* v. *Baker* (1870) 7 Bombay High Court Reports (Original Civil Jurisdiction) 186.

hire of goods, where Holt, following Bracton and Justinian's Institutes, had demanded a very high degree of care but Jones had said that only ordinary care was required and liability should be imposed for ordinary negligence.[67] English case-law here expressly followed Jones in preference to *Coggs* v. *Barnard*. In *Cooper* v. *Barton*,[68] Le Blanc J. held at the Lancaster Assizes that it was incumbent on the plaintiff in an action on a contract of hire to show that the hirer had been negligent, but that Jones's analysis of the standard of care was correct rather than that described in *Coggs* v. *Barnard* or Buller's *Nisi Prius*. More demonstrably, and perhaps more importantly, Jones's work had left its mark in American case-law, and this had in its turn been picked up by Story and later writers. The *Essay* directly influenced subsequent works, too, and even where their authors disagreed with Jones's analysis it none the less stood as a point of reference for other lawyers. Moreover, the structure imposed on the Common law by Jones – or locked in place by him after its introduction by Holt C.J. in *Coggs* v. *Barnard* – was substantially adopted by his successors, and the organisation of the law in terms of different degrees of care required of different types of bailees survived in English law until 1962, when it was finally superseded by a standard which, it was said, varied infinitely according to the circumstances of each particular case.[69] Even the most modern treatise on the subject is shot through with Jones's influence, both in concrete references to his work and in its continued adoption of the classical terminology of depositum, mandatum, and commodatum.[70]

Less predictably, Jones's work played its part more generally in the development of the law of tort and contract.

In tort, the *Essay*, together with the judgment in *Coggs* v. *Barnard*, was centrally important in the emergence of the tort of negligence in the

[67] *Bailments*, [117]-[119].
[68] (1810) 3 Camp. 5n. *Cf. Mackenzie* v. *Cox* (1840) 9 C. & P. 632 to the same effect; and in America *Platt* v. *Hibbard* (1827) 7 Cowen 497 (New York Supreme Court). Jones's line was adopted by Kent (*Commentaries on American Law*, 2.256) and Story (*Commentaries on the Law of Bailments*, 264).
[69] *Houghland* v. *R. R. Low (Luxury Coaches) Ltd.* [1962] 1 Q.B. 694, especially at 698. The newer approach has resonances of Jones's own analysis in *Bailments*, [5].
[70] N. E. Palmer, *Bailment* (2nd edn., London, 1991).

nineteenth century.[71] The development of negligence as a unitary tort can be described in terms of the weaving together of two strands of cases, those where there was a pre-existing relationship between the parties and those where there was not. The former category consisted largely of cases arising out of bailments. Whereas Roman law, and in its wake the Natural lawyers, classified actions against defaulting bailees as contractual, an analysis picked up in *Coggs* v. *Barnard* and by Jones, in English law such claims were formally indistinguishable from claims in tort. From the early nineteenth century, primarily for very technical reasons of procedural convenience, it became more normal to treat them as a part of the law of torts, thereby facilitating their integration into the tort of negligence.[72] Already the legal responsibility of the bailee was expressed in terms of variable duties to take care, language more naturally suited to contractual than tortious thinking;[73] and this was carried over from the contractual context into the tortious, helping to concretise the language of the duty of care as the most distinctive feature of the Common law of negligence. It was in the law of bailments, too, that the standard of liability was moulded around the degree of care which would be taken by a reasonable person, the Roman lawyers' *diligens paterfamilias*. This contrasts with the unanthropomorphised standard of reasonable care more generally found in the non-relationship strand of cases woven into the tort of negligence.[74] Jones has therefore been described as 'the true inventor of the standard of the reasonable man',[75]

[71] D. J. Ibbetson, 'The Tort of Negligence in the Common Law in the Nineteenth and Twentieth Centuries', in E. J. H. Schrage, ed., *Negligence: The Comparative Legal History of the Law of Torts* (Berlin, 2001), 229, 230-231.

[72] M. J. Prichard, *Scott v. Shepherd (1773) and the Emergence of the Tort of Negligence* (London, 1976), 22-29. The importance of the bailment cases is already noted by F. Wharton, *A Treatise on the Law of Negligence* (Philadelphia, 1874), v.

[73] *Cp*. Roman law, where the analysis of duties was dealt with at length in the context of the real contracts and ignored completely in the context of the law of delict: W. W. Buckland, 'The Duty to Take Care' (1935) 51 *Law Quarterly Review* 637.

[74] Technically, we might say, the 'reasonable man' standard fixes the level by reference to the care which people of the relevant class habitually do take, whereas the standard of 'reasonable care' leaves it to the jury (in the eighteenth- and nineteenth-century context) to determine what standard of care the defendant ought to have taken.

[75] P. Birks, 'Negligence in the Eighteenth Century Common Law', in Schrage, *Negligence*, 173, 194.

though others, especially Holt C.J., played their part too; and bailment-based reasoning was at the core of the establishment of the reasonable or prudent man as the metwand of tortious liability in the seminal case of *Vaughan* v. *Menlove*,[76] effectively committing the Common law to a framework of negligence modelled on the eighteenth-century bailment rules.

If the influence of the *Essay* on the law of tort was the result of bailment cases having been recategorised as tortious, it followed that there was less scope for it to influence the law of contract directly. Indirectly, though, it was to prove crucial. Its great importance lay in the fact that it introduced to English lawyers the works of Pothier, which were to play a central part in the reformulation of the rules of the law of contract in England in the first half of the nineteenth century.[77] Most importantly, under the influence of Pothier's writings, the classical English law of contract which emerged in this period came to be expressed in terms of the agreement between the parties and not in terms of unilateral promises, as might otherwise have occurred given the fact that the pleadings in the main contractual action, the action of assumpsit, used the language of promising. It was through this route, in particular, that the rules relating to the formation of contract came to be framed in terms of offer and acceptance, that the interpretation of contractual terms came to depend on an evaluation of the intention of the parties, and that damages were assessed by reference to the circumstances reasonably in the contemplation of the parties at the time of entering into the contract. In addition, more tortuously, Jones's use of Pothier had an indirect effect on English contract law through his introduction of it to India. It is known that he had Pothier's works with him when in Calcutta,[78] and they were later to form the basis of Henry Colebrooke's

[76] (1837) 3 Bing. N. C. 468.

[77] A. W. B. Simpson, 'Innovation in Nineteenth Century Contract Law' (1975) 91 *Law Quarterly Review* 247; Ibbetson, *Historical Introduction to the Law of Obligations*, 220-232. For Pothier's influence in general, See B. Rudden, 'Pothier et la *Common Law*', in J. Monéger, J.-L. Sourioux, and A. Terrasson de Fougères, *Robert-Joseph Pothier; d'Hier à Aujourd'hui* (Paris, 2001), 91.

[78] B.L. MS Add 8885 f.1, dated 16th January 1784, listing twenty volumes of Pothier in his desk, together with Blackstone's *Commentaries* and 'Roccus', presumably Francesco Rocco's treatise on maritime law and insurance.

short treatise on the Anglo-Indian law on the subject.[79] A generation later, ideas which had developed in an Indian context on the basis of Pothier's theories were introduced into England and immediately taken up by English writers: it is to Pothier, indirectly, that the Common law owes its basic rules of contractual mistake and the analysis of fraud and duress in terms of impaired consent.[80]

[79] H. T. Colebrooke, *Treatise on Obligations and Contracts* (London, 1818).
[80] Ibbetson, *Historical Introduction to the Law of Obligations*, 227-228, 234-235. The crucial channel appears to have been the Indian Law Commission's Report on Contract of 1866 (P.P. HC 1867-8 xlix. 603).

EXCURSUS: THE HISTORY OF THE BAILEE'S STANDARD OF CARE

It is impossible to make any sense of the contorted history of the law of bailments[1] before the eighteenth century except in terms of the counterpoint between legal practice, as evidenced through the cases, and the frameworks of legal doctrine propounded principally by Glanvill, Bracton and St. German. The case law is very messy: frequently uncertain, substantially under-theorised, and pulled in different directions by a variety of competing pragmatic considerations. By contrast, the doctrinal writings give an impression of order and clarity, if not always complete coherence, largely as a result of adopting without much thought the analysis of Roman law found in Justinian's Institutes. The two lines did not run wholly independently of each other – sometimes practice seems to have been influenced by theory, sometimes vice versa – but it was not until the decision of the Court of King's Bench in *Coggs* v. *Barnard* in 1703 that they ran wholly together. *Coggs* v. *Barnard* constituted the major watershed in the development of the Common law on the subject; for this reason, as well as because Jones described his *Essay on the Law of Bailments* as essentially a commentary on the case, it marks the end-point of the present study.

Glanvill, Bracton, and the Early History of the Law of Bailments

Before the middle of the twentieth century, legal historians wrote a good deal about the early history of bailment, much of which depended on the theoretical preconceptions of the writer rather than historical evidence.[2] Subsequently, writers have paid less attention to the subject. Perhaps typifying the modern approach, Milsom has seen it as something which can only sensibly be described when English trial process was sufficiently so-

[1] I use this terminology for no other reason than that it was the terminology used by Jones. Whether there could be said to be a law of bailment(s) as such before *Coggs* v. *Barnard* is not really clear, and we might prefer to speak of the law *relating to* bailments.

[2] S. Stoljar, 'The Early History of Bailment' (1957) 1 *American Journal of Legal History* 1, with earlier references at note 1. Of the earlier works, E. G. M. Fletcher, *The Carrier's Liability* (London, 1932), remains of considerable value. For an undogmatic overview see G. W. Paton, *Bailment in the Common Law* (London, 1952), 66-90.

phisticated or 'rational' that the questions which needed to be answered could actually be asked.[3] This, though, is too narrow. Given the interplay between doctrinal writings and legal practice, we should not dismiss the former as something extra-legal simply because they raised questions which could not be thrown up in any formal way within the legal process.

The earliest text on which any reliance can be placed is in Glanvill (*c*1187), in that part of the treatise dealing with the generic writ of debt, a claim for money or goods (as yet not sub-divided into debt and detinue as it would be from the thirteenth century). The analysis proceeds by looking at five specific *causae* out of which a debt could arise: *mutuum*; *commodatum*; *emptio venditio*; *locatio conductio*; and *depositum*.[4] The dependence on Roman law for these *causae* is obvious, and unsurprisingly what is said about them is substantially based on Roman law. It is therefore unexpected that the brief statement about *commodatum*, the loan of goods for use, is very different from the rule of Roman law. Where the Romans had regarded liability in *commodatum* as fault-based, for Glanvill it was strict:

> The cause of a debt is sometimes a loan for use, as when I gratuitously lend you some thing of mine to make use of in your service. When the service has been accomplished, you are bound to restore my thing to me in its original condition, if it still exists; but if the thing has perished or been damaged in any way while in your keeping you are strictly bound to pay me a reasonable price...[5]

It may be, as van Caenegem has suggested, that Glanvill simply failed to see the distinction between *mutuum* and *commodatum*, the loan for consumption and the loan for use, and ignorantly applied the rule of the former in the latter;[6] but it seems implausible that an author who was familiar

[3] S. F. C. Milsom, *Historical Foundations of the Common Law* (2nd edn., London, 1981), 264-265.

[4] Glanvill (ed. G. D. G. Hall, London, 1965), X.3 (*depositum* is not further discussed); H. Kaufmann, 'Causa Debendi und Causa Petendi bei Glanvill' (1961) 17 *Traditio* 107.

[5] Glanvill X.13 (ed. Hall, 128): Ex causa quoque comodati solet res aliqua quandoque deberi, ut si rem meam tibi gratis commodem ad usum inde percipiendum in seruitio tuo. Expleto quidem seruitio, rem meam mihi teneris reddere sine deterioratione si extet. Sin autem res ipsa interierit uel deperdita fuerit quocumque modo in custodia tua, omni modo teneris ad racionabile precium mihi restituendum. For the Roman law, see above, 38-39, 47-48.

[6] R. van Caenegem, *Royal Writs from the Conquest to Glanvill* (71 S.S.), 381.

enough with the Roman categories to use them as the organising device for his whole discussion of the writ of debt should have so disastrously failed to understand the distinction which is very clearly drawn in Justinian's Institutes. Alternatively, perhaps, he was deliberately altering the Roman law rule since it was incompatible with English law. Oliver Wendell Holmes saw this as the continuation of a supposed Germanic principle of absolute liability,[7] but the evidence for this principle is thin and we should be reluctant to accept an explanation dependent on it in the absence of a stronger factual base. It is altogether more likely that Glanvill's text was reproducing a version of Roman law which was current in twelfth-century England: we know from the *Liber Pauperum* of Vacarius that, contrary to the orthodox Roman rule, some believed that the borrower and the pledgee should be strictly liable if the property was lost (although Vacarius himself rejected that view).[8] We must, though, remain agnostic as to whether or not his statement represented the practice of the English courts.[9]

Bracton's analysis of the bailee's liability, probably dating from the second quarter of the thirteenth century, is even more heavily dependent on

[7] O. W. Holmes, *The Common Law* (ed. M. DeWolfe Howe, London, 1968), 131-132, 138-142; followed by F. Pollock and F. W. Maitland, *History of English Law* (2nd edn., reissued, Cambridge, 1968), 2.203.

[8] F. de Zulueta, ed., *The Liber Pauperum of Vacarius* (44 S.S.), 4.21, ad C.4.24.5 (p.129) (*pignus*); 4.20, ad D.13.6.5.2 (p.127) (equating *commodatum* with *pignus*); P. Stein, *The Teaching of Roman Law in England around 1200* (S.S. Supp. Ser., 8), lxxiv. The normal approach of the glossators was to require a very high degree of care, *exactissima diligentia*: H.-J. Hoffmann, *Die Abstufung der Fahrlässigkeit in der Rechtsgeschichte* (Berlin, 1968), 42-43.

[9] *Cf. Maltravers* v. *de Turberville* (1200) 1 C.R.R. 273 (= 3 S.S. 3 pl. 8) (discussed by Fletcher, *Carrier's Liability*, 6). A claim for detinue of charters was met by a plea that the defendant had held them but that they had been burned by robbers, to which the plaintiff responded that this only happened after the action had been initiated. This might suggest that robbery or arson would normally have been a good defence. The case, however, may not have involved a contractual bailment at all: the defendants were the mother and step-father of the plaintiff, and we know that there was other litigation about the mother's right to dower as well as an assize of mort d'ancestor hinging on whether the father had died seised in demesne of land now in the possession of the mother and step-father: 1 C.R.R. 244, 271. It is possible, therefore, that the charters had simply been retained by the defendants after the death of the father.

Roman law than Glanvill's. The two sections of the treatise dealing with it are copied almost verbatim from Justinian's Institutes. The hirer of property is required to show a very high degree of care, that of a *diligentissimus paterfamilias*; to which is added the observation that it is not sufficient to take the same care as one takes in one's own affairs.[10] In the case of a loan for consumption (*mutuum*) the borrower is liable for all eventualities;[11] a depositee is only liable for deliberate wrongdoing, *dolus*;[12] and since a pledge is of benefit to both parties the pledgee has to show *exacta diligentia*, equivalent to taking the care of a *bonus paterfamilias*.[13] It is only when dealing with the loan for use, *commodatum*, that Bracton clearly departs from the substance of the Roman model. According to the Institutes the borrower here was required to show *exacta diligentia*, to take reasonable care (and not, it is noted in passing, only the care which he showed in his own affairs), expressly contrasting this with the absolute liability in *mutuum*. Bracton's text follows that of the Institutes closely, but instead of saying that in *mutuum* the borrower is liable even if the property is lost by fire, earthquake or the like, he says that this is so in *commodatum*, thereby applying to it the same absolute liability rule as was found in *mutuum*:

> He to whom a thing is given for use is also bound by the thing lent him. But there is a great difference between a loan for consumption and a loan for use, for he who has taken a loan for use is bound to restore the very thing, or its value if it is consumed or lost by fire, earthquake or shipwreck, or stolen or carried away by thieves or enemies. He is not excused if he shows as much care in its safekeeping as he ordinarily bestows on his own goods if another could have safeguarded the thing with greater care, [but] he is not held liable

[10] Bracton f.62b (ed. Thorne, 2.184), closely derived from Inst. 3.24.6.

[11] Bracton, f.99 (ed. Thorne, 2.284), closely derived from Inst. 3.14.pr.

[12] Bracton, f.99b (ed. Thorne, 2.284), derived from Inst. 3.14.3. There is a slight but perhaps significant variation in wording between the Institutes and Bracton. Where the former reads that the depositee is bound to return the thing, but liable to an action only if he is guilty of fraud ('de ea re quam accepit restituenda tenetur. Sed is ex eo solo tenetur, si quid dolo commiserit …'), Bracton seems to say that he is bound to return the thing, and also to compensate for any loss which he causes fraudulently ('de ea re quam accepit restituenda tenetur, et etiam ad id si quid in re deposita dolo commiserit…'). It may be therefore that the Bractonian text is pointing to a strict duty to restore in *depositum*, as also more clearly in *commodatum* (discussed immediately below).

[13] Bracton, f.99b (ed. Thorne, 2.284), closely derived from Inst. 3.14.4.

> for force majeure or accidents unless there has been culpa, as where he takes on a journey a thing lent him for use at home and loses it in an attack of enemies or thieves or by shipwreck; he is then clearly liable.[14]

The similarity of the beginning of this text to Glanvill's description of the liability of the borrower for use makes it possible that this is a deliberate distortion of Roman law in order to bring it into line with the (supposedly) English law of the earlier work;[15] but this downplays or ignores the statement that there is a 'great difference' between the loan for consumption and the loan for use, and the fact that the text continues by saying that the borrower for use is not liable for *force majeure* or accident unless his fault has contributed to it, reproducing accurately the law of the Institutes and wholly undermining the rule of absolute liability which has just been stated. It is perhaps more likely that the unsatisfactory form of the text as it stands is the consequence of an early copyist having mangled a more coherent original version.[16] But whether we attribute the change of Justinian's text to

[14] Bracton, f.99-99b (ed. Thorne, 2.284, but rejecting Thorne's emendations reflected in his translation), derived from Inst. 3.14.2 (for word-by-word comparison, see F. W. Maitland, *Bracton and Azo* (8 S.S.), 146): Sed magna differentia est inter mutuum commodatumque, quia is qui rem commodatam accepit ad ipsam restituendam tenetur vel eius pretium, si forte incendio, ruina, naufragio, aut latronum hostiumve incursu, consumpta fuerit vel deperdita, subtracta vel ablata. Et qui rem utendam accepit, non sufficit ad rei custodiam quod talem diligentiam adhibeat qualem suis rebus propriis adhibere solet, si alius eam diligentius potuit custodire. Ad vim autem maiorem vel casus fortuitos non tenetur quis nisi culpa sua intervenerit, ut si rem sibi domi commodatam secum detulerit cum peregre profectus fuerit, et illam incursu hostium vel prædonum vel naufragio amiserit, non est dubium quin ad rei restitutionem teneatur.

[15] Holmes, *Common Law*, 139; Maitland, *Bracton and Azo* (8 S.S.), 147.

[16] Thorne draws attention to the 'rough handling' of this (Romanised) part of the treatise (Bracton, 3.xlv n.8). The most plausible emendation is that suggested by E. Genzmer, reading 'nisi forte' for 'si forte' in the first sentence, and so reversing the meaning of the second clause (B. Biondi, ed., *Conferenze Romanistiche* (Milan 1960), 140 n.37). H. Kantorowicz, *Bractonian Problems* (Glasgow 1941), 94-97, emends *rem commodatam* to *rem mutuo datam*, accusing an early copyist of 'putting a group of four letters with eight strokes in place of a group of four partly different letters with again eight strokes'. But this will not do: the relevant clause of the Institutes is dealing with *commodatum*, and the statement that the borrower must return the thing itself or its price – making no mention of equivalent property – is accurate for *commodatum* and inaccurate for *mutuum*. Nor can we accept

the original author of Bracton or to a copyist, we may be sure of one thing: at least somebody in the middle of the thirteenth century believed, like the author of Glanvill, that the borrower for use was liable strictly to return the borrowed goods or their value.

Traces of the same rule are still found at the end of the thirteenth century, though by this time they are only traces. Fleta, for example, at one point simply reproduces Bracton's text.[17] Yet elsewhere, dealing with the question whether a shepherd should be liable for the death of a sheep in his charge, he draws the sharp distinction between cases where the sheep has died through bad custody (*mala custodia*) and those where the death was an accident (*casus fortuitus*), the loss in the former case being borne by the shepherd and in the latter by the owner of the sheep.[18] 'No one is responsible for *force majeure* or accident, unless some fault of his own has contributed to it.'[19] Britton, more tellingly, reverses Bracton's error: the loan for consumption and the loan for use are governed by the same rule, but for him it is a rule of liability for fault rather than strict liability.[20]

The Developed Mediaeval Law

By 1300 the case law – largely absent for most of the thirteenth century – is pointing also to a rule of fault liability. In *Bydeford* v. *Aunfrey*,[21] for example, an action of detinue was brought against a shepherd after sheep which he had been guarding died. He admitted that they had been bailed to him, but pleaded that he should be exonerated since they had not died through his fault (*defectus*), but because the land on which they were grazing had been flooded, as a result of which they drowned together with

Thorne's solution, transposing the clause relating to liability for fire and the like out of the section dealing with *commodatum* into that concerned with *mutuum* (Bracton, 2.284; 1.xl n.81): the words are found in the section on *commodatum* in the Institutes (albeit there referring to *mutuum* by way of contrast), and it is difficult to suppose that an ignorant copyist should have taken the offending clause away from the place to which the original author had moved it and restored it to exactly the place where it would have appeared in the Institutes.

[17] Fleta 2.56 (72 S.S. 186-187).

[18] Fleta 2.72 (72 S.S. 243).

[19] *Ibid*: ad vim autem maiorem vel ad casus fortuitos non tenetur quis nisi sua culpa interuenerit. And see also 2.56 (72 S.S. 187).

[20] Britton, 1.29.3 (ed. F. M. Nichols (Oxford 1865), 1.157).

[21] P.R.O. CP 40/90 m.53 (1291).

other sheep which had been there. Issue was joined on the question whether or not the death of the sheep was the result of his fault and bad custody (*defectus et mala custodia*). Nowhere here is there any attempt to suggest that liability should have been strict. Indeed, so far are we from the Romanised world of Bracton's text that it is never said whether the defendant was being paid for his keeping: there is no hint that it might matter whether or not the contract was one of *depositum* or *locatio conductio*.

Against this background we must consider the case of *Bowdon* v. *Pelleter*, otherwise known as *Bonion's Case*.[22] This was an action of detinue for goods which had been bailed by the plaintiff to the defendant. The defendant said that the goods had been bailed to her in a chest which had been locked by the plaintiff, who had taken away the key; that the chest had been stolen, together with goods of her own; and that the thieves had broken open the chest and carried off its contents. According to the more elaborate version of the report, the defendant demanded judgment whether she could be liable, seeing that her own goods were taken as well as the plaintiff's chest. The plaintiff, in his turn, denied that the goods had been bailed in a chest or in any locked container, and denied that they had been taken by thieves as alleged by the defendant; and issue was joined on this. From the doctrinal standpoint the case is frustratingly elusive – the parties' stories are so far apart from each other that we cannot see any sharp issue at the heart of the case, and it is never explained why it might have been important whether the goods were bailed in a locked chest – but we can make three observations. First, the defendant must have thought it relevant that her goods had been taken at the same time as the plaintiff's, pointing in the direction of a subjective standard approximating to Roman law's *diligentia quam in suis rebus*, at least in some cases. The fact that the plaintiff took issue on whether the bailed goods were stolen at all, ignoring the question whether the defendant's goods were stolen at the same time, may perhaps suggest that this was not an uncontroversially accepted view; but since exactly the same defence is made, and apparently accepted as pertinent by the other party, in an action of 1299,[23] it would be a mistake to dismiss it out of

[22] YB P. 8 Edw. II (41 S.S.) 136, elaborating the Vulgate version YB P. 8 Edw. II f.275 (Fitz. Abr., *Detinue* 59); *cf.* the remarks of Dr. Bolland at 41 S.S. xxiii.

[23] *Prior of Brinkburn* v. *William of Whelpinton* (1299), in W. Page, ed., *The Chartulary of Brinkburn Priory* (Surtees Society, vol. 90; Durham, 1893), 105; dis-

hand. Secondly, as in *Bydeford* v. *Aunfrey*, it is nowhere said whether or not the defendant was to be paid. That the distinction between *depositum* and *locatio conductio* is once again not drawn suggests that it was probably not relevant. Thirdly, the arguments of both plaintiff and defendant centred on the circumstances of the loss (whether by theft or not), and not on whether the defendant had taken the requisite amount of care: nowhere in the reports or the record of the case is there explicit mention of fault in any form.

The focus on the reason why the defendant should not be liable, as seen in *Bowdon* v. *Pelleter*, was largely a consequence of the logic of the form of action, detinue. Here the plaintiff was claiming his property from the defendant, property which she was bound to hand over to him since he had bailed it to her.[24] Provided the plaintiff could show that the bailment had been made and the goods not returned, he would prima facie succeed in his claim; it therefore fell to the defendant to show why the action should not succeed. At the end of the thirteenth century, it seems, it might have been sufficient for the defendant to say that the goods need not be returned because they had been destroyed without his fault,[25] but it later became more normal to describe with greater precision why he should not be charged. Fourteenth-century cases show that these excusing conditions would have included the burning down of the house in which bailed goods were being kept,[26] the goods being taken by thieves (at least if the bailee's goods were taken along with them),[27] or the sudden death from natural causes of a bailed animal.[28] Analogous principles applied in the writ of account, where it was an open question whether a factor would be liable when

cussed by Maitland in Pollock and Maitland, *History of English Law*, 2.171 n.6). A similar observation might be made about *Bydeford* v. *Aunfrey*, above.

[24] For the proprietary basis of the claim, see Milsom, *Historical Foundations*, 257-275, D. J. Ibbetson, *A Historical Introduction to the Law of Obligations* (Oxford, 1999), 1-2, 17-21, 33-34. The distinction between claims based on bailments and claims based on the simple fact of the defendant's possession was firmly drawn in YB T. 29 Edw. III f.38 (1355).

[25] As in *Bydeford* v. *Aunfrey*, above n.21, though even there the faultlessness was further elaborated.

[26] YB 12 & 13 Edw. III (R.S.) 245 (1339).

[27] YB 29 Lib. Ass. 163 pl. 28 (1355).

[28] YB H. 40 Edw. III f.5 pl. 11 (1366).

the plaintiff's goods had to be jettisoned during a storm at sea.[29] Here, though, the situation was confused by the need to distinguish between circumstances which could be pleaded in bar of the action, thereby excusing the defendant from making an account at all, and circumstances which could be shown before the auditors in determining what if anything was owed to the plaintiff.

We should not exaggerate the significance of this apparent move away from explicitly fault-based reasoning. Liability was still in substance based on fault, though what constituted fault was becoming more crystallised. The language of blameworthiness was not extirpated,[30] but it was subordinated to the analysis of excusing conditions. Moreover, if the claim was not for the loss of the property but for damage to it, where the appropriate form of action after the middle of the fourteenth century would have been trespass on the case,[31] the question for the jury would have been simply and directly whether the defendant had been at fault or, in a non-technical sense, negligent.[32]

This shift of focus onto a set of excusing conditions may not significantly have changed the substantive liability of the bailee, but it had one very important consequence: it meant that where the property was lost it was not open to the jury to decide whether, on consideration of all the facts, the defendant was to blame. By taking the question away from the jury it was turned into a matter of law for the judges, and as a matter of law it became liable to change in ways that are visible to the historian. Such a change, making the bailee's liability progressively stiffer, can be discerned in the first half of the fifteenth century. It came to be said that he would not be liable if the goods were stolen, a case in 1431 assuming that such a situation would inevitably be attributable to the bailee's failure to keep

[29] YB M. 41 Edw. III f.3 pl. 8 (1367).

[30] See for example YB H. 40 Edw. III f.5 pl. 11 (1366); *Veel* v. *Wygryme*, YB H. 11 Ric. II (A.F.) 163 (1388); YB M. 10 Hen. VI f.21 pl. 69 (1431); YB H. 33 Hen. VI f.1 pl. 3 (1455).

[31] The defendant could avoid paying damages in detinue by handing over the goods to the lender, hence the inappropriateness of the form of action in cases of damaged goods: *Prior of Lenton* v. *Shaldeford*, YB 4 Edw. II (42 S.S.) 134, 135 (1311).

[32] YB H. 2 Hen. VII f.11 pl. 9 (B.&M. 398); Ibbetson, *Historical Introduction to the Law of Obligations*, 62-63; J. H. Baker, *Oxford History of the Laws of England, Volume 6* (Oxford, 2003), 757-760.

proper guard over them.[33] In that case the distinction was made between simple theft, for which the bailee was liable, and robbery, for which he was not; but thirty years later it was coming to be said that he was liable in the case of robbery too.[34]

One reason for making the bailee liable for theft, and eventually perhaps for robbery, was that he had in his turn a right of action against the thief or robber. That he could bring the appeal of robbery was clear in the thirteenth century,[35] and at the end of the century *The Mirror of Justices* described this rule as applying to larceny too;[36] and slightly later than this it was clear law that he could bring a writ of trespass.[37] The bailee's right of action and his liability to the bailor were clearly interdependent, though we cannot easily say that one was the cause of the other.[38] In the second half of the fifteenth century it was several times said that the bailee had his action against the third party *because* he was himself liable over to the bailor,[39] with the corollary that if for some reason he was not liable to the bailor he would not himself have an action.[40] On the other hand, in an analogous case of 1455 – a case which was to be influential in later discussions – the causation moved in the opposite direction.[41] The defendant was gaoler of the Marshalsea prison. A debtor, imprisoned at the suit of the plaintiff, escaped,

[33] YB M. 10 Hen. VI f.21 pl. 69 (1431); but *cp.* YB M. 9 Edw. IV f.40 pl. 22 (1469), where Serjeant Jenney argued that the bailee would not be liable in case of theft, though Danby C.J.denied this was the law.
[34] YB M. 2 Edw. IV f.15 pl. 7 (1462).
[35] Bracton, f.103b (ed. Thorne, 2.295), f.146 (ed. Thorne, 2.412-413).
[36] *The Mirror of Justices* (7 S.S.), 57.
[37] YB T. 48 Edw. III f.20 pl. 8 (1374); YB M. 11 Hen. IV f.17 pl. 39 (1409); YB M. 11 Hen. IV f.23 pl. 46 (1409). The Chancery refused to allow a writ in which it was expressly stated that the plaintiff was a bailee (YB T. 48 Edw. III f.20 pl. 8 (1374), *per* Cavendish C.J.; YB M. 11 Hen. IV f.23 pl. 46 (1409), *per* Colpeper J.), so no formal distinction could be drawn between the bailee's claim and that of the owner.
[38] P. Bordwell, 'Property in Chattels' (1916) 29 *Harvard Law Review* 731, 733-734, 737-739.
[39] YB M. 2 Edw. IV f.15 pl. 7, at f.16 (1462); YB T. 8 Edw. IV f.6 pl. 5 (1468); YB M. 9 Edw. IV f.33 pl. 9, at f.34 (1469); YB T. 3 Hen. VII f.4 pl. 16 (1488).
[40] YB M. 9 Edw. IV f.33 pl. 9, at f.34 (1469); YB T. 3 Hen. VII f.4 pl. 16 (1488).
[41] YB H. 33 Hen. VI f.1 pl. 3 (1455).

and the plaintiff brought an action of debt against the gaoler.[42] It was apparently accepted that if the escape had been the result of a sudden tempest (or perhaps a fire) or the act of enemy aliens, then the gaoler would not be liable. If, however, the prisoner had been allowed to escape by the act of the King's subjects – even if it was not known who they were – it would have been different: here, at least in theory, the gaoler would have had an action against them, so he ought to be liable to the plaintiff. Although the priority between the two ideas is obscure, there is a clear link between them; the fixing in place of the increasingly strict liability of the bailee in the fifteenth century can only be understood against the background of the concurrence of these rules.

A second, more general, legal phenomenon may have played some part as well. In the fourteenth and fifteenth centuries liability in contract generally became strict, in the sense that once it was shown that the defendant had contracted to do something he would be liable unless he could show some good reason why he should not be.[43] As with the bailment cases, the acceptable reasons for non-performance became more restricted in the fifteenth century, essentially reducing to the act of the plaintiff, act of God, and the act of third parties against whom the defendant could not have any remedy. Since most, if not all, bailments were contractual, it would not be surprising if there was a direct linkage between these cases and the law of bailments. Something like this assumption perhaps lies behind *Veel* v. *Wygryme*.[44] Account was brought against a carrier of money from Somerset to London, who had been robbed on the journey. His plea was that he had agreed to take the money on the condition that he would look after it as he looked after his own, and the plaintiff denied that there had been any such condition.[45] The contract to carry the money to London, it appears, would be construed strictly, so that the defendant would in principle be liable for failing to get it there. If he wanted to be held to a lower standard of accountability he should ensure that such a term was incorporated into the agreement. By the end of the fifteenth century the distinction between gen-

[42] For the gaoler's liability, see R. B. Pugh, *Imprisonment in Medieval England* (Cambridge, 1968), 242-245.

[43] D. J. Ibbetson, 'Absolute Liability in Contract: the Antecedents of *Paradine* v. *Jayne*', in F. D. Rose, ed., *Consensus ad Idem* (London, 1996), 1, 13-22.

[44] YB H. 11 Ric. II (A.F.) 163 (1388).

[45] *Veel* v. *Wygryme*, YB H. 11 Ric. II (A.F.) 163, 164, 166 (1388).

eral bailments and special bailments (*i.e.* bailments containing some specific term allocating risk) was clear; in the former the stringent default terms would apply, in the latter it was open to the parties themselves to determine where the risk fell.[46] A bailee who wanted to specify that he should only be liable should he fail to keep the goods as his own, or that the risk of loss should be borne by the bailor, was advised insist on a term to that effect,[47] as was a bailor who wanted all the risk of loss to fall on the bailee.[48]

Perhaps the most notable feature of the post-Bractonian case-law relating to bailments is just how un-Roman it all is. There is nothing approaching the Romans' sub-divisions into different classes of bailment, still less anything to suggest that the bailee's duties might have varied according to any such categorisation. Behind the cases is a common theme that the bailee would either be strictly liable or required to take the same care of the bailed goods as he took of his own, nothing like the Roman standard of the *diligens paterfamilias*. If there was any sub-division it was perhaps between carriers and other sorts of bailees,[49] but it requires imagination to see even this before the sixteenth century.

Doctor and Student and the Sixteenth Century

Doctrinal writing, largely absent between 1300 and 1500 began to revive in the early years of the sixteenth century with the publication of Christopher St. German's *Doctor and Student*.[50] The view of the law presented here is very different from that which we see unfolding in the Common law courts. His entire framework is Roman, distinguishing the standard of care owed by the bailee according to the category of bailment. The borrower of a horse, he says, will be liable if it is killed by a house falling on it if this house was likely to fall, since this would be attributed to his fault; but if it blew down in a tempest the borrower would not be liable. The case – one of *commodatum*, though erroneously described by St. Ger-

[46] YB T. 3 Hen. VII f.4 pl. 16 (1488).
[47] *Veel* v. *Wygryme*, YB H. 11 Ric. II (A.F.) 163 (1388); YB M. 9 Edw. 4 f.40 pl. 22 (1469); YB T. 3 Hen. VII f.4 pl. 16 (1488).
[48] *Note* (*c*1530) 121 S.S. 391.
[49] Baker, *Oxford History of the Laws of England, Volume 6*, 760; see below, 87-89.
[50] C. St. German, *Doctor and Student*, 2.38 (ed. T. F. T. Plucknett and J. L. Barton (91 S.S.), 259-261).

man as a case of *depositum* – is taken from the Canonist *Summa Rosella*,[51] but St. German is very careful to say explicitly that the Common law is the same. He continues by elaborating the rule, for the 'ordering of conscience': in a loan for consumption (*mutuum*) the borrower is liable for all casualties; in a loan for use (*commodatum*) the borrower will be liable if the loss was caused by his fault, though if he used the thing in a way different from that which had been allowed by the contract he should also bear the risk of accidental loss; if the bailee was to receive payment (a case of *locatio conductio*) and had promised to bear all the risks he should be held to this, but such a term agreed to by a gratuitous bailee would have had no effect since he was not bound by such a naked promise; and a finder was liable for wilful negligence, but not otherwise. The only aspect of this exposition that can be regarded as English rather than Roman law is the explanation that a gratuitous bailee could not be liable for all risks since his promise to bear them was (in our terms) not supported by consideration; but St. German's views on consideration were themselves slightly precocious and it might therefore be a mistake to treat this explanation as an uncontroversial statement of the position of the depositee or commodatary in English law.[52] None the less, in drawing the distinction between the terms imposed by law and those agreed to by contract, St. German gave expression to the division which was by his time fundamental in the Common law. In addition, reflecting what might have been an emerging distinction, he dealt separately with the liability of the common carrier, saying in effect that he should be liable if the goods were damaged, destroyed or lost by his fault. This was a good deal more generous to the carrier than were the contemporary Common law judges, though St. German balanced this with the statement – erroneous as a matter of English law – that the carrier was not allowed to exclude his liability.

Although the trajectory of the law in the later Middle Ages was fairly clear, there was a good deal of uncertainty in points of detail. This uncertainty was added to by St. German's attempts in *Doctor and Student* to reincorporate Romanised elements into English law. Was the bailee's liability

[51] B. Trovamala, *Summa Roselle* (Strasbourg, 1516), 28v, sub tit. *Casus Fortuitus*, quoted by Jones at *Bailments*, [145], where St. German's error is noted.
[52] *Doctor and Student*, 2.24 (91 S.S. 228-233). See Barton, 91 S.S. lv-lix; Baker, *Oxford History of the Laws of England, Volume 6*, 863-864. The point was to take on real force later: below, 90-91, 97-98, 101-102.

strict, in the sense that loss was borne by him or her unless there was some excusing circumstance, as the cases of the fifteenth century were suggesting, or did the bailor have to allege and prove fault as St. German described the law? If it was strict, what circumstances excused? And if it was fault-based, did the level of care required of the bailee vary according to the type of bailment?

These questions are most easily answered where the defendant was a carrier for reward. Here, by at least the 1520s, there is strong evidence that liability was strict, the risk of loss being borne prima facie by the carrier unless there was a term in the contract to the contrary.[53] Cases in the second half of the century consistently followed this line: it was not open to a carrier to claim that the goods were lost through the negligence of an innkeeper, that his boat had sunk or been overthrown by a violent tempest, or that the goods had been taken by robbers or captured by a foreign warship.[54] Since such carriers were likely to be commercial traders there might be good sense in having a black-and-white default rule against the background of which the parties could allocate their own risks,[55] and in practice we find quite elaborate clauses doing this. One contract for the sale of wine, to be carried by the buyer from Dieppe to Newcastle, for example, provided that the risks of the sea and of Scottish or Easterling pirates should be borne

[53] Baker, *Oxford History of the Laws of England, Volume 6*, 760-764. It is not clear what risks, if any, would be borne by the consignor, but we may be fairly certain that the carrier would avoid liability at the very least where loss was attributable to the consignor's fault.

[54] *Hatch* v. *Thorne* (1557) P.R.O. KB 27/1183 m.193 (Baker, *Oxford History of the Laws of England, Vol. 6*, 762 n.31); *Taylor's Case* (1584) 4 Leon. 31; *Thomson* v. *Miles* (1591) Ro. Abr., *Conditions* G (9), C.U.L. MS Ee 6.12 f.91, Exeter College Oxford MS 126 f.7v, B.L. MS Add. 25197 f.25v; *Woodlife* v. *Curties* (1597) Moo. 462, Owen 57, Ro. Abr., *Action sur le Case* C (4); *Sherington and Wintrope* v. *Leman* (1578) P.R.O. KB 27/1265 m.27. The rule in the Court of Admiralty was different, liability being imposed only for fault: Ibbetson, 'Absolute Liability in Contract', 27-28.

[55] Hence perhaps the doubts shown in *Anon* (1553) Dal. 8, where the Court of Common Pleas was reluctant to impose absolute liability on a 'common' carrier. Since he was under an obligation to carry goods he may not have been in a position to negotiate to avoid this liability.

by the seller while the buyer carried the risk of capture by Englishmen.[56] In the case of carriage by sea, too, if the goods were to be insured it would be the shipmaster who did so: the custom of London, it was said in 1562, was for him to take out a policy over goods 'apperteyninge to him or to whatsoever other personne they doo perteyne', and in the event of any claim being made he would recover the value of the goods whether they were his own or another's.[57] The connection between the rule of near-absolute liability (subject to contractual variance) and the practice of insurance was to be made in argument in *Williams* v. *Hide* in 1628,[58] and it may be that this relationship had a long history behind it.

The situation with regard to other bailees is far more confused. We may be sure that they were not as a matter of course subjected to the same regime of near-absolute liability as carriers, but it is impossible to say with any certainty what the law was. The question arose in two inconclusive cases in the 1590s, *Woodlife* v. *Curtis*[59] and *Mosley* v. *Fosset*,[60] neither of which is particularly well reported. The principal distinction, outlined by Popham C.J. in *Woodlife* v. *Curtis*,[61] seems to have been between the ordinary bailee on the one hand and the paid bailee who had undertaken to care safely for the goods on the other; the latter would be liable on the same basis as the carrier, the former would not.[62] This distinction was picked up in *Mosley* v. *Fosset*. The plaintiff had bailed his horse to the defendant to be pastured, whence it was carried off by persons unknown. An action of assumpsit was brought, to which the defendant demurred. With clear overtones of St. German's analysis,[63] it was agreed that the success of the action

[56] *Piquet* c. *Brandelyn* (1533) *Select Pleas in the Court of Admiralty, volume 2* (11 S.S.), 64.

[57] *Select Pleas in the Court of Admiralty, volume 2* (11 S.S.), 52; J. S. Kepler, 'The Operating Potential of London Marine Insurance in the 1570's' (1975) 17 *Business History* 44; G. Malynes, *Consuetudo vel Lex Mercatoria* (London, 1622), 150-156.

[58] *Williams* v. *Hide* (1628) Palmer 548.

[59] (1597) Moo. 462, Owen 57, Ro. Abr., *Action sur le Case* C (4).

[60] (1598) Moo. 543, Harvard Law School MS 1004c f.3; C.U.L. MS Dd 8.48 p.19; P.R.O. KB 27/1347 m.83.

[61] See the report at Owen 57.

[62] A rather different argument was put forward by Gawdy J., that all depended on whether the bailee had an action over against a third party (*cf.* above, 83-84); but this was denied by Popham C.J.

[63] Above, 85-86.

depended on whether there had been a 'special assumpsit' – a contract – to guard the horse safely; if there had not been, the defendant would have been no more than a 'common bailee' and not responsible for the theft of the bailed property. Behind this lay the more abstract distinction between a claim in contract and a claim in tort, which was coming to replace the older distinction dependent on the form of action.[64] Contracts were interpreted strictly, so an agreement to keep property safely and redeliver it to the bailor would be treated as an undertaking to bring about a result; whereas in the absence of such a contract the bailee would be liable only if he was at fault.[65] This was easy to state, less easy to apply in practice. Since the same form of action, assumpsit, could be used whether the claim was analytically contractual or tortious, it might be impossible to tell from the pleadings which approach to liability should be adopted. This seems to have been the fundamental problem in *Mosley* v. *Fosset*: it had been alleged that the defendant had undertaken to look after the horse safely, but whether there had been a genuine 'special assumpsit' to do so it was quite impossible to say. Probably following Bracton,[66] John Stevens, counsel for the plaintiff, argued that the fact that the bailee was being paid imposed on him the duty to take a high level of care, that of 'a most diligent paterfamilias', since 'special consideration implye special care et charge';[67] but he does not seem to have gone so far as to argue that the receipt of consideration would in itself have been enough to trigger the contractual rule of near-absolute liability. We do not know whether the argument would have succeeded, for no judgment was given.[68]

[64] By this time the action on the case, in the form of assumpsit, was commonly being used for all claims arising out of contracts not under seal, so the formal distinction between claims in case and claims in detinue (and similar actions) was becoming no longer tenable.

[65] Above, 84-85. See in particular *Mountford* v. *Catesby* (1573) Dyer 328, 3 Leon. 43, B.L. MS Add. 25211 f.52 for the sixteenth-century approach.

[66] Bracton f.62b (ed. Thorne, 2.184).

[67] C.U.L. MS Dd 8.48 p.19.

[68] The case was continued from term to term until Michaelmas 1600, when it was discontinued with the consent of the plaintiff.

A further twist was given by the Court of King's Bench three years later, in *Southcote* v. *Bennet.*[69] Here the plaintiff had bailed a christening robe to the defendant to be looked after safely and restored to him on request. When the goods were not returned the plaintiff brought a writ of detinue. The defendant pleaded that they had been feloniously carried off by one Thomas Laughing; the plaintiff replied that Laughing was the defendant's servant; to which the defendant demurred. The pleadings here reflect the assumption which lay behind *Mosley* v. *Fosset*, that in the absence of a special contract the bailee would not in principle be liable if the goods were stolen; on any other assumption the defendant's plea would have amounted to an admission of liability and the plaintiff's replication would have been redundant. This is reflected in the argument of John Dodderidge, counsel for the defendant.[70] Drawing the distinction between a general and a special bailment, he said that it was only where the bailee specifically undertook to keep goods at his peril that he would be liable if they were stolen. Without such a special undertaking he would be liable only to look after the bailor's goods as he looked after his own, and so would be discharged if the goods were taken by thieves. Hugh Pine, for the plaintiff, seems to have advanced two lines of argument. First, apparently accepting the legal point in Dodderidge's argument, he treated this case as if it involved a form of special bailment: the defendant, according to the pleadings, had received the goods to look after safely, and so he ought to keep them at his peril. Secondly, even if the bailee would normally have been discharged if the goods had been stolen, this was not so where the thief was his servant; his servants were his responsibility, so this was 'a default in him which shall not turn to the disadvantage of the plaintiff.' Presumably, given the focus of the pleadings, it was the latter argument which was his main one; but it was the former which seems primarily to have moved the court. Since it was said that the goods had been bailed to keep safely, it was taken to follow that the defendant who had received them on these terms had accepted to keep them at his peril; and this, according to Coke's report, was so even if he was acting gratuitously. This final point was crucial. No longer could it be said

[69] (1601) 4 Co. Rep. 83b (from B.L. MS Harl. 6686 f.445v); Cro. El. 815; J. H. Beale, 'Southcott *v.* Bennett' (1899) 13 *Harvard Law Review* 43 (from Thomas Coventry's report); P.R.O. KB 27/1362 m.500d.
[70] The arguments appear only in Coventry's report: 13 *Harvard Law Review* 43-44. A little imagination is needed to reconstruct them.

that a 'special bailment' required a special contract, since in the absence of consideration there could not be any legally enforceable contract unless the parties had put their agreement under seal.[71] Nor, as Coke pointed out,[72] was it realistic to draw a fine line between a bailment to look after goods and a bailment to look after goods safely. Hence, although retaining the distinction between general and special bailment which lay at the heart of *Mosley* v. *Fosset*, the rule was inverted: in the argument of the earlier case the 'special assumpsit' or 'special consideration' served to subject the bailee to a more stringent duty, whereas the basis of the decision in *Southcote* v. *Bennet* was that the bailee was subject to the more stringent rule of liability unless he had accepted the goods on special terms that he should only be required to hold to some lower standard of care. Coke himself might have been schizophrenic about this. In the manuscript of his report, though not in his printed text, there is a side-note reference to *Doctor and Student*, where both the fault principle and the distinction between bailments for value and gratuitous bailments were drawn;[73] and at the end of the manuscript report is a quotation from Justinian's Institutes, perhaps taken from Bracton, that the person who bails a thing to a negligent friend has only himself to blame.[74]

What was the more stringent liability rule imposed by *Southcote* v. *Bennet*? According to Coventry's report, Gawdy J. held that what was important on the facts of the case was whether the bailee had an action over against the wrongdoer (effectively therefore excusing the bailee where the goods had been destroyed or taken by enemy aliens but not by other strangers), following the line taken in the Year Book case of 1455.[75] A year later the King's Bench was, unsurprisingly, to hold that the act of the plaintiff himself would equally excuse the defendant,[76] thereby moving the bailee's

[71] As had been seen by St. German: above, 86.

[72] It seems at this time to have been absolutely standard in pleadings in detinue to say that the defendant had received the goods to keep safely, and not merely to keep: W. Rastell, *Collection of Entrees* (London, 1596), *Detinew*, *passim*.

[73] Above, 86.

[74] B.L. MS Harl. 6686 f.445v.

[75] Above, 83-84. He had made the same point in *Woodlife* v. *Curtis* (above, n.62), but on that occasion had been slapped down by Popham C.J. Popham was not present for the argument in *Southcote* v. *Bennet*.

[76] *Shilbury* v. *Scotsford* (1602) L.I. MS Misc. 492 f.488v.

liability further into line with the general rule coming to be applied for the breach of a contract. The one point still to be settled was whether the bailee would be liable for an Act of God. The contract rule was that a person who had agreed to do something bore the risk of an Act of God making it impracticable or impossible, and in *Williams* v. *Hide*[77] an attempt was made to apply this rule to the bailee too. The plaintiff had bailed a horse to the defendant, which the defendant had failed to redeliver to him. An action of assumpsit was brought, the defendant pleaded that the horse had died, to which the plaintiff demurred. Much was made in argument of the practice of the marine insurance market, so it is safe to surmise that the analogy with the case of carriage of goods, with its default rule of near-absolute liability, was being pressed; none the less – with good sense – the King's Bench refused to adopt such a line and gave judgment for the defendant. In the absence of any special term excusing him the bailee might take the risk of theft or robbery, except probably by enemy aliens, but he was not to be answerable for every accident which might befall the bailed property.

The Seventeenth Century: Bailees and Common Carriers

Williams v. *Hide* effectively drove a wedge between the case of the professional carrier and that of the ordinary bailee. This was already implicit in the development of the form of action against a common carrier in which the plaintiff counted explicitly on a custom of the realm that the carrier should take such care of the goods that no harm come to them. The paradigm case was that of the carrier by land, but it extended also to hoymen, wharfingers, lightermen and other inland carriers by water.[78] Unless otherwise agreed, such common carriers transported the goods at their own peril, and they were liable if the goods were lost in any way,[79] except

[77] (1628) W. Jones 179, Palmer 548.

[78] *Rich* v. *Kneeland* (1614) Hob. 17, Cro. Jac. 330; *Symons* v. *Darknoll* (1628) Palm. 523; *Nicholls* v. *More* (1661) 1 Sid. 36; *Mors* v. *Slue* (1672) 2 Keb. 866, 3 Keb. 72, 3 Keb. 112, 3 Keb. 136, 1 Mod. 85, T. Raym. 220, 1 Vent. 190, 1 Vent. 238, 2 Lev. 69; *Boson* v. *Sandford* (1689) 1 Sho. 29, 1 Sho 101, 2 Sho. 478, 3 Lev. 258, 1 Freem. 499, 2 Salk. 440, 3 Salk. 203, 3 Mod. 321, Carthew 58, Comb. 116.

[79] *Symons* v. *Darknoll* (1628) Palm. 523; *George* v. *Wiburn* (1638) 1 Ro. Abr. 6; *Kenrig* v. *Eggleston* (1648) Aleyn 93.

(probably) by act of God or act of the King's enemies.[80] In 1614 it was said that it was unnecessary to mention any such custom, since it was no more than the Common law,[81] but it became the ordinary form by the second half of the seventeenth century.[82] In substance the liability of the common carrier under the custom of the realm was the same as liability in contract; the only benefit of bringing the action under the custom was that there was no need for the plaintiff to refer explicitly to the contract. Carriers by sea fell outside this custom; though since in such cases there would practically always be a written contract, whether the action was brought in the Admiralty or at Common law the precise terms of the contract would govern the case.[83]

Where the defendant was an ordinary bailee, not a common carrier, the plaintiff's action might take two forms. Most simply, it might be said that the property had been delivered to him to be redelivered, without alleging that there had been any contract, and that he had so negligently looked after the property that it had been lost or damaged. Such an action would be treated as tortious,[84] and it would be essential for the plaintiff to prove that the defendant had been guilty of some fault.[85] Alternatively, and probably more commonly, the action could be pleaded contractually in assumpsit,

[80] *Gravenor* v. *Prest* (1637), in H. Winch, *Le Beau-Pledeur* (London 1680), 28; *Chester* v. *Hawkins* (*c*1666), in A. Vidian, *The Exact Pleader* (London 1684), 37; W. Sheppard, *Actions upon the Case for Deeds* (London, 1675), 293 (based on *Doctor and Student*), 373, 377.

[81] *Rich* v. *Kneeland* (1614) Hob. 17; *Matthew* v. *Hopkins* (1665) 1 Sid. 244 (unnecessary to cite custom, but good practice to do so).

[82] J. Herne, *The Pleader* (London, 1657), 76; R. Aston, *Placita Latine Rediviva* (London, 1661), 62; *Liber Placitandi* (London, 1671), 34; Vidian, *Exact Pleader*, 37; R. Brownlow, *Latine Redivivus* (London, 1693), 11.

[83] Aston, *Placita Latine Rediviva*, 50, 61; *Pickering* v. *Barkley* (1648) Style 132; Fletcher, *Carrier's Liability*, 122-133. In the absence of relevant written terms the Common law courts appear to have adopted the normal rules for contractual bailees, the Admiralty to have treated liability as fault-based.

[84] The precise boundary between tortious and contractual actions was problematic. See for example *Symons* v. *Darknoll* (1628) Palm. 523; *Boson* v. *Sandford* (1689) 1 Sho. 29, 1 Sho. 101, 2 Sho. 478, 3 Lev. 258, 1 Freem. 499, 2 Salk. 440, 3 Salk. 203, 3 Mod. 321, Carthew 58, Comb. 116.

[85] *Rives* v. *Moxham* (1617) Hob. 187; *Whyte* v. *Rysden* (1625) Cro. Car. 20; *Bingloe* v. *Morrice* (1676) 1 Mod. 210.

where it was essential that there should have been some consideration: either some payment received by the bailee or some other benefit received by him (which would include a benefit stemming from the use of the property).[86] Here, following *Williams* v. *Hide*, and substantially in line with the normal rules for breach of contract,[87] the default rule was that the defendant would be liable for all loss not arising from act of God, act of the plaintiff, or the act of third parties against whom he could have no remedy. The contract, though, might have allocated the risks differently. In contracts of carriage, for example, the normal practice seems to have been for the carrier to bear the risk of accidental loss, so much so that such a term might have been implied,[88] but it is likely that this was limited to contracts of carriage, leaving other cases of bailment for reward to be governed by the default rule where the risk rested with the bailor.[89]

The vagaries of contractual practice make it impossible to articulate clear rules, but as a rough generalisation it could be said that gratuitous bailees were liable for losses only if they had been at fault; carriers for reward were liable for all losses except those stemming from the fault of the bailor, act of God or the acts of third parties against whom they could have no action; while other bailees for reward were liable in the same way as carriers except in so far as the contract had provided otherwise.

Yet again, two points need to be made. First, absolutely no Roman law influence can be discerned on the Common law of this period; the only case

[86] *Rogers* v. *Head* (1610) Cro. Jac. 262; *Nicholls* v. *More* (1661) 1 Sid. 36; *Rogers* v. *Pack* (1688), in H. Clift, *A New Book of Declarations* (London, 1703), 64; *Middleton* v. *Fowler* (1698) 1 Salk. 282, Holt 130, Skinner 625; R. Brownlow, *Declarations and Pleadings in English* (London, 1659), 214; W. Browne, *Formulae Bene Placitandi* (London, 1674), 21, 77; *Liber Placitandi*, 14, 25; T. Robinson, *Book of Special Entries* (London, 1684), 29; Brownlow, *Latine Redivivus*, 67.

[87] *Paradine* v. *Jane* (1647) Aleyn 26, Style 47, B.L. MS Harg. 42 f.74v, Harvard Law School MS 145a p.30. Ibbetson, 'Absolute Liability in Contract', 30-37.

[88] The point is put succinctly in *Laws Concerning Travelling* (London, 1718), 23: … if the party to whom such money or goods is delivered is to have no consideration allowed him for his trouble and care, he shall not be responsible for the loss if he is robbed ... But whoever is to receive a profit for the safekeeping of goods or money, it is agreed shall be answerable if they miscarry.

[89] See for example the precedents in Robinson, *Book of Special Entries*, 29, 30, 50, 69.

in which the civilian rules are clearly at work is *Mors* v. *Slue*,[90] where the whole point of the (unsuccessful) argument was that the Common law should *not* be applied on the facts of the case. Secondly, except in so far as it was the consequence of the consideration rules, the Common law did not distinguish between different types of bailment in determining what standard of care was demanded of the bailee.

Coggs v. Barnard

Against this background there arose the pivotal case of *Coggs* v. *Barnard*,[91] 'a case of great consequence'.[92] The defendant, it was said, had assumed *salvo et secure* to lift several barrels of brandy from a cellar, and then *salvo et secure* to deposit them in another cellar;[93] he had carried out this task so negligently and improvidently that as a result of his lack of care one of the barrels was broken and 150 gallons of brandy lost.[94] After verdict for the plaintiff, it was argued in arrest of judgment that the claim was ill framed, since it was alleged in the declaration neither that the defendant

[90] (1672) 3 Keb. 72, 3 Keb. 112, 1 Vent. 238.

[91] (1703) 2 Lord Raym. 909, 3 Lord Raym. 163, 1 Salk. 26, 2 Salk. 735, 3 Salk. 11, 268, 1 Com. 133, Holt 13, 131, 528, B.L. MS Add. 34125 f.111, L.I. MS Coxe 64 ff. 39, 56, L.I. MS Hill 52 f.10v. The fullest printed report is that in 2 Lord Raym. 909, originally the work of the Inner Templar Herbert Jacob (see B.L. MS Harg. 66 f.44 (attribution at f.1v.), Harvard Law School MS 2136 f.81 (attribution of volume)). This report needs to be read in conjunction with what appears to be Holt C.J.'s own draft of his judgment in B.L. MS Add. 34125 f.111 (copied in B.L. MS Add. 35981 f.122v). The briefer notes in L.I. MS Coxe 64 and L.I. MS Hill 52 are useful supplements; though largely confirmatory of 2 Lord Raym. 909 they are our only source of information about the arguments of counsel and the judgment of Powys J.

[92] 2 Lord Raym. 909.

[93] The words *salvo et secure*, anglicised as safely and securely, are underlined by Holt C.J.: B.L. MS Add. 34125 f.111.

[94] For the pleadings, see 3 Lord Raym. 163, 2 Salk. 725, B. & M. 370 (from P.R.O. KB 122/5 m.435). The price of brandy at this time was in the region of ten shillings per gallon (J. E. Thorold Rogers, *A History of Agiculture and Prices in England* (Oxford, 1866-1902), 5.450, 6.421, 7(1).353), and damages were ultimately assessed at only £10; it is likely therefore that the jury found that the spillage was less substantial than alleged. Interestingly, perhaps, the version of the record at 2 Salk. 735 refers to the loss of 150 bottles of brandy, which would equate rather better with the £10 awarded.

was to be paid for his labour nor that he was a common porter (in which case the payment would be implied).[95] On the face of it, this was an argument without much merit. There were cases in the Year Books in which apparently gratuitous bailees had been held liable for damaging goods,[96] the Register of Writs contained a number of precedents of claims against bailees who had damaged or lost property where there was no consideration alleged,[97] and a case reported in Rolle's *Abridgment* had expressly held that there was no need to allege consideration in such an action;[98] but it was said that by 'long and antient practise' these had not been followed.[99] Whereas all of these situations would have been analysed as tortious, the court in *Coggs* v. *Barnard* consistently stressed the contractual nature of the claim.[100] It may be that this was because the carelessness of the defendant had been described insufficiently precisely if it was the essence of the action, *a fortiori* if it was to be argued that a bailee doing a good turn for a friend should be held to a lower standard of care than one acting for reward;[101] or, perhaps, it might have been thought that the older law had been superseded by the relatively recent decision in *Boson* v. *Sandford*, where the fundamentally contractual nature of the claim against the common carrier had been stressed.[102] A third possibility, signalled by the repeated references to 'reason' in the judgment of Powell J. and 'natural reason' in the

[95] According to Holt C.J. it had been found at the trial (over which he had presided) that the defendant was in fact a common porter: L.I. MS Coxe 64 f.39. One William Barnard, a fishmonger's porter, of the parish of St. Dunstan's in the East, who died in 1706 (Lambeth Palace Library, VH/94/4/924), may perhaps be identified as the defendant.

[96] *E.g. Waldon* v. *Mareschal*, YB M. 43 Edw. III f.33 pl.38 (B.&M. 359); *Stratton* v. *Swanlond*, YB H. 48 Edw. III f.6 pl.11 (B.&M. 360).

[97] *Registrum Omnium Brevium* (London, 1687), f.110.

[98] *Powtney* v. *Walton* (1597) 1 Ro. Abr. 10 (B.&M. 370).

[99] B.L. MS Add. 34125 f.111, at f.111v. A generation before *Coggs* v. *Barnard*, William Sheppard displayed no doubt as to the validity of these cases: *Actions upon the Case for Deeds*, 372.

[100] *Cf.* L.I. MS Coxe 64 f.39, where plaintiff's counsel is reported as arguing that the claim was in fact in tort, and accepting that had it been contractual it might have been objectionable.

[101] See in particular the judgment of Powell J. at 2 Lord Raym. 909, 910.

[102] *Boson* v. *Sandford* (1689) 1 Sho. 29, 1 Sho. 101, 2 Sho. 478, 3 Lev. 258, 1 Freem. 499, 2 Salk. 440, 3 Salk. 203, 3 Mod. 321, Carthew 58, Comb. 116.

judgment of Holt C.J.,[103] is that English lawyers were beginning to be influenced by the Natural law writers, for whom these cases were paradigmatically contractual.[104]

The judges agreed on three things. Most important was that the declaration was well-founded and that the plaintiff should win. Secondly, the clear division between contractual misperformance and contractual non-performance was firmly reiterated: in a claim for non-performance lack of consideration would be fatal, but not in an action for misperformance. Thirdly, it was agreed that the decision in *Southcote's Case* was too harsh. A simple receipt of goods to look after, without any special undertaking to keep them safe and secure, should not make the bailee chargeable if the goods were stolen from him. At a more sophisticated level, though, a distinction has to be drawn between the judgments of Holt C. J. on the one hand and Gould, Powell and (probably) Powys JJ. on the other.

The puisnes grounded their judgments on the orthodox Common law question, whether there had been an undertaking to keep the goods safely. If there had not been, the gratuitous bailee would not be liable, except perhaps for gross neglect.[105] On the other hand, if there had been an undertaking to look after the goods safely, it was perfectly appropriate to hold the bailee to that undertaking and make him liable for losses except those caused by Act of God and the Queen's Enemies; this was, in effect exactly what had been held in *Williams* v. *Hide*.[106] It was necessary to decide, therefore, in which category *Coggs* v. *Barnard* fell. On the pleadings there had been a promise to carry the goods *salvo et secure*; hence, on the face of the matter, it fell into the second group. This placed the undertaking at the heart of the case – in the words of Powell J. it was the gist of the action[107] – bringing to the fore the central question, whether it followed from the fact that the undertaking was central to the defendant's liability that it was essential to show that there had been good consideration for the promise. Both Gould J. and Powell J. held not. To reach this conclusion, both judges exploited ambiguities around the edge of contractual liability. Gould J. several times referred to the 'trust' reposed in the gratuitous bailee, echoing the

[103] 2 Lord Raym. 909, 910-912; B.L. MS Add. 34125 f.111, at f.113v.
[104] Above, 23-26.
[105] 2 Lord Raym. 909 (Gould J., based on *Doctor and Student*).
[106] (1628) W. Jones 179, Palmer 548; above, 91-92.
[107] 2 Lord Raym. 909, 910.

language of the English translation of Pufendorf's *De Officio Hominis et Civis* where the Latin '*depositum*' had been rendered as 'trust'.[108] An express trust required no consideration, but the trustee was none the less liable if his neglect to carry it out caused loss to the beneficiary. Powell J. drew on a different analogy, that of a warranty.[109] Just as a warranty of quality would be actionable without any allegation of consideration,[110] on the basis that the plaintiff had trusted in the defendant's word, so here the bailee would be liable since the bailor had trusted him with the goods and relied on him to look after them. Each of these arguments could be used to justify giving judgment for the plaintiff, even if each required an extension beyond the normal range of contractual liability. More to the point, though, they had at their core essentially the same problem which had been faced in *Southcote's Case*, that on the facts of any case it would commonly be quite impossible to say whether there had been a simple undertaking to carry the goods or look after them or an undertaking to do so safely.

Though the fundamental basis for his judgment on the facts of the case was similar to that of Gould J., that the bailor had trusted the bailee and this was sufficient consideration, Holt C.J. struck out on his own in fixing this conclusion into the wider context of the different types of bailment. Given the obscurity of much of the case-law he can hardly be criticised for doing so, though the effect of his way of proceeding was to restructure English law along the Romanised lines of Bracton and St. German.

Taking Roman law as his model, in conjunction with the text of Bracton, he identified six different sorts of bailment, each with its own liability rules. First was *depositum*, where one person gratuitously looked after goods for the benefit of the bailor. In the draft of his judgment he held that

[108] S. Pufendorf, *On the Whole Duty of Man according to the Law of Nature* (trans. A. Tooke, London, 1691), 1.15.7 (p.178). For the ambiguously contractual nature of the trust at this time, see in particular M. Macnair, 'The Conceptual Basis of Trusts in the Later 17th and Early 18th Centuries', in R. Helmholz and R. Zimmermann, eds., *Itinera Fiduciae* (Berlin, 1998), 207. William Sheppard had included the carrier's liability under his heading 'Actions upon the Case for Breach of Trust', and elsewhere used the language of trust to describe the bailee's liability: *Actions upon the Case for Deeds*, 292, 314.

[109] 2 Lord Raym. 909, 911; L.I. MS Hill 52 f.10v, f.11.

[110] For the form of pleading on breach of warranty, see for example, R. Aston, *Placita Latine Rediviva* (London, 1661), 35-37.

the bailee was here liable only for *dolus*, deliberate wrongdoing, though (reflecting the ordinary rule of Roman law) gross negligence was to be treated as *dolus*. This, he said, had been stated as the rule of English law by Bracton, expressed by using the words of Justinian.[111] Lord Raymond's report is rather different. According to this, the English rule, again purportedly based on Bracton, was that if the depositee exercised the same standard of care as he normally took of his own goods this would be evidence that he had not acted dishonestly; and such a rule was now contrasted with the rule of Roman law.[112] It is not easy to make sense of the argument, for (as is made clear in the draft judgment) Bracton's words are to all intents and purposes identical to Justinian's; but since the same conclusion is reported independently elsewhere[113] it is likely that it is a fair reflection of the final form of the judgment. If this is so, in coming to interpret Bracton in this way Holt must have been tacitly moving towards the Common law focus on the subjective standard of fault which was found in the Year Books.[114] Whatever the explanation, the difference between the draft judgment and the judgment as reported suggests that there was a degree of uncertainty in Holt's mind on the matter. A second point at which we can perceive ambivalence on Holt's part is his discussion of the effect of an express undertaking to look after the goods safely. In the draft judgment he at first allowed that such an undertaking might oblige the bailee to look after the goods with the 'utmost care and diligence', though it could not be interpreted as making him liable for the acts of third parties which he could not prevent;[115] but a paragraph or so later there is an interpolated section derived from *Doctor and Student* holding that this type of gratuitous undertaking would be of no effect since in the absence of consideration it was no more than an unenforceable *nudum pactum*.[116] In the final judgment, as reported in Lord Raymond, the second of these had come to prevail: lacking

[111] B.L. MS Add. 34125 f.111, at f.118, describing the rule also as 'the Law of the world' and 'common and naturall justice'. Bracton f.99b (ed. Thorne, 2.284); Inst. 3.14.3.
[112] 2 Lord Raym. 909, 914-915.
[113] 1 Com. 133, 134; L.I. MS Hill 52 10v, 11v.
[114] Above, 80, 84-85.
[115] B.L. MS Add. 34125 f.111, at f.116.
[116] B.L. MS Add. 34125 f.111, at ff.117-116v.

consideration, the undertaking would be wholly ineffective.[117] Perhaps reflecting this, Holt referred expressly to the fact that he had only slowly come to the conclusion that *Southcote* v. *Bennet*, the principal reported case dealing with the effect of this sort of undertaking, was in fact wrong.[118] The second category was *commodatum*, the gratuitous loan for use. In line with the Institutes and with his interpretation of Bracton, Holt held that the bailee was liable for the slightest neglect, and was hence chargeable if the goods were stolen only if it was shown that this had occurred through his fault.[119] Third was the hire of goods, *locatio conductio*. Here, it was said, the bailee was also bound to take the utmost care, again following Bracton (who in his turn had followed Justinian).[120] It is likely that Holt meant this to represent the same standard of care as for *commodatum*: the 'also' points strongly in that direction.[121] It would follow that again the hirer would not be liable if the goods were stolen without his fault.[122] Fourth was pledge, pawn, where the pledgee was bound only to use 'true diligence', equated by Holt to 'ordinary care'. Once more, this test was drawn directly from Bracton.[123] The fifth category was things handed over to a bailee to be car-

[117] 2 Lord Raym. 909, 915.

[118] 2 Lord Raym. 909, 914. *Cf.* B.L. MS Add. 34125 f.111, at f.114v, noting that he had thought *Southcote* v. *Bennet* to be law.

[119] 2 Lord Raym. 909, 915. According to this report (both in print and in manuscript) he misquoted Bracton's text (quoted above, 77-78) at the crucial point, reading *rem mutuam* for *rem commodatam*, and so reversing the apparent sense of the text but restoring to it the meaning found in Justinian's Institutes. The text is referred to but not quoted in the draft judgment: B.L. MS Add. 34125 f.111, at f.119.

[120] Bracton, f.62b (ed. Thorne, 2.184); Inst. 3.24.5.

[121] 2 Lord Raym. 909, 916. The point is clearer in the draft of the judgment: in *commodatum* the borrower must use 'utmost care and diligence', in *locatio conductio* 'utmost or most exact care' (B.L. MS Add. 34125 f.111, at f.119 and f.120).

[122] There is an ambiguity in the printed report (2 Lord Raym. 909, 916) between robbery and theft, but the more plausible interpretation of the words of Holt C.J. is that he was treating them as equivalent, and exonerating the blameless hirer from liability for both. The point is again made more clearly in the draft judgment, where it is said that he need not 'warrant against thieves and robbers': B.L. MS Add. 34125 f.111, at f.121.

[123] 2 Lord Raym. 909, 917, B.L. MS Add. 34125 f.111, at f.123. Bracton f.99b (ed. Thorne, 2.284).

ried or otherwise worked on for reward. This would have constituted a form of *locatio conductio* for the Romans – *locatio conductio operis faciendi* – but it is noticeable that Holt did not himself make this connection. His treatment here, in clear contrast with the previous four forms, was strongly rooted in more modern English law. A basic division was drawn between those exercising a public employment and private persons. The former, in line with the case-law on common carriers, were liable for all eventualities apart from Act of God and Act of the Queen's enemies; the latter were required 'to do the best they can' or to exercise their own 'personal care and diligence', seemingly a subjective standard though perhaps equivalent to taking reasonable care.[124]

Finally he came to the sixth type of case, where a person undertook gratuitously to carry goods or do other work on them, the type of agreement in issue in *Coggs* v. *Barnard* itself.[125] This was equated to the Romans' contract of *mandatum*,[126] though Holt himself preferred the English term 'commission'. The person undertaking the commission was said to be obliged to 'diligent management' or required to take the 'utmost care and diligence'.[127] This was not a rule which could easily be derived from Roman law, and it was not at all clear why a higher standard of care should be applied where the bailee was gratuitously doing something for the benefit of the bailor than where he was merely passively looking after the bailor's goods. In so far as Holt justified it he used logically weak arguments: either that the failure to use reasonable care was a deceit since the plaintiff had only trusted him because he had pretended that he would take care, or that it was a matter of definition that a person who undertook to look after the affairs of another must necessarily imply that he would take care in doing so.[128] Even if these had been good arguments, which they were not, it would have been necessary to address the central point which had been raised against the action, that the defendant could not be liable in assumpsit in the absence of any consideration. The solution offered was that the bailor

[124] 2 Lord Raym. 909, 917-918, B.L. MS Add. 34125 f.111, at ff.124-125.
[125] 2 Lord Raym. 909, 918-920, B.L. MS Add. 34125 f.111, at ff.125-130.
[126] Citing Inst. 3.26, together with the elegant definition given by Vinnius in his commentary on the title, and Bracton f.100b (ed. Thorne, 2.287).
[127] 2 Lord Raym. 909, 919; B.L. MS Add. 34125 f.111, at f.126.
[128] 2 Lord Raym. 909, 919; B.L. MS Add. 34125 f.111, at f.127. For the Roman law, see Zimmermann, *Obligations*, 426-430.

had trusted the bailee, and that this trust constituted good consideration. It is very probable that the word 'trust' here was at heart being used to connote a genuine trust of the sort that would have been enforced by the Chancery: the starting point of the argument, as appears from the draft judgment, was the sixteenth-century decision in *Megod's Case*,[129] where it had been held that the existence of such a trust entitled the beneficiary to bring an action of assumpsit against the trustee. A similar argument could be used to explain why a promise by a bailee to return the bailed goods to the bailor should be enforceable, as it had been held that it was;[130] and within the same principle, according to Holt, there could be brought all the cases of contractual misperformance in which an action on the case had been held to lie in the absence of any consideration.[131] This last step was a step too far: it was one thing to say that assumpsit would lie on a promise to do that which one was already bound to do (*e.g.* to carry out a trust, to return property to its owner), and hence that the existing duty constituted good consideration for that promise, and something completely different to say that an existing duty to do one thing could be treated as good consideration for a promise to do something else.[132] Merely to say that one had been trusted to do a job was nowhere near enough to support this extension of the law. It is important to note the nuanced difference between Holt's approach and that of Gould and Powell JJ.: where the two puisnes had seemingly argued that in cases like this there was no need for consideration, the Chief Justice had said that there was in fact good consideration, thereby underscoring the genuinely contractual nature of the claim.

This led on to a final point in his draft argument, a point made also by Gould and Powell JJ.,[133] that it was only because of the express undertaking

[129] (1586) Godb. 64; B.L. MS Add. 34125 f.111, at f.127. See N. G. Jones, 'Uses, Trusts, and a Path to Privity' [1997] *Cambridge Law Journal* 175, 192-198.
[130] *Wheatley* v. *Low* (1623) Cro. Jac. 668; *cf. Bailments*, [75].
[131] Above, 96. Note B.L. MS Add. 34125 f.111, at ff. 129 and 128v: the original text reads that the misfeasance cases in the Register were of great weight, into which is interpolated the explanation that there is a consideration implied in them.
[132] D. J. Ibbetson, 'Consideration and the Theory of Contract in Sixteenth Century Common Law', in J. Barton, ed., *Towards a General law of Contract* (Berlin, 1990), 67, 69-72; W. Swain, 'The Changing Nature of the Doctrine of Consideration, 1750-1850' (2005) 26 *Journal of Legal History* 47, 53-56.
[133] Above, 97.

to carry and stow the brandy safely and securely that he was bound to observe the utmost diligence,[134] in effect contradicting his earlier point that this was the standard of care to be demanded in all mandates or commissions.[135] The printed reports make no reference to this argument, and it may be that it had been abandoned in the final version of the judgment, but it underlines the real uncertainty in Holt's mind about the true basis of the defendant's liability.[136] This perhaps explains the somewhat defensive sentiment expressed at the end of Lord Raymond's report:

> I have said thus much in this case, because it is of great consequence, that the law should be settled in this point, but I don't know whether I may have settled it, or may not rather have unsettled it. But however that happen, I have stirred these points, which wiser heads in time may settle.[137]

Uncertainties there may have been in the underlying argument, but Holt's conclusions were firmly enough stated that later lawyers largely took them at face value, treating them as settled law. By the time that Jones was writing his *Essay on the Law of Bailments* some eighty years later they represented the established and unquestioned starting-point for the analysis of English law.

[134] B.L. MS Add. 34125 f.111, at f.130. Cf. also f.111, where in the note of the plaintiff's declaration the words 'safely and securely' are underlined.
[135] Above, 101.
[136] The shift might have flowed from his adoption of St. German's analysis of these undertakings as ineffective in the absence of consideration (above, 86); though this is not easy to square with his conclusion that the trusting of the bailee in fact constituted good consideration.
[137] 2 Lord Raym. 909, 920.

AN ESSAY ON THE LAW OF BAILMENTS

SIR WILLIAM JONES

NOTES ON THE EDITION

This edition follows the the text of the edition of 1781, the only one seen through the press by Jones. I have inserted paragraph numbers for reference in the margins, indicating original page breaks and numbering by asterisks in the text. Punctuation, italicisation and capitalisation follow the original.

Alphabetical footnotes are Jones's; numerical footnotes are editorial additions.

AN ESSAY ON THE LAW OF BAILMENTS

1. HAVING lately had occasion to examine with some attention the nature and properties of that contract, which lawyers call BAILMENT, or, *A delivery of goods on a condition, expressed or implied, that they shall be restored by the bailee to the bailor, or according to his directions, as soon as the purpose, for which they were bailed, shall be answered*, I could not but observe with surprise, that a title in our ENGLISH law, which seems the most generally interesting, should be the least generally understood, and the least precisely ascertained. Hundreds and thousands of men pass through life, without knowing, or caring to know, any of the numberless niceties, which attend our abstruse, though elegant, system of [*2] real property, and without being at all acquainted with that exquisite logick, on which our rules of special pleading are founded; but there is hardly a man of any age or station, who does not every week and almost every day contract the obligations or acquire the rights of a *hirer* or a *letter to hire*, of a *borrower* or a *lender*, of a *depositary* or a person *depositing*, of a *commissioner* or an *employer*, of a *receiver* or a *giver*, in *pledge*; and what can be more absurd, as well as more dangerous, than frequently to be bound by duties, without knowing the nature or extent of them, and to enjoy rights, of which we have no just idea? Nor must it ever be forgotten, that the contracts abovementioned are among the principal springs and wheels of civil society; that, if a want of mutual confidence, or any other cause, were to weaken them or obstruct their motion, the whole machine would instantly be disordered or broken to pieces: preserve them, and various accidents may still deprive men of happiness; but destroy them, and the whole species must infallibly be miserable. It seems therefore astonishing, that so important a branch of jurisprudence should have been so long and so strangely unsettled in a great commercial country; and that, from the reign of ELIZABETH to the reign of ANNE, *the doctrine of bailments* should have produced more contradictions and confusion, more diversity of opinion and inconsistency of argument, than any [*3] other part,

perhaps, of juridical learning; at least, than any other part equally simple.

2. Such being the case, I could not help imagining, that a short and perspicuous discussion of this title, an exposition of all our ancient and modern decisions concerning it, an attempt to reconcile judgements apparently discordant, and to illustrate our laws by a comparison of them with those of other nations, together with an investigation of their true spirit and reason, would not be wholly unacceptable to the student of *English* law; especially as our excellent BLACKSTONE, who of all men was best able to throw the clearest light on this, as on every other, subject, has comprised the whole doctrine in three paragraphs, which, without affecting the merit of his incomparable work, we may safely pronounce the least satisfactory part of it; for he represents *lending* and *letting to hire*, which are *bailments* by his own definition, as contracts of *a distinct species*; he says nothing of employment by *commission*; he introduces the doctrine of a *distress*, which has an analogy to a *pawn*, but is not properly *bailed*; and, on the great question of *responsibility for neglect*, he speaks so loosely and indeterminately, that no fixed ideas can be collected from his words[a]. His commentaries are the most correct and beautiful outline, that ever was exhibited of any human [*4] science; but they alone will no more form a lawyer, than a general map of the world, how accurately and elegantly soever it may be delineated, will make a geographer: if, indeed, all the titles, which he professed only to sketch in elementary discourses, were filled up with exactness and perspicuity, *Englishmen* might hope at length to possess a digest of their laws, which would leave but little room for controversy, except in cases depending on their particular circumstances; a work, which every lover of humanity and peace must anxiously wish to see accomplished. The following essay (for it aspires to no higher name) will explain my idea of

[a] 2. Comm. 452, 453, 454.[1]

[1] Blackstone, *Commentaries*, 2.452, 453, 454.

supplying the omissions, whether designed or involuntary, in the Commentaries on the Laws of ENGLAND.

3. I propose to begin with treating the subject *analytically*, and, having traced every part of it up to the first principles of natural reason, shall proceed *historically*, to show with what perfect harmony those principles are recognised and established by other nations, especially the ROMANS, as well as by our ENGLISH courts, when their decisions are properly understood and clearly distinguished; after which I shall resume *synthetically* the whole learning of *bailments*, and expound such rules, as, in my humble apprehension, will prevent any farther perplexity on this interesting title, except in cases very peculiarly circumstanced.

4. [*5] From the obligation, contained in the definition of bailment, *to restore the thing bailed at a certain time*, it follows, that the bailee must *keep* it, and be *responsible* to the bailor, *if it be lost or damaged*; but, as the bounds of justice would in most cases be transgressed, if he were made answerable for the loss of it *without his fault*, he can only be obliged to keep it with a degree of *care proportioned to the nature of the bailment*, and the investigation of this *degree* in every particular contract is the problem, which involves the principal difficulty.

5. There are infinite shades of *care* or *diligence* from the slightest momentary thought, or transient glance of attention, to the most vigilant anxiety and solicitude; but *extremes* in this case, as in most others, *are inapplicable to practice*: the first extreme would seldom enable the bailee to perform the condition, and the second ought not in justice to be demanded; since it would be harsh and absurd to exact the same anxious care, which the greatest miser takes of his treasure, from every man, who borrows a book or a seal. The degrees then of care, for which we are seeking, must lie somewhere between these extremes; and, by observing the different manners and characters of men, we may find a certain standard, which will greatly facilitate our enquiry; for, although some are excessively careless, and others excessively vigilant, and some through life, others only at par-[*6]ticular times, yet we may perceive, that *the generality of rational men* use nearly the same degree of diligence in the conduct of *their*

own affairs; and this care, therefore, which *every person of common prudence and capable of governing a family* takes of *his own* concerns, is a proper measure of that, which would uniformly be required in performing every contract, if there were not strong reasons for *exacting* in some of them a *greater*, and *permitting* in others a *less*, degree of attention. Here then we may fix a constant determinate point, on each side of which there is a series consisting of variable terms tending indefinitely towards the abovementioned extremes, in proportion as the case admits of indulgence or demands rigour: if the construction be *favourable*, a degree of care *less* than the standard will be sufficient; if *rigorous*, a degree *more* will be required; and, in the first case, the measure will be that care, which *every man of common sense, though absent and inattentive*, applies to his own affairs; in the second, the measure will be that attention, which a man *remarkably exact and thoughtful* gives to the securing of his personal property.

6. The fixed mode or standard of diligence I shall (for want of an apter epithet) invariably call ORDINARY; although that word is equivocal, and sometimes involves a notion of degradation, which I mean wholly to exclude; but the unvaried use of the word in one sense will pre-[*7]vent the least obscurity. The degrees on each side of the standard, being indeterminate, need not be distinguished by any precise denomination: the first may be called LESS, and the second, MORE, THAN ORDINARY diligence.

7. *Superlatives* are exactly true in mathematicks; they approach to truth in abstract morality; but in practice and actual life they are commonly false: they are often, indeed, used for mere *intensives*, as *the* MOST *diligent* for VERY *diligent*; but this is a rhetorical figure; and, as rhetorick, like her sister poetry, delights in fiction, her language ought never to be adopted in sober investigations of truth: for this reason I would reject from the present inquiry all such expressions as *the utmost care*, *all possible*, or *all imaginable, diligence*, and the like, which have been the cause of many errors in the code of ancient ROME, whence, as it will soon be demonstrated, they have been introduced into our books even of high authority.

8. Just in the same manner, there are infinite shades of *default* or *neglect*, from the slightest inattention or momentary absence of mind to the most reprehensible supineness and stupidity: these are the omissions of the before-mentioned degrees of diligence, and are exactly correspondent with them. Thus the omission of that care, *which every prudent man takes of his own property*, is the determinate point of negligence, on each side of which is a series of variable [*8] modes of default infinitely diminishing, in proportion as their opposite modes of care infinitely increase; for the want of extremely great care is an extremely little fault, and the want of the slightest attention is so considerable a fault, that it almost changes its nature, and nearly becomes in theory, as it exactly does in practice, a breach of trust and a deviation from common honesty. This known, or fixed, point of negligence is therefore a mean between *fraud* and *accident*; and, as the increasing series continually approaches to the first extreme, without ever becoming precisely equal to it, until the last term melts into it or vanishes, so the decreasing series continually approximates to the second extreme, and at length becomes nearer to it than any assignable difference: but the last terms being, as before, excluded, we must look within them for modes applicable to practice; and these we shall find to be the omissions of such care as *a man of common sense, however inattentive*, and of such as a *very cautious and vigilant* man, respectively take of *their own possessions*.

9. The constant, or fixed, mode of *default* I likewise call ORDINARY, not meaning by that epithet to diminish the culpability of it, but wanting a more apposite word, and intending to use this word uniformly in the same sense: of the two variable modes the first may be called GREATER, and the second, LESS, THAN ORDI-[*9]NARY, or the first GROSS, and the other, SLIGHT neglect.

10. It is obvious, that a bailee of common honesty, if he also have common prudence, would not be *more* negligent *than ordinary* in keeping the thing bailed: such negligence (as we before have intimated) would be a violation of good faith, and a proof of an intention to defraud and injure the bailor.

11. It is not less obvious, though less pertinent to the subject, that infinite degrees of *fraud* may be conceived increasing in a series from the term, where *gross neglect* ends, to a term, where positive *crime* begins; as *crimes* likewise proceed gradually from the lightest to the most atrocious; and, in the same manner, there are infinite degrees of *accident* from the limit of extremely slight neglect to a *force irresistible* by any human power. Law, as a practical science, cannot take notice of melting lines, nice discriminations, and evanescent quantities; but it does not follow, that *neglect*, *deceit*, and *accident*, are to be considered as indivisible points, and that *no degrees whatever* on either side of the standard are admissible in legal disquisitions.

12. Having discovered the several modes of *diligence*, which may justly be demanded of contracting parties, let us inquire in what particular cases a bailee is by natural law bound to use them, or to be answerable for the omission of them.

13. [*10] When the contract is *reciprocally beneficial to both parties*, the obligation hangs in an even balance; and there can be no reason to recede from the standard: nothing more, therefore, ought in that case to be required than *ordinary diligence*, and the bailee should be responsible for no more than *ordinary neglect*; but it is very different, both in reason and policy, when *one* only of the contracting parties derives advantage from the contract.

14. If the *bailor only* receive benefit or convenience from the bailment, it would be hard and unjust to require any particular trouble from the bailee, who ought not to be molested unnecessarily for his obliging conduct: if more, therefore, than *good faith* were exacted from such a person, that is, if he were to be made answerable for less than *gross* neglect, few men, after one or two examples, would accept goods on such terms, and social comfort would be proportionably impaired.

15. On the other hand, when the *bailee alone* is benefited or accommodated by his contract, it is not only reasonable, that he, *who receives the benefit, should bear the burden*[1], but, if he were not obliged to be *more than ordinarily* careful, and bound to an-

[1] Coke, *Second Institute*, 489: Qui sentit commodum sentire debet et onus (from *Liber Sextus*, 5.13.55: Qui sentit onus sentire debet commodum, et econtra).

swer even for *slight neglect*, few men (for acts of pure generosity and friendship are not here to be supposed) would part with their goods for the mere advantage of another, and much convenience would consequently be lost in civil society.

16. [*11] This distinction is conformable not only to natural reason, but also, by a fair presumption, to the *intention of the parties*, which constitutes the genuine law of all contracts, when it contravenes no maxim of morals or good government; but, when a different intention is *expressed*, the rule (as in devises) yields to it; and a bailee without benefit may, by a special undertaking, make himself liable for *ordinary*, or *slight*, neglect, or even for inevitable *accident*: hence, as an agreement, *that a man may safely be dishonest*, is repugnant to decency and morality, and, as no man shall be *presumed* to bind himself against *irresistible force*, it is a just rule, that *every* bailee is responsible for *fraud*, even *though* the contrary be stipulated, but that *no* bailee is responsible for *accident*, *unless* it be most expressly so agreed.

17. The plain elements of natural law, on the subject of responsibility for neglect, having been traced by this short analysis, I come to the second, or *historical*, part of my essay; in which I shall demonstrate, after a few introductory remarks, that a perfect harmony subsists on this interesting branch of jurisprudence in the codes of nations most eminent for legal wisdom, particularly of the ROMANS and the ENGLISH.

18. Of all known laws the most ancient and venerable are those of the JEWS; and among the *Mosaick* institutions we have some curious rules on the very subject before us; but, as they are [*12] not numerous enough to compose a system, it will be sufficient to interweave them as we go along, and explain them in their proper places: for a similar reason, I shall say nothing here of the *Attick* laws on this title, but shall proceed at once to that nation, by which the wisdom of ATHENS was eclipsed, and her glory extinguished.

19. The decisions of the old *Roman* lawyers, collected and arranged in the sixth century by the order of JUSTINIAN, have been for ages, and in some degree still are, in bad odour among *Englishmen*: this is an honest prejudice, and flows from a laudable

source; but a prejudice, most certainly, it is, and, like all others, may be carried to a culpable excess.

20. The constitution of ROME was originally excellent; but, when it was *settled*, as historians write, by AUGUSTUS, or, in truer words, when that bare dissembler and cold-blooded assassin *C. Octavius* gave law to millions of honester, wiser and braver men than himself by the help of a profligate army and an abandoned senate, the new form of government was in itself absurd and unnatural; and the *lex regia*, which concentrated in the prince all the powers of the state both executive and legislative, was a tyrannous ordinance, with the name only, not the nature, of a law[b]; had it even been voluntarily conceded, as it was in truth forcibly extorted, it [*13] could not have bound the *sons* of those who consented to it; for "a renunciation of *personal* rights, especially rights of the highest nature, can have no operation beyond the *persons* of those, who renounce them." Yet, iniquitous and odious as the *settlement* of the constitution was, ULPIAN only spoke in conformity to it, when he said that "the will of the prince had the force of law;"[1] that is, as he afterwards explains himself, *in the* ROMAN *empire*; for he neither meaned, nor could be mad enough to mean, that the proposition was just or true as a general maxim. So congenial, however, was this rule or sentence, ill understood and worse applied, to the minds of our early NORMAN kings, that some of them, according to Sir JOHN FORTESCUE, "were not pleased with their own laws, but exerted them to introduce the civil laws of *Rome* into the government of ENGLAND[c];" and so hateful was it to our sturdy ancestors, that, if JOHN of SALISBURY be credited, "they burned and tore all such books of civil and

[b] D.1.4.1.[2]
[c] *De* Laud. Leg. Angl. c.33. 34.[3]

[1] D.1.4.1.pr.
[2] D.1.4.1.pr: Quod principi placuit, legis habet vigorem: utpote cum lege regia, quae de imperio eius lata est, populus ei et in eum omne suum imperium et potestatem conferat.
[3] Fortescue, *De Laudibus Legum Anglie* (ed. S. B. Chrimes, Cambridge, 1942), 79.

canon law as fell into their hands[d]:" but this was intemperate zeal; and it would have been sufficient to improbate the *publick*, or *constitutional*, maxims of the *Roman* imperial law, as absurd in themselves as well as inapplicable to our free government, without [*14] rejecting the whole system of *private* jurisprudence as incapable of answering even the purpose of illustration. Many *positive* institutions of the *Romans* are demonstrated by FORTESCUE, with great force, to be far surpassed in justice and sense by our own immemorial customs; and the rescripts of SEVERUS or CARACALLA, which were laws, it seems, at *Rome*, have certainly no kind of authority at *Westminster*; but, in questions of *rational* law, no cause can be assigned, why we should not shorten our own labour by resorting occasionally to the wisdom of ancient jurists, many of whom were the most ingenious and sagacious of men. What is good sense in one age must be good sense, all circumstances remaining, in another; and pure unsophisticated reason is the same in ITALY and in ENGLAND, in the mind of a PAPINIAN and of a BLACKSTONE.

21. Without undertaking, therefore, in all instances to reconcile NERVA with PROCULUS, LABEO with JULIAN, and GAIUS either with CELSUS or with himself, I shall proceed to exhibit a summary of the *Roman* law on the subject of *responsibility for neglect*.

22. The two great sources, whence all the decisions of civilians on this matter must be derived, are *two* laws of ULPIAN; the first of which is taken from his work on *Sabinus*, and the second from his tract on the Edict: of both these laws I shall give a verbal translation accord-[*15]ing to my apprehension of their obvious meaning, and shall then state a very learned and interesting controversy concerning them, with the principal arguments on each side, as far as they tend to elucidate the question before us.

23. "Some contracts, says the great writer on *Sabinus*, make the party responsible for DECEIT ONLY; some, for both DECEIT AND

[d] Seld. *in* Fort. c.33.[1]

[1] *De Laudibus Legum Angliae*, with notes by John Selden (London, 1727), 74; John of Salisbury, *Polycraticus* 8.22 (ed. C. J. Nederman, Cambridge, 1990, 215).

NEGLECT. Nothing more than *responsibility for* DECEIT *is demanded* in DEPOSITS and POSSESSION AT WILL; both DECEIT AND NEGLECT *are inhibited* in COMMISSIONS, LENDING FOR USE, CUSTODY AFTER SALE, TAKING IN PLEDGE, HIRING; also in PORTIONS, GUARDIANSHIPS, VOLUNTARY WORK: (among these some *require* even *more than ordinary* DILIGENCE). PARTNERSHIP and UNDIVIDED PROPERTY make *the partner and joint-proprietor* answerable for both DECEIT AND NEGLIGENCE[e]."

24. "In contracts, says the same author in his other work, we are sometimes responsible for DECEIT ALONE; sometimes, for NEGLECT ALSO; for DECEIT ONLY in DEPOSITS; be-[*16]cause, since NO BENEFIT accrues to the depositary, he can justly be answerable for no more than DECEIT; but, if a REWARD happen to be given, then *a responsibility* for NEGLECT ALSO is required; or, if it be agreed at the time of the contract, that the depositary shall answer both for NEGLECT and for ACCIDENT: but, where A BENEFIT accrues to BOTH parties, as in KEEPING A THING SOLD, as in HIRING, as in PORTIONS, as in PLEDGES, as in PARTNERSHIP, both DECEIT AND NEGLECT make the party liable. LENDING FOR USE, indeed, is for the most part BENEFICIAL to the BORROWER ONLY; and, for this reason, the better opinion is that of Q. MUCIUS, who thought, that HE should be responsible not only for NEGLECT, but even for the omission of *more than ordinary* DILIGENCE[f]."

[e] Contractûs quidam DOLUM malum DUNTAXAT recipiunt; quidam, et DOLUM ET CULPAM. DOLUM tantùm DEPOSITUM et PRECARIUM; DOLUM ET CULPAM, MANDATUM, COMMODATUM, VENDITUM, PIGNORI ACCEPTUM, LOCATUM; item DOTISDATIO, TUTELAE, NEGOTIA GESTA: (in his QUIDAM ET DILIGENTIAM). SOCIETAS et RERUM COMMUNIO et DOLUM ET CULPAM recipit. D.50.17.23.

[f] In contractibus interdum DOLUM SOLUM, interdum ET CULPAM, praestamus; DOLUM IN DEPOSITO; nam, quia NULLA UTILITAS ejus versatur, apud quem deponitur, merito DOLUS praestatur SOLUS; nisi fortè et MERCES accessit, tunc enim, ut est et constitutum, ETIAM CULPA exhibetur; aut, si hoc ab initio convenit, ut et CULPAM et PERICULUM praestet is, penes quem deponitur: sed, ubi UTRIUSQUE UTLITAS vertitur, ut in EMPTO, ut in LOCATO, ut in DOTE, ut in PIGNORE, ut in SOCIETATE, et DOLUS ET CULPA praestatur. COMMODATUM autem plerumque SOLAM UTILITATEM continet ejus, CUI COMMODATUR; et ideò verior est Q. MUCII sententia existimantis et CULPAM praestandam et DILIGENTIAM. D.13.6.5.2.

25. [*17] One would scarce have believed it possible, that there could have been two opinions on laws so perspicuous and precise, composed by the same writer, who was indubitably the best expositor of his own doctrine, and apparently written in illustration of each other; the first comprising the rule, and the second containing the reason of it: yet the single passage extracted from the book on SABINUS has had no fewer than twelve particular commentaries in *Latin*[g], one or two in *Greek*[h], and some in the *modern* languages of Europe, besides the general expositions of that important part of the digest, in which it is preserved. Most of these I have perused with more admiration of human sagacity and industry than either solid instruction or rational entertainment; for these authors, like the generality of commentators, treat one another very roughly on very little provocation, and have the art rather of

[g] BOCERUS,[1] CAMPANUS,[2] D'AVEZAN,[3] DEL RIO,[4] LE CONTE,[5] RITTERSHUSIUS,[6] GIPHANIUS,[7] J. GODEFROI,[8] and others.

[h] The scholium on *Harmenopulus*, l 6. tit. de Reg. Jur. n.55. may be considered as a commentary on this law.[9]

[1] H. Bocer, *Commentarii in Celebrem L Contractus 23 D De Regulis Iuris* (Speyer, 1587).

[2] H. Cinus Campanus, *Ad Utilissimam l. Contractus ff. De Regulis Iuris* (Paris, 1574).

[3] J. D'Avezan, *Contractuum Liber Prior*, in *Novus Thesaurus Juris Civilis et Canonici* (The Hague, 1752), 4.49-64 (earlier edition, Arles, 1644).

[4] M. A. Del Rio, *Repetitio L. Transigere C. de Transactionibus. Eiusdem Exercitatio ad L. Contractus 23 de Diversis Regulis Iuris Antiqui Totam Culpae Praestandae Materiae Comprehendens* (Lyons, 1606), 113-292.

[5] A. Le Conte (Contius), *Ad L. Contractus de Diversis Regulis Iuris Antiqui Dictatae Praelectiones* (Bourges, 1574).

[6] C. Rittershusius, *Commentarius Novus Pulcherrimus et Utilissimus: in Celeberrimam Legem XXIII Contractus Digesti De Regulis Juris Antiqui* (Strasbourg, 1616).

[7] H. Giphanius, *Commentarii in Titulum Digestorum de Diversis Regulis Iuris Antiqui* (Frankfurt, 1606), pp. 121-134.

[8] J. Godefroy (Gothofredus), *In Titulum Pandectarum De Diversis Regulis Iuris Antiqui Commentarius* (Geneva, 1652), pp. 97-147.

[9] Constantine Harmenopulus, *Manuale Legum sive Hexabiblos* (ed. G. Heimbach, Leipzig, 1841), 786-793 (earlier edition, Cologne, 1566, 664-670).

clouding texts in themselves clear, than of elucidating passages, which have any obscurity in the words or the sense of them. CAMPANUS, indeed, who was both a lawyer and a poet, has turned the first law of *Ulpian* into *Latin* hexameters;[1] and his authority, both in [*18] prose and verse, confirms the interpretation, which I have just given.

26. The chief causes of all this perplexity have been, first, the vague and indistinct manner in which the old *Roman* lawyers, even the most eminent, have written on the subject; secondly, the loose and equivocal sense of the words DILIGENTIA and CULPA; lastly, and principally, the darkness of the parenthetical clause IN HIS QUIDAM ET DILIGENTIAM, which has produced more doubt, as to its true reading and signification, than any sentence of equal length in any author *Greek* or *Latin*. Minute as the question concerning this clause may seem, and dry as it certainly is, a short examination of it appears absolutely necessary.

[1] Cinus Campanus, *Ad Utilissimam l. Contractus ff. De Regulis Iuris*, 3:
Contractus quosdam solum dolus afficit, urget
Quosdam alios dolus ac culpa, at dolus arctat eum, quem
Penes depono, precibus quique accipit usu,
Mandatum accipiens culpaque, doloque tenetur,
Tempore quin usu certo, rem detinet, et qui
Vendicat, aut capit in pignus, caute locat, aut dat
In dotem impuberes fidei recipitque tuendos
Sive ad amicorum curanda negocia ventum est,
Hos inter quidam studium praestare iubentur
At socii, atque alii quibus est fortuna bonorum.
Communis caveant culpamque dolumque subire,
Sed minus interdum nonnunquam ad plura tenemur
Ceu placitis varie contractibus addita lex est
Nam latam primum servari iure decens est
Excipit at Celsus nunquam illud posse valere
Hi praestare dolum curent ea pactio iniqua.
Nempe fidem offendit, iamdudum hoc iure receptum est
Infausti a miseris casus mortalibus, ut sunt
Funera, servorumque fugae iniustaeque rapinae,
Seditio in populis, miseranda incendia, aquarum
Impetus, atque incursus praedonum excipiuntur.

27. The vulgate edition of the pandects, and the manuscripts, from which they were printed, exhibit the reading above set forth; and it has accordingly been adopted by CUJAS[1], P. FABER[2], LE CONTE[3], DONELLUS[4], and *most* others, as giving a sense both perspicuous in itself and consistent with the second law; but the FLORENTINE copy has *quidem*, and the copies, from which the *Basilica* were translated three centuries after JUSTINIAN, appear to have contained the same word, since the *Greeks* have rendered it by a particle of similar import[5]. This variation in a single letter makes a total alteration in the whole doctrine of ULPIAN; for, *if* it be agreed, that *diligentia* means, by a figure of speech, *a more* [*19] *than ordinary degree of diligence*, the common reading will imply, conformably with the second law before cited, that "SOME of the preceding contracts demand that higher degree;" but the *Florentine* reading will denote, in contradiction to it, that "ALL of them require more than ordinary exertions."

28. It is by no means my design to depreciate the authority of the venerable manuscript preserved at *Florence*; for, although few civilians, I believe, agree with POLITIAN, in supposing it to be one of the *originals*, which were sent by *Justinian* himself to the principal towns of *Italy*[i], yet it may *possibly* be the very book, which the Emperor LOTHARIUS II. is *said* to have found at *Amalfi* about the year 1130, and gave to the citizens of PISA, from whom it was taken, near three hundred years after, by the *Florentines*, and has

[i] Epist.x.4.[6] Miscell. cap. 41.[7] See Gravina, lib. 1. § 141.[8]

[1] J. Cujas, *Recitationes Solemnes*, ad D.50.17.23 (*Opera* (Prato, 1838), 6.1869).
[2] P. Faber, *Ad Titulum de Diversis Regulis Iuris Antiqui Commentarium* (Paris, 1585), 107, 127.
[3] *ad L. Contractus de Diversis Regulis Iuris Antiqui Dictatae Praelectiones*, 7.
[4] *Commentariorum de Iure Civili*, 16.7.34 (*Opera* (Florence, 1842), 4.733-734).
[5] Bas. 2.3.23 (ed. Heimbach, 1.66): *ἐν τούτοις δὲ καὶ ἐπιμέλεια* (translated as *in his autem et diligentia*).
[6] Angelus Politianus, *Epistulae*, 10.4 (in *Angeli Politiani Opera*, vol. 1 (Lyons, 1528), 293-296).
[7] Angelus Politianus, *Miscellaneorum Centuria Una*, c.41 (in *Angeli Politiani Opera*, vol. 1, 568).
[8] J. V. Gravina, *Origines Iuris Civilis* (Leipzig, 1708), 1.141 (p.170).

been kept by them with superstitious reverence[k]: be that as it may, the copy deserves the highest respect; but, if any proof be requisite, that it is *no faultless* transcript, we may observe, that, in the very law before us, *accedunt* is erroneously written for *accidunt*; and the whole phrase, indeed, in which that word occurs, is different from the copy used by the *Greek* interpreters, and conveys a meaning, as BOCERUS[1] and others [*20] have remarked, not supportable by any principle or analogy.

29. This, too, is indiputably clear; that the sentence, *in his* QUIDEM *et diligentiam*, is ungrammatical, and cannot be construed according to the interpretation, which some contend for. What verb is understood? *Recipiunt*. What noun? *Contractûs*. What then becomes of the words *in his*, namely *contractibus*, unless *in* signify *among*? And, in that case, the difference between QUIDEM and QUIDAM vanishes; for the clause may still import, that "AMONG the preceding contracts (that is, *in* SOME *of them*), more than usual diligence is exacted:" in this sense the *Greek* preposition seems to have been taken by the scholiast on HARMENOPULUS;[2] and it may here be mentioned, that *diligentia*, in the nominative, appears in some old copies, as the *Greeks* have rendered it; but ACCURSIUS, DEL RIO,[3] and a few others, consider the word as implying no more than diligence *in general*, and distinguish it into various *degrees* applicable to the several contracts, which ULPIAN enumerates. We may add, that one or two interpreters thus explain the whole sentence, "in his *contractibus* quidam *jurisconsulti* et diligentiam *requirunt*," but this interpretation, if it could be admitted, would entirely destroy the authority of the clause, and imply, that *Ulpian* was of a different opinion. As to the last conjecture, that

[k] Taurelli, Praef. ad Pand. Florent.[4]

[1] The point seems not to be made by Bocer.
[2] Harmenopulus, *Manuale Legum sive Hexabiblos* (ed. Haenel), 789.
[3] Accursius, gl. ad D.50.17.23; Del Rio, *Exercitatio ad L. Contractus 23 de Diversis Regulis Iuris Antiqui*, 132, 228.
[4] Taurelli, *Digestorum seu Pandectarum Libra Quinquaginta*, f.ii[v].

only *certain cases* and *circumstances* are meaned by the word [*21] QUIDAM, it scarce deserves to be repeated. On the whole, I strongly incline to prefer the vulgate reading, especially as it is not conjectural, but has the authority of manuscripts to support it; and the mistake of a letter might easily have been made by a transcriber, whom the prefaces, the epigram prefixed, and other circumstances, prove to have been, as *Taurelli* himself admits, a *Greek*.[1] Whatever, in short, be the genuine words of this much-controverted clause, I am persuaded, that it ought by no means to be strained into an inconsistency with the *second* law; and this has been the opinion of most foreign jurists from AZO and ALCIAT down to HEINECCIUS and HUBER; who, let their dissension be, on other points, ever so great, think alike in distinguishing three degrees of neglect, which we may term *gross*, *ordinary*, and *slight*, and in demanding responsibility for those degrees according to the rule before expounded.

30. The law then on this head, which prevailed in the ancient *Roman* empire, and still prevails in *Germany*, *Spain*, *France*, *Italy*, *Holland*, constituting, as it were, a part of the law of nations, is in substance what follows.

31. GROSS neglect, *lata culpa*, or, as the *Roman* lawyers most accurately call it, *dolo proxima*, is in practice considered as equivalent to DOLUS, or FRAUD, itself; and consists, according to the best interpreters, in the *omission* of that care, *which even inattentive and thoughtless men never* [*22] *fail to take of their own property*: this fault they justly hold a violation of *good faith*.

32. ORDINARY neglect, *levis culpa*, is the *want* of that diligence, which the *generality of mankind use in their own concerns*; that is, of *ordinary care*.

33. SLIGHT neglect, *levissima culpa*, is the *omission* of that CARE, which *very attentive and vigilant persons take of their own goods*, or, in other words, of *very exact diligence*.

34. Now, in order to ascertain the degree of neglect, for which a man, who has in his possession the goods of another, is made responsible by his contract, either *express* or *implied*, civilians establish *three* principles, which they deduce from the law of *Ul*-

[1] Taurelli, *Digestorum seu Pandectarum Libra Quinquaginta*, f.ii^{v}.

pian on the *Edict*; and here it may be observed, that they frequently distinguish this law by the name of *Si ut certo*, and the other by that of *Contractus*[l]; as many poems and histories in ancient languages are denominated from their *initial* words.

35. First: In contracts, which are beneficial *solely* to the owner of the property holden by another, no more is demanded of the holder than *good faith*, and he is consequently responsible for nothing less than *gross* neglect: this, therefore, is the general rule in DEPOSITS: but, in regard to COMMISSIONS, or, as foreigners call them, MAN-[*23]DATES, and the *implied* contract *negotiorum gestorum*, a certain care is requisite from *the nature of the thing*; and, as *good faith* itself demands, that such care be proportioned to the exigence of each particular case, the law *presumes*, that the mandatary or commissioner, and, by parity of reason, the *negotiorum gestor*, engaged at the time of contracting to use a degree of diligence *adequate to the performance of the work undertaken*[m].

36. Secondly: In contracts *reciprocally* beneficial to *both* parties, as in those of SALE, HIRING, PLEDGING, PARTNERSHIP, and the contract implied in JOINT-PROPERTY, such care is exacted, as *every prudent man commonly takes of his own goods*; and, by consequence, the *vendor*, the *hirer*, the *taker in pledge*, the *partner*, and the *co-proprietor*, are answerable for *ordinary* neglect.

37. Thirdly: In contracts, from which a benefit accrues *only* to him, who has the goods in his custody, as in that of LENDING FOR USE, an *extraordinary* degree of care is demanded; and the *borrower* is, therefore, responsible for *slight* negligence.

38. This had been the learning generally, and almost unanimously, received and taught by the doctors of *Roman* law; and it is very remarkable, that even ANTOINE FAVRE, or *Faber*, who [*24] was

[l] Or l. 5. § 2. ff. *Commod.* and l. 23. ff *de reg. jur*. Instead of *ff*, which is a barbarous corruption of the initial letter of *πανδέκται*, many write D, for *Digest*, with more clearness and propriety.

[m] *Spondet diligentiam*, say the *Roman* lawyers, *gerendo negotio parem.*[1]

[1] Pothier, *Observation Générale* (*Oeuvres*, 1.280). *Cf. Traité du Contrat de Mandat*, c.46: Spondet diligentiam et industriam negotio gerendo parem.

famed for innovation and paradox, who published two ample volumes *De Erroribus Interpretum*[1], and whom GRAVINA justly calls *the boldest of expositors and the keenest adversary of the practisers*[n], discovered no error in the common interpretation of two celebrated laws, which have so direct and so powerful an influence over social life, and which he must repeatedly have considered: but the younger GODEFROI of *Geneva*, a lawyer confessedly of eminently learning, who died about the middle of the last century, left behind him a regular *commentary* on the law *Contractus*[2], in which he boldly combats the sentiments of all his predecessors, and even of the ancient *Romans*, and endeavours to support a new system of his own.

39. He adopts, in the first place, the *Florentine* reading, of which the student, I hope, has formed by this time a decided opinion from a preceding page of this essay.

40. He censures the rule comprised in the law *Si ut certo* as weak and fallacious, yet admits, that the rule, which He condemns, had the approbation and support of MODESTINUS[3], of PAULUS[4], of AFRICANUS[5], of GAIUS[6], and of the great PAPINIAN[7] himself; nor does he satisfactorily prove the *fallaciousness*, to which he objects, unless every rule be fallacious, to which there are some exceptions. He understands by DILIGENTIA that care, which *a very attentive and* [*25] *vigilant man* takes of his own property; and he demands this care in *all* the eight contracts, which immediately precede the disputed clause: in the *two*, which follow it, he requires no more than *ordinary* diligence.[8] He admits, however, the

[n] Orig. Jur. Civ. lib. i. § 183.[9]

[1] A. Faber, *De Erroribus Pragmaticorum et Interpretum Iuris* (Lyons, 1658).
[2] J. Godefroy (Gothofredus), *In Titulum Pandectarum De Diversis Regulis Iuris Antiqui Commentarius* (Geneva, 1652), 97-147.
[3] *Mosaicarum et Romanarum Legum Collatio*, 10.2.1.
[4] Perhaps PS. 2.4.3.
[5] D.30.108.12.
[6] Perhaps D.13.6.18.pr.
[7] Unidentified.
[8] Godefroy, *In Titulum Pandectarum De Diversis Regulis Iuris Antiqui Commentarius*, 107, 125-126.
[9] Gravina, *Origines Iuris Civilis*, 1.183 (p.228).

three degrees of neglect above stated, and uses the common epithets *levis* and *levissima*; but, in order to reconcile his system with many laws, which evidently oppose it, he ascribes to the old lawyers the wildest mutability of opinion, and is even forced to contend, that ULPIAN himself *must have changed his mind.*[1]

41. Since his work was not published, I believe, in his life-time, there may be reason to suspect, that he had not completely settled *his own* mind; and he concludes, indeed, with referring the decision of every case on this head to that most dangerous and most tremendous power, the *discretion of the judge*[o].

42. The *triple* division of neglects had also been highly censured by some lawyers of reputation. ZASIUS had very justly remarked, that neglects differed in *degree*, but not in *species*; adding, "that he had no objection to use the words *levis* and *levissima*, merely as terms of practice adopted in courts, for the more easy distinction between the different degrees of [*26] care exacted in the performance of different contracts[p]:" but DONELLUS, in opposition to his master *Duaren*, insisted that *levis* and *levissima* differed in sound only, not in sense; and attempted to prove his assertion triumphantly by a regular syllogism[q]; the minor proposition of which is raised on the figurative and inaccurate manner, in which positives are often used for superlatives, and conversely, even by the best of the old *Roman* lawyers. True it is, that, in the law *Contractus*, the division appears to be *twofold* only, DOLUS and CULPA; which differ in *species*, when the first means *actual*

[o] "Ego certè hac in re censentibus accedo, vix quidquam generaliùs definiri posse; remque hanc ad *arbitrium judicis*, prout res est, referendam." p. 141.[2]

[p] Zas. *Singul. Resp*. lib. i. cap. 2.[3]

[q] "Quorum definitiones eaedem sunt, ea inter se sunt eadem; *levis* autem culpae et *levissimae* una et eadem definitio est; utraque igitur culpa eadem." Comm. Jur. Civ. lib. xvi. cap. 7.[4]

[1] *Ibid.*, 132, 133, 141.

[2] *Ibid.*, 141.

[3] U. Zasius, *Singularium Responsorum Libri Duo*, 1.2, esp. ad no. 9 (in *Opera Omnia* (Lyons, 1550), 5.32-42, at 34).

[4] H. Donellus, *Commentariorum de Iure Civili*, 16.7.16-17 (*Opera* (Florence, 1840-47), 4.710-713, quote at 710).

fraud and malice, but in *degree* merely, when it denotes no more than *gross neglect*; and, in either case, the second branch, being capable of *more* and *less*, may be subdivided into *ordinary* and *slight*; a subdivision, which the law *Si ut certo* obviously requires: and thus are both laws perfectly reconciled.

43. We may apply the same reasoning, changing what should be changed, to the *triple* division of *diligence*; for, when *good faith* is considered as implying at least the exertion of *slight* attention, the other branch, *Care*, is subdivisible into *ordinary* and *extraordinary*; which brings us back [*27] to the number of degrees already established both by the analysis and by authority.

44. Nevertheless, a system, in one part entirely new, was broached in the present century by an advocate in the parliament of PARIS, who may, probably, be now living, and, possibly, in that professional station, to which his learning and acuteness justly entitle him. I speak of M. LE BRUN, who published, not many years ago, an *Essay on Responsibility for Neglect*[r], which he had nearly finished, before he had seen the commentary of *Godefroi*, and, in all probability, without ever being acquainted with the opinion of *Donellus*.

45. This author sharply reproves the *triple* division of neglects, and seems to disregard the rule concerning a benefit arising to *both*, or to *one*, of the contracting parties; yet he charges *Godefroi* with a want of due clearness in his ideas, and with a palpable misinterpretation of several laws. He reads *in his quidEm et diligentiam*; and that with an air of triumph; insinuating, that *quidAm* was only an artful conjecture of *Cujas* and *Le Conte*, for the purpose of establishing *their* system; and he supports *his own* reading by the authority of the BASILICA; an authority, which, on another occasion, he depreciates[2]. He derides the absurdity of *permitting* [*28] *negligence* in any contract, and urges, that such *permission*, as he calls it, is against express law: "now, says he, where a contract is beneficial to both parties, the doctors permit *slight* negligence,

[r] *Essai sur la Prestation des Fautes*, à Paris, chez Saugrain, 1764.[1]

[1] D. Le Brun, *Essai sur la Prestation des Fautes* (Paris, 1764).
[2] *Essai sur la Prestation des Fautes*, 66, 70.

which, how slight soever, is still *negligence*, and ought always be to inhibited."[1] He warmly contends, that the ROMAN laws, properly understood, admit only *two* degrees of diligence; one, measured by that, which *a provident and attentive father of a family* uses in his own concerns; another, by that care, which the *individual party*, of whom it is required, *is accustomed to take of his own possessions*; and he, very ingeniously, substitutes a new rule in the place of that, which he rejects; namely, that, *when the things in question are the* SOLE *property of the person, to whom they must be restored*, the holder of them is obliged to keep them with the *first* degree of diligence; whence he decides, that a *borrower* and a *hirer* are responsible for precisely the same neglect; that a vendor, who retains for a time the custody of the goods sold, is under the same obligation, in respect of care, with a man, who undertakes to manage the affairs of another, either *without* his request, as a *negotiorum gestor*, or *with* it, as a *mandatary*: "but, says he, *when the things are the* JOINT *property of the parties contracting*, no higher diligence can be required than the second degree, or that, which the *acting party* commonly uses in *his own* affairs; and it is [*29] sufficient, *if he keep them, as he keeps his own*."[2] This he conceives to be the distinction between the *eight* contracts, which precede, and the *two*, which follow, the words *in his quidem et diligentiam*.

46. Throughout his work he displays no small sagacity and erudition, but speaks with too much confidence of his own decisions, and with too much asperity or contempt of all other interpreters from BARTOLUS to VINNIUS.

47. At the time when this author wrote, the learned M. POTHIER was composing some his admirable *treatises* on all the different species of express, or implied, *contracts*; and here I seize with pleasure an opportunity of recommending those treatises to the *English* lawyer, exhorting him to read them again and again; for, if his great master LITTLETON has given him, as it must be presumed, a taste for luminous method, apposite examples, and a clear manly style, in which nothing is redundant, nothing defi-

[1] *Essai sur la Prestation des Fautes*, 50-51.
[2] *Essai sur la Prestation des Fautes*, 37, 71-73, 146.

cient, he will surely be delighted with works, in which all those advantages are combined, and the greatest portion of which is law at *Westminster* as well as at *Orleans*[s]: for my own part, I am so charmed with them, that, if my undissembled fondness for the study of jurisprudence were never to produce any greater [*30] benefit to the publick, than barely the introduction of POTHIER to the acquaintance of my countrymen, I should think that I had in some measure discharged the debt, which *every man*, according to lord COKE, *owes to his profession*[1].

48. To this venerable professor and judge, for he had sustained both characters with deserved applause, LE BRUN sent a copy of his little work; and M. POTHIER honoured it with a short, but complete, answer in the form of a *General Observation on his Treatises*[t]; declaring, at the same time, that *he would not enter into a literary contest*, and apologizing for his fixed adherence to the ancient system, which he politely ascribes to *the natural bias of an old man in favour of opinions formerly imbibed*. This is the substance of his answer: "that he can discover no kind of absurdity in the usual division of *neglect* and *diligence*, nor in the *rule*, by which different *degrees* of them are applied to different contracts; that to speak with strict propriety, negligence is not *permitted* in any contract, but *a less rigorous construction* prevails in some than in others; that a *hirer*, for instance, is not considered as *negligent*, when he takes the same care of the goods hired, which the generality of mankind take of their own; that the *letter to hire*, who has his reward, must be presumed to have [*31] demanded at first no higher degree of diligence, and cannot justly complain of that *inattention*, which in another case might have been culpable;

[s] *Oeuvres de M. Pothier*, à Paris, chez DEBURE: 28 volumes in *duodecimo*, or 6 in *quarto*. The illustrious author died in 1772.

[t] It is printed apart, in *fourteen* pages, at the end of his treatise on the *Marriage-contract*.[2]

[1] Identified in later editions as Coke, *Eighth Report*, Preface p.34.

[2] *Observation Générale sur le Précédent Traité, et sur les Suivans*. In most editions it is printed at the end of the *Traité des Obligations*. I have used that in *Oeuvres de R.-J. Pothier* (Brussels, 1831), 1.280-283.

for a *lender*, who has *no* reward, may fairly exact from the borrower that *extraordinary* degree of care, which *a very attentive person of his age and quality* would certainly have taken; that the diligence, which *the* INDIVIDUAL *party commonly uses in his own affairs*, cannot properly be the object of judicial inquiry; for *every* trustee, administrator, partner, or co-proprietor, must be *presumed* by the court, auditors, or commissioners, before whom an account is taken, or a distribution or partition made, to use in *their own* concerns such diligence, as is commonly used by *all prudent men*; that it is a violation of *good faith* for any man to take less care of another's property, which has been intrusted to him, *than of his own*; that, consequently, the author of the new system demands no more of a *partner* or a *joint-owner* than of a *depositary*, who is bound to keep the goods deposited *as he keeps his own*; which is directly repugnant to the indisutable and undisputed sense of the law *Contractus*."[1]

49. I cannot learn, whether M. LE BRUN ever published a reply, but am inclined to believe, that his system has gained very little ground in *France*, and that the old interpretation continues [*32] universally admitted on the continent both by theorists and practisers.

50. Nothing material can be added to POTHIER'S argument, which, in my humble opinion, is unanswerable; but it may not be wholly useless to set down a few general remarks on the controversy: particular observations might be multiplied without end.

51. The only *essential* difference between the systems of GODEFROI and LE BRUN relates to the *two* contracts, which follow the much-disputed clause; for the *Swiss* lawyer makes the partner and co-proprietor answerable for *ordinary* neglect, and the *French* advocate demands no more from them than *common honesty*: now, in this respect, the error of the *second* system has been proved to demonstration; and the author of it himself confesses

[1] Pothier, *Observation Générale* (*Oeuvres*, 1.282).

ingenuously, that the other part of it fails in the article of *Marriage-portions*[u].

52. In regard to the division of neglect and care into *three* degrees or *two*, the dispute appears to be merely verbal; yet, even on this head, LE BRUN seems to be self-confuted: he begins with engaging to prove "that only *two* degrees of fault are distinguished by the laws of *Rome*," and ends with drawing a conclusion, that they acknowledge but *one* degree[1]: now, though this might be only a slip, yet the whole tenor of his book established *two* modes of [*33] *diligence*, the *omissions* of which are *as many* neglects; exclusively of *gross* neglect, which he likewise admits, for the *culpa levissima* is only that, which he repudiates. It is true, that he gives no epithet or name to the omission of his *second* mode of care; and, had he searched for an epithet, he could have found no other than *gross*; which would have demonstrated the weakness of his whole system[v].

53. The disquisition amounts, in fact, to this: from the barrenness or *poverty*, as LUCRETIUS calls it, of the *Latin* language[2], the single word CULPA includes, as a generick term, various degrees or shades of *fault*, which are sometimes distinguished by epithets, and sometimes left without any distinction; but the *Greek*, which is rich and flexible, has a term expressive of almost every shade, and the translators of the law *Contractus* actually use the words *ῥᾳθυμία* and *ἀμέλεια,* which are by no means synonymous, the former implying a certain *easiness of mind* or *remissness of attention*, while the second imports a higher and more culpable de-

[u] See p. 71. *note*. and p. 126.
[v] See pages 32. 73. 74. 149.

[1] Le Brun, *Essai sur la Prestation des Fautes*, 149.
[2] Lucretius, *De Rerum Natura*, 1.136-140:

> Nec me animi fallit Graiorum obscura repeta
> difficile inlustrare Latinis versibus esse,
> multa novis verbis praesertim cum sit agendum
> propter egestatem linguae et rerum novitatem.

gree of *negligence*[w]. This observation, indeed, seems [*34] to favour the system of *Godefroi*; but I lay no great stress on the mere words of the translation, as I cannot persuade myself, that the *Greek* jurists under BASILIUS and LEO were perfectly acquainted with the niceties and genuine purity of their language; and there are invincible reasons, as, I hope, it has been proved, for rejecting all systems but that, which POTHIER has recommended and illustrated.

54. I come now to the laws of our own country, in which the same distinctions and the same rules, notwithstanding a few clashing authorities, will be found to prevail; and here I might proceed chronologically from the oldest *Year-book* or *Treatise* to the latest adjudged *Case*; but, as there would be a most unpleasing dryness in that method, I think it better to examine separately every distinct *species* of bailment, observing at the same time, under each head, a kind of historical order. It must have occurred to the reader, that I might easily have taken a wider field, and have extended my inquiry to every possible case, in which a man *possesses for a time the goods of another*; but I chose to confine myself within certain limits, lest, by grasping at too vast a subject, I should at last be compelled, as it frequently happens, by accident

[w] *Basilica*, 2. 3. 23.[1] See *Demosth.* 3 Phil. *Reiske's* edit I. 112. 3.[2] For *levissima culpa*, which occurs but once in the whole body of *Roman* law, *ῥᾳθυμία* seems the proper word in *Greek*; and it is actually so used in the *Basilica*, 60. 3. 5. where mention is made of the *Aquilian* law, *in quâ*, says ULPIAN, *et levissima culpa venit.* D.9.2.44.[3]

[1] G. E. Heimbach, ed., *Basilicorum Libri LX* (Leipzig, 1833), 1.66 (where mandate, *commodatum*, sale, pledge, *locatio conductio*, *dotis datio*, *tutela* and *negotiorum gestio* are said to lead to liability for *ῥᾳθυμία* (translated by Heimbach as *culpa*), while societas carries liability for *ἀμέλεια*, translated as *negligentia*).

[2] J. J. Reiske, *Oratorum Graecorum* (Leipzig, 1770), 1.112; Demosthenes, *Third Philippic*, 5: But in fact it is your indifference (*ῥᾳθυμία*) and carelessness (*ἀμέλεια*) that Philip has conquered.

[3] Heimbach, *Basilicorum Libri LX*, 5.265 (translating the *culpa* of D.9.2.5.1 as *ῥᾳθυμία*); but *cp.* Bas. 60.3.44 (Heimbach, 5.314), translating *culpa* in D.9.2.44 (the only Roman text where *culpa levissima* is found) as *ἀμέλεια*).

or want of leisure, to leave the whole work unfinished: it will be sufficient to remark, that the rules are in general the same, [*35] by whatever means the goods *are legally* in the hands of the possessor, whether by delivery from the owner, which is a proper *bailment*, or from any other person, by finding[x], or in consequence of some distinct contract.

55. Sir JOHN HOLT, whom every *English* man should mention with respect, and from whom no *English* lawyer should venture to dissent without extreme diffidence, has taken a comprehensive view of this whole subject in his judgement on a celebrated case, which shall soon be cited at length; but, highly as I venerate his deep learning and singular sagacity, I shall find myself constrained, in some few instances, to differ from him, and shall be presumptuous enough to offer a correction or two in part of the doctrine, which he propounds in the course of his argument[y].

56. His division of bailments into *six* sorts appears, in the first place, a little inaccurate; for, in truth, his *fifth* sort is no more than a branch of his *third*, and he might, with equal reason, have added a *seventh*, since the fifth is capable of another subdivision. I acknowledge, therefore, but *five* species of bailment; which I shall now enumerate and define, with all the *Latin* names, one or two of which lord *Holt* has omitted. 1. DE-[*36]POSITUM, which is a naked bailment, without reward, of goods to be *kept* for the bailor. 2. MANDATUM, or *commission*; when the mandatary undertakes, without recompence, to *do some act* about the thing bailed, or simply to *carry* them; and hence Sir HENRY FINCH divides bail-

[x] Doct. and Stud. dial. 2. ch. 38.[1] Lord Raym. 909. 917.[2] See Ow. 141. 1 Leon 224. 1 Cro. 219. *Mulgrave* and *Ogden*.[3]

[y] Lord Raym. 912.[4]

[1] St. German, *Doctor and Student*, 2.38 (91 S.S. 259-261).

[2] *Coggs* v. *Barnard* (1703) 2 Lord. Raym 909, 917.

[3] *Mulgrave* v. *Ogden* (1591) Owen 141, 1 Leon. 224, Cro. El. 219.

[4] *Coggs* v. *Barnard* (1703) 2 Lord. Raym. 909, 912. A version of the judgment of Holt C.J., attributed to the whole court, can be found at 1 Com. 133.

ment into *two* sorts, to *keep*, and to *employ*[z]. 3. COMMODATUM, or *loan for use*; when goods are bailed, without pay, to be *used* for a certain time by the bailee. 4. PIGNORI ACCEPTUM; when a thing is bailed by a debtor to his creditor in *pledge*, or as a security for the debt. 5. LOCATUM, or *hiring*, which is always for a *reward*; and this bailment is either, 1. *locatio rei*, by which the hirer gains the temporary use of *the thing*; or, 2. *locatio operis faciendi*, when *work* and *labour*, or *care* and *pains*, are to be performed or bestowed on the thing delivered; or, 3. *locatio operis mercium vehendarum*, when goods are bailed for the purpose of being *carried* from place to place, either to a *publick* carrier, or to a *private* person.

57. I. The most ancient case, that I can find in our books, on the doctrine of DEPOSITS (there were others, indeed, a few years earlier, which turned on points of pleading) was adjudged in the eighth of Edward II. and is abridged by *Fitzherbert*[a]. It may be called BONION'S case, [*37] from the name of the plaintiff, and was, in substance, this: An action of detinue was brought for *seals*, *plate*, and *jewels*, and the defendant pleaded, "that the plaintiff had bailed to him a chest *to be kept*, which chest was *locked*; that the bailor himself took away the key, *without informing the bailee of the contents*; that robbers came in the NIGHT, *broke open the defendant's chamber*, and carried off the chest into the fields, where they forced the lock, and took out the *contents*; that the defendant was robbed at the same time of his own goods." The plaintiff replied, "that the jewels were delivered, in a chest *not locked*, to be restored at the pleasure of the bailor," and *on this*, it is said, *issue was joined*.

58. Upon this case lord *Holt* observes, "that he cannot see, why the bailee should not be charged with goods *in* a chest as well as with goods *out of* a chest; for, says he, the bailee has as little

[z] Law, B. 2. Ch. 18.[1]
[a] Mayn. Edward II. 275. Fitzh. Abr, *tit*. Detinue, 59.[2]

[1] H. Finch, *Law, or a Discourse Thereof* (London, 1627), 2.18 (p.179).
[2] YB P. 8 Edw. II f.275; Fitz. Abr., *Detinue*, 59. *Bowdon* v. *Pelleter*, YB P. 8 Edw. II (41 S.S.) 136.

power over them, as to any benefit, that he might have from them, and as great power to defend them, in one case as in the other[b]." The very learned judge was dissatisfied, we see, with Sir *Edward Coke's* reason, "that, when the jewels were locked up in a chest, the bailee was not in fact trusted with them[c]." Now there was diversity of opinion, upon this very point, among the greatest [*38] lawyers of *Rome*; for "it was a question, whether, if a box sealed up had been deposited, the box only should be demanded in an action, or the clothes, which it contained, should also be specified; and TREBATIUS insists, that the box only, not the particular contents of it, must be sued for; unless the things were previously shown, and then deposited: but LABEO asserts, that he, who deposits the box, deposits the contents of it; and ought, therefore, to demand the clothes themselves. What then, if the depositary *was ignorant of the contents*? It seems to make no great difference, since he took the charge upon himself; and I am of opinion, says *Ulpian*, that, although the box was sealed up, yet an action may be brought for what it contained[d]." This relates chiefly to the form of the libel; but, surely, cases may be put, in which the difference may be very material as to the *defence*. Diamonds, gold, and precious trinkets, ought, *from their nature*, to be kept with peculiar care under lock and key: it would, therefore, be *gross* negligence in a depositary to leave such a deposit in an open antichamber, and *ordinary* neglect, at least, to let them remain on his table, where they might possibly tempt his servants; but no man can proportion his care to the *nature* of things, without knowing them: perhaps, therefore, it [*39] would be no more than *slight* neglect, to leave out of a drawer a box or casket, which was neither known, nor could justly be suspected, to contain diamonds; and DOMAT, who prefers the opinion of *Trebatius*, decides, "that, in such a case, the depositary would only be obliged to restore the

[b] Lord Raym. 914.[1]
[c] 4 Rep. 84.[2]
[d] D.16.3.1.41.

[1] *Coggs* v. *Barnard* (1703) 2 Lord. Raym 909, 914.
[2] *Southcote* v. *Bennet* (1601) 4 Co. Rep. 83b, 83b-84a.

casket, as it was delivered, without being responsible for the contents of it[1]." I confess, however, that, anxiously as I wish on all occasions to see authorities respected, and judgements holden sacred, BONION'S case appears to me wholly incomprehensible; for the defendant, instead of having been *grossly* negligent (which alone could have exposed him to an action), seems to have used at least *ordinary* diligence; and, after all, the loss was occasioned by a *burglary*, for which no bailee can be responsible without a very special undertaking. The plea, therefore, in this case was good, and the replication, idle; nor could I ever help suspecting a mistake in the last words *alii quòd non*; although *Richard de Winchedon*, or whoever was the compiler of the *table* to this Year-book, makes a distinction, that, "if jewels be bailed to me, and *I put them* into a casket, and *thieves rob me of them in the night time*, I am answerable; not, if they be *delivered* to me in a chest *sealed up*[2];" which could never have been law, for the next oldest case, in the book of *Assise*, contains the opinion of chief justice THORPE, that "a general bailee *to keep* is not responsible, *if the goods be stolen*, with-[*40]out his *gross* neglect[e];" and it appears, indeed, from *Fitzherbert*, that the party was driven to this issue, "whether the goods were taken away by *robbers*[3]."

59. By the *Mosaick* institutions, "if a man delivered to his neighbour MONEY or STUFF *to keep*, and it was *stolen* out of his house, and the thief could not be found, the master of the house was to be brought before the judge, and to be discharged, if he could swear, that he had not *put his hand* unto his neighbour's goods[f]," or, as the *Roman* author of the LEX DEI translates it, *Nihil se*

[e] 29 Ass. 28. Bro. Abr. *tit.* Bailment, pl. 7.[4]
[f] Exod. xxii. 7, 8.[5]

[1] Domat, *The Civil Laws in their Natural Order*, 1.7.1.17. Jones appears to have used the French original, *Les Loix Civiles dans leur Ordre Naturel* (Paris, 1689).
[2] YB Edw. II, Table, sub verb *Detinue de Fait*. For the attribution to John de Winchedon, see YB Edw. II (London, 1678), Preface.
[3] Fitz. Abr., *Barre*, 304.
[4] YB 29 Lib. Ass. f.163 pl. 28; Bro. Abr., *Bailment*, 7 (1355).
[5] Exodus 22. 7-8.

nequiter gessisse[g]; but a distinction seems to have been made between a stealing by *day* and a stealing by *night*[h]; and "if CATTLE were bailed and stolen (by *day*, I presume), the person, who had the care of them, was bound to make restitution to the owner[i];" for which the reason seems to be, that, when *cattle* are delivered *to be kept*, the bailee is rather a *mandatary* than a depositary, and is, consequently, obliged to use a degree of diligence *adequate to the charge*: now sheep can hardly be stolen in the *day-time* without some neglect of the shepherd; and we find that, when JACOB, who was, for a long time at least, [*41] a bailee of a different sort, *as he had a reward*, lost any of the beasts intrusted to his care, LABAN made him answer for them "whether stolen by day or stolen by night[k]."

60. Notwithstanding the high antiquity as well as the manifest good sense of the rule, a contrary doctrine was advanced by Sir EDWARD COKE in his *Reports*, and afterwards deliberately inserted in his *Commentary on* LITTLETON, the great result of all his experience and learning; namely, "that a depositary is responsible, if the goods be stolen from him, unless he accept them specially *to keep as his own*," whence he advises all depositaries to make such a special acceptance[l]. This opinion, so repugnant to natural reason and the laws of all other nations, he grounded partly on

[g] Lib. 10. De Deposito. This book is printed in the same volume with the *Theodosian* Code, Paris, 1586.[1]
[h] Gen. xxxi. 39.[2]
[i] Exod. xxii. 12.[3]
[k] Gen. xxxi. 39.[4]
[l] 4 Rep. 83. b. 1 Inst. 89. a. b.[5]

[1] *Mosaicarum et Romanarum Legum Collatio* (ed. F. Mommsen), 10.1.1; in S. Riccobono, *Fontes Iuris Romani Anteiustiniani*, 1.567: nihil se nequiter egisse. The same reading, with *egisse* rather than *gessisse*, is found in the text referred to by Jones: *Codex Theodosiani Libri XVI* (Paris, 1586), [2].113.
[2] Genesis 31.39
[3] Exodus 22.12.
[4] Genesis 31.39.
[5] *Southcote* v. *Bennet* (1601) 4 Co. Rep. 83b; Co. Litt. 89. The point cited is at Co. Litt. 89b.

some broken cases in the Year-books, mere conversations on the bench or loose arguments at the bar; and partly on SOUTHCOTE'S case, which he has reported, and which by no means warrants his deduction from it. As I humbly conceive that case to be law, though the doctrine of the learned reporter cannot in all points be maintained, I shall offer a few remarks on the pleadings in the cause, and the judgement given on them.

61. SOUTHCOTE declared in detinue, that he had delivered goods to BENNET, *to be by him* SAFELY [*42] *kept*: the defendant confessed SUCH delivery, but pleaded in bar, that a certain person STOLE them out of his possession; the plaintiff replied, protesting that he had not been robbed, that the person named in the plea was a SERVANT of the defendant, and demanded judgement; which, on a general demurrer to the replication, he obtained. "The reason of the judgement, says lord *Coke*, was, because the plaintiff had delivered the goods to be SAFELY kept, and the defendant had taken the charge of them upon himself, by accepting them on SUCH a delivery." Had the reporter stopped here, I do not see what possible objection could have been made; but his exuberant erudition boiled over, and produced the frothy conceit, which has occasioned so many reflections on the case itself; namely, "that *to* KEEP and *to keep* SAFELY are one and the same thing;" a notion which was denied to be law by the whole court in the time of chief justice *Holt*[m].

62. It is far from my intent to speak in derogation of the great commentator on *Littleton*; since it may truly be asserted of him, as *Quintilian* said of CICERO, that *an admiration of his works is a sure mark of some proficiency in the study of the law*; [1] but it must be allowed, that his profuse learning often ran wild, and that he

[m] Ld. Raym. 911. *margin.*[2]

[1] Quintilian, *Institutio Oratoria*, 10.1.112: *Ille se proficisse sciat, si Cicero valde placebit.*

[2] *Coggs* v. *Barnard* (1703) 2 Lord Raym. 909, 911 (3rd edn., 1775): "That notion in Southgate's case, 4 Rep. 83b. that a general bailment and a bailment to be safely kept is all one, was denied to be law by the whole Court, ex relatione m'ri Bunbury."

has injured many a good case by the vanity of thinking to improve them.

63. [*43] The pleader, who drew the replication in *Southcote's* case, must have entertained an idea, that the *blame* was *greater*, if a *servant* of the depositary stole the goods, than if a mere *stranger* had purloined them; since the defendant ought to have been more on his guard against a person, who had so many opportunities of stealing; and it was his own fault, if he gave those opportunities to a man, of whose honesty he was not morally certain: the court, we find, rejected this distinction, and also held the replication informal, but agreed, that no advantage could be taken on a *general* demurrer of such informality, and gave judgement on the substantive badness of the plea[n]. If the plaintiff, instead of replying, had demurred to the plea in bar, he might have insisted in argument, with reason and law on his side, "that, although a *general* bailee *to keep* be responsible for GROSS neglect *only*, yet *Bennet* had, by a *special* acceptance, made himself answerable for ORDINARY neglect *at least*; that it was *ordinary* neglect, to let the goods be *stolen* out of his possession, and he had not averred, that they were stolen *without his default*; that he ought to have put them into a *safe* place, according to his undertaking, and have kept the key of it himself; that the *special* bailee was reduced to the class of a *conductor operis*, or a workman *for hire*; and that a tailor, to whom his employer has delivered lace for [*44] a suit of clothes, is bound, if the lace be *stolen*, to restore the value of it[o]."

[n] 1 Cro. 815.[1]

[o] "Alia est *furti* ratio; id enim *non casui*, sed *levi culpae*, fermè ascribitur." *Gothofr*. Comm. in L. *Contractus*, p.145.[2] See D.17.2.52.3. where says the annotator, "Adversùs *latrones* parùm prodest custodia; adversus *furem* prodesse potest, si quis advigilet."[3] See also POTH. *Contrat de Louage*, n. 429.[4] and *Contrat de Pret à usage*, n. 53.[5] So, by justice *Cottesmore*, "Si jeo grante byens a un home a garder a mon oeps, si les byens per *son mesgarde* sont *embles*, il sera charge a moy de mesme les byens, mez s'il soit *robbe* de mesme les byens, il est excusable per le ley." 10 Hen. VI. 21.[6]

[1] *Southcote* v. *Bennet* (1601) Cro. El. 815.

[2] Godefroy, *In Titulum Pandectarum De Diversis Regulis Iuris Antiqui Commentarius*, 145.

This reasoning would not have been just, if the bailee had pleaded, as in *Bonion's* case, that he had been *robbed by violence*, for no degree of *care* can in general prevent an open robbery: *impetûs praedonum*, says ULPIAN, *à nullo praestantur*.[1]

64. Mr. Justice POWELL, speaking of *Southcote's* case, which he denies to be law, admits, that, "if a man *does* undertake *specially* to keep goods SAFELY, that is a warranty, and will oblige the bailee to keep them safely against perils, where *he has a remedy over*, but *not* against those where he has *no* remedy over[p]." One is unwilling to suppose, that this learned judge had not read lord *Coke's* report with attention; yet the case, which he puts, is precisely that which he opposes, for Bennet *did* undertake "to keep the goods SAFELY;" and, with submission, *the* [*45] *degree of care demanded*, not *the remedy over*, is the true measure of the obligation; for the bailee might have his *appeal of robbery*, yet he is not bound to keep the goods against *robbers* without a most express agreement[q]. This, I apprehend, is all that was meaned by St. GERMAN, when he says, "that, if a man *have nothing* for keeping the goods bailed, and promise, at the time of the delivery, to restore them *safe at his peril,* he is not responsible for *mere* casualties[r];" but the rule extracted from this passage, "that *a special* acceptance *to keep* SAFELY will not charge the bailee against the

[3] D. Gothofredus, gl. *furibus* ad D.17.2.52.3.
[4] Pothier, *Traité du Contrat de Louage*, s.429.
[5] Pothier, *Traité du Prêt à Usage et du Précaire*, s.53.
[6] YB M. 10 Hen. VI f.21 pl. 69.

[p] Ld. Raym. 912.[2]
[q] 2 Sho. pl. 166.[3]
[r] Doct. and Stud. dial. 2. chap. 38.[4]

[1] D.50.17.23, *in fin.*
[2] *Coggs* v. *Barnard* (1703) 2 Lord Raym. 909, 912.
[3] *R.* v. *Sheriff of Hertford* (1681) 2 Sho. 172 pl. 164 (noted as 2 Show. pl. 166 in Vin. Abr., *Bailment*, A.12).
[4] St. German, *Doctor and Student*, 2.38 (91 S.S. 260).

acts of *wrongdoers*[s]," to which purport HOBART also and CROKE are cited[1], is too general, and must be confined to acts of *violence*.

65. I cannot leave this point, without remarking, that a *tenant at will*, whose interest, when he has it rentfree, the *Romans* called PRECARIUM, stands in a situation exactly parallel to that of a depositary; for, although the contract be for *his benefit*, and, in some instances, for his benefit *only*, yet he has an *interest* in the land till the will is determined, "and, our law adds, it is the folly of the lessor, if he do not restrain him by a special condition:" thence it was adjudged, in the *Countess of Shrewsbury's* case, "that an [*46] action will not lie against a tenant at will *generally*, if the house be burned through his neglect[t];" but, says justice *Powell*, "had the action been founded on a *special* undertaking, as that, in consideration that the lessor would let him live in the house, he would deliver it up *in as good repair as it then was in*, such an action would have been maintainable.[u]"

66. It being then established, that a bailee of the *first* sort is answerable only for a *fraud*, or for *gross* neglect, which is considered as evidence of it, and not for such *ordinary* inattentions as may be compatible with *good faith*, if the depositary be himself *a careless and inattentive* man; a question may arise, whether, if proof be given, that he is, in truth, *very thoughtful and vigilant in his own concerns*, he is not bound to restitution, if the deposit be lost through his neglect, either *ordinary* or *slight*; and it seems easy to support the affirmative; since in this case the measure of diligence is *that, which the bailee uses in his own affairs*. It must however be confessed, that the character of the individual de-

[s] Com. 135. Ld. Raym. 915.[2]
[t] 5 Rep. 13 b.[3]
[u] Ld. Raym. 911[4]

[1] *Tisdale* v. *Essex* (1615) Hob. 34, *Andrew's Case* (1591) Cro. El. 214; cited *Coggs* v. *Barnard* (1703) 2 Lord Raym. 909, 915. Both cases deal with the liability of the lessor of land on a covenant for quiet enjoyment.
[2] *Coggs* v. *Barnard* (1703) 1 Com. 133, 134; 2 Lord Raym. 909, 915.
[3] *Countess of Shrewsbury's Case* (1600) 5 Co. Rep. 13b.
[4] *Coggs* v. *Barnard* (1703) 2 Lord Raym. 909, 911.

positary can hardly be an object of judicial discussion; if he be *slightly* or even *ordinarily* negligent in keeping the goods deposited, the favourable presumption is, that he is equally neglectful of his own property; but this presumption, like all others, may be repelled; and, if it be proved, [*47] for instance, that, his house being on fire, he saved his own goods, and, having time and power to save also those deposited, suffered them to be burned, he shall restore the worth of them to the owner[w]. If, indeed, he have time to save only one of two chests, and one be a deposit, the other his own property, he may justly prefer his own; unless that contains things of small comparative value, and the other be full of much more precious goods, as fine linen or silks; in which case he ought to save the more valuable chest, and has a right to claim indemnification from the depositor for the loss of his own. Still farther; if he commit even a *gross* neglect in regard to his own goods *as well as* those bailed, by which *both* are lost or damaged, *he cannot be said to have violated good faith*, and the bailor must impute to his own folly the confidence which he reposed in so improvident and thoughtless a person[x].

67. To this principle, that a depositary is answerable *only* for *gross* negligence, there are some exceptions.

68. First, as in *Southcote's* case, where the bailee, by a *special* agreement, has engaged to answer for less[1]: "Si quid nominatim convenit," says the *Roman* lawyer, "vel plus vel minus in sin-[*48]gulis contractibus, hoc servabitur quod initiò convenit; legem enim contractui dedit[y];" but the opinion of CELSUS, that an agreement *to dispense with deceit* is void, as being contrary to

[w] POTH. *Contrat de Dépôt*, n. 29.[2] Stiernh. *de Jure Sueon*. l. 2. c. 5.[3]
[x] Bract. 99. b.[4] Justin. Inst. l. 3. tit. 15.[5]
[y] l. *Contractus*, 23. D. *de reg. jur.*[6]

[1] Text: more. Corrected by corrigendum and in subsequent editions.
[2] Pothier, *Traité du Contrat de Dépôt*, s.29.
[3] J. O. Stiernhöök, *De Jure Sveonum et Gothorum* (Stockholm 1672), 257.
[4] Bracton, *De Legibus et Consuetudinibus Angliae*, 99b (ed. Thorne, 2.284).
[5] Inst. 3.14.3.
[6] D.50.17.23. The penultimate word should read *contractus* rather than *contractui*.

good morals and decency, has the assent both of *Ulpian* and our *English* courts[z].

69. Secondly; when a man spontaneously and officiously proposes to keep the goods of another, *he may prevent the owner from intrusting them with a person of more approved vigilance*; for which reason *he takes upon himself*, according to JULIAN, *the risk of the deposit, and becomes responsible at least for ordinary neglect, but not for mere casualties*[a].

70. Where things are deposited through necessity on any sudden emergence, as a fire or shipwreck, M. LE BRUN insists, "that the depositary must answer for *less than gross* neglect, how careless soever he may be in his own affairs; since the preceding remark, that *a man, who reposes confidence in an improvident person, must impute any loss to his own folly*, is inapplicable to a case, where the deposit was not optional; and *the law ceases with the reason of it*[b];" but that is not the *only* reason; and, though it is an additional misfortune, for a man in extreme haste and deep distress to light upon a stupid or [*49] inattentive depositary, yet I can hardly persuade myself, that more than perfect *good faith* is demanded in this case, although a violation of that faith be certainly more criminal than in other cases, and was therefore punished at *Rome* by a forfeiture of the double value of the goods deposited.

71. In these circumstances, however, a benevolent *offer* of keeping another's property for a time would not, I think, bring the case within *Julian's* rule before-mentioned, so as to make the person offering answerable for *slight*, or even *ordinary*, negligence; and my opinion is confirmed by the authority of LABEO, who requires no more than *good faith* of a *negotiorum gestor*, when "affectione coactus, ne bona mea distrahantur, negotiis se meis obtulerit[1]."

[z] Doct. and Stud. dial. 2. chap. 38.[2]
[a] D.16.3.1.35.
[b] De la Prestation des Fautes, p. 77.[3]

[1] D.3.5.3.9.
[2] St. German, *Doctor and Student*, 2.38 (91 S.S. 261); D.50.17.23, D.16.3.1.7.
[3] Le Brun, *Essai sur la Prestation des Fautes*, 77-78.

72. Thirdly; when the bailee, improperly called a *depositary*, either *directly* demands and receives a reward *for his care*, or takes the charge of goods, *in consequence of* some *lucrative* contract, he becomes answerable for *ordinary* neglect; since, in truth, he is in both cases a *conductor operis*, and *lets out* his mental labour at a just price: thus, when clothes are left with man, who is paid for the use of his bath, or a trunk with an inn-keeper or his servants, or with a ferryman, the bailees are as much bound to indemnify the owners, if the goods be lost or damaged through their want of *ordinary* circumspection, as if they were to receive a stipulated recompense *for their* [*50] *attention and pains*; but of this more fully, when we come to the article of *hiring*.

73. Fourthly; when the *bailee alone* receives advantage from the deposit, as, if a thing be borrowed on a future event, and deposited with the intended borrower, until the event happens, because the owner, perhaps, is likely to be absent at the time, such a depositary must answer even for *slight* negligence; and this bailment, indeed, is rather a *loan* than a deposit, in whatever light it may be considered by the parties. Suppose, for example, that *Charles*, intending to appear at a masked ball expected to be given on a future night, requests *George* to lend him a dress and jewels for that purpose, and that *George*, being obliged to go immediately into the country, desires *Charles* to keep the dress till his return, and, if the ball be given in the mean time, to wear it; this seems to be a regular *loan*, although the original purpose of borrowing be future and contingent.

74. Since, therefore, the two last cases are not, in strict propriety, *deposits*, the exceptions to the general rule are reduced to two only; and the second of them, I conceive, will not be rejected by the *English* lawyer, though I recollect no decision or dictum exactly conformable to the opinion of *Julian*.

75. Clearly as the obligation to *restore* a deposit flows from the nature and definition of this contract, yet, in the reign of ELIZABETH, [*51] when it had been adjudged, consistently with common sense and common honesty, "that an action on the case lay against a man, who had not performed his promise of redelivering, or delivering over, things bailed to him," that judgement

was *reversed*; and, in the sixth year of JAMES, judgement for the plaintiff was arrested in a case exactly similar[c]: it is no wonder, that the profession *grumbled*, as lord HOLT says, at so absurd a reversal; which was itself most justly reversed a few years after, and the first decision solemnly established in the house of peers[d1].

76. Among the curious remains of *Attick* law, which philologers have collected, very little relates to the contracts, which are the subject of this essay; but I remember to have read of DEMOSTHENES, that he was advocate for a person, with whom *three* men had deposited some valuable utensil, of which they were joint-owners; and the depositary had delivered it to *one* of them, of whose knavery he had no suspicion; upon which the other *two* brought an action, but were nonsuited on their own evidence, that there was a *third* bailor, whom they had not joined in the suit; for, the truth not being proved, *Demosthenes* insisted, *that his client could not legally restore the deposit, unless all three pro-* [*52]*prietors were ready to receive it*; and this doctrine was good at *Rome* as well as at *Athens*, when the thing deposited was in its nature incapable of partition: it is also law, I apprehend, in Westminster-hall[e].

77. The obligation to return a deposit faithfully was, in very early times, holden sacred by the *Greeks*, as we learn from the story of GLAUCUS, who, on consulting the oracle, received this answer, "that it was criminal even *to harbour a thought* of with-holding

[c] Yelv. 4. 50. 128.[2]
[d] 2 Cro. 667. *Wheatly* and *Low*.[3]
[e] D.16.3.1.36.[4] Bro. Abr. *tit*. Bailment, pl. 4.[5]

[1] Corrigendum deletes 'in the house of peers'; words omitted in second and subsequent editions.
[2] *Riches* v. *Brigges* (1602) Yelv. 4; *Game* v. *Harvie* (1604) Yelv. 50; *Pickas* v. *Guile* (1608) Yelv. 128.
[3] *Wheatley* v. *Low* (1623) Cro. Jac. 668.
[4] D.16.3.1.36: Sed si res sunt, quae dividi non possunt, omnes debebit tradere satisdatione idonea a petitore ei praestanda in hoc, quod supra eius partem est. The Roman rule was, in fact, the reverse of that which Jones described.
[5] Bro. Abr., *Bailment*, 4, abridging YB H. 12 Hen. IV f.18 pl. 19.

deposited goods from the owners, who claimed them[f];" and a fine application of this *universal* law is made by an *Arabian* poet contemporary with JUSTINIAN, who remarks, "that life and wealth are only *deposited* with us by our creator, and, *like all other deposits*, must in due time be restored[1]."

78. II. Employment by COMMISSION was also known to our ancient lawers; and BRACTON, the best writer of them all, expresses it by the *Roman* word, *Mandatum*; now, as the very essence of this contract is the *gratuitous* performance of it by the bailee, and as the term *commission* is also pretty generally applied to bailees, who receive *hire* or *compensation* for their attention and trouble, I shall not scruple to adopt the word MANDATE as appropriated *in a limited sense* to the species of bailment now before us; [*53] nor will any confusion arise from the common acceptation of the word in the sense of a judicial command or precept, which is in truth only a *secondary* and inaccurate usage of it. The great distinction then between one sort of *mandate* and a *deposit* is, that the former *lies in fesance*, and the latter, simply *in custody*: whence, as we have already intimated, a difference often arises between the degree of care demanded in the one contract and in the other; for, the mandatary being considered as having engaged himself, to use *a degree of diligence and attention adequate to the performance of his undertaking*, the omission of such diligence may be, according to the nature of the business, either *ordinary*, or *slight*, neglect; although a bailee of this species ought regularly to be answerable only for a violation of *good faith*. This is the common doctrine taken from the law of ULPIAN; but there seems, in reality, to be no exception in the present case from the general rule; for, since *good faith* itself obliges every man *to perform his actual engagements*, it of course obliges the mandatary to exert himself in proportion to the exigence of the affair in hand, and

[f] Herod. VI. 86.[2] Juv. *Sat*. XIII. 199.[3]

[1] Probably *Mufaddalīyāt* XXVII.27-28 (C. J. Lyall, ed., *The Mufaddalīyāt* (Oxford, 1918), 1.302, 2.103).
[2] Herodotus, *Histories*, 6.86.
[3] Juvenal, *Satires*, 13.199-202.

neither to *do* any thing, how minute soever, by which his employer may sustain damage, nor *omit* any thing, however inconsiderable, which the nature of the act requires[g]: nor will a want of ability [*54] to perform the contract be any defence for the contracting party; for, though the law *exacts no impossible things*[1], yet it may justly require, that every man shall know his own strength, before he undertakes to do an act, and that, if he delude another by false pretensions to skill, he shall be responsible for any injury, that may be occasioned by such delusion. If, indeed, an unskilful man yield to the pressing instances of his friend, who could not otherwise have his work performed, and engage reluctantly in the business, no higher degree of diligence can be demanded of him than a fair exertion of his capacity.

79. It is almost needless to add, that a mandatary, as well as a depositary, may bind himself by a *special* agreement to be answerable even for casualties; but that neither the one nor the other can exempt himself by any stipulation from responsibility for *fraud*, or, its equivalent, *gross* neglect.

80. A distinction seems very early to have been made in out law between the *non*fesance, and the *mis*fesance, of a *conductor operis*, and, by equal reason, of a mandatary; or, in other words, between a total failure of performing an executory undertaking and a culpable neglect in executing it; for, when an action on the case was brought against a carpenter, who, having undertaken to build a new house for the plaintiff within a certain time, *had not built it*, the [*55] court gave judgement of nonsuit; but agreed, that, if the defendant had built the house negligently and spoiled the timber, an action against him would have been maintainable[h]. However, in a subsequent reign, when a similar action was commenced against one WATKINS for *not building* a mill according to his undertaking, there was a long conversation between the judges

[g] Lord Raym. 910.[2]
[h] Yearb. 11. Hen. IV. 33.[3]

[1] D.50.17.185; *Liber Sextus*, 5.13.6.
[2] *Coggs* v. *Barnard* (1703) 2 Lord Raym. 909, 910.
[3] YB M. 11 Hen. IV f.33 pl. 60.

and the bar, which chief justice *Babington* at length interrupted by ordering the defendant's counsel either to plead or to demur; but serjeant *Rolf* chose to plead specially, and issue was taken on a *discharge* of the agreement[i]. Justice *Martin* objected to the action, because no tort was alledged; and he persisted warmly in his opinion, which seems not wholly irreconcilable to that of his two brethren; for in the cases, which they put, a special injury was supposed to be occasioned by the non-performance of the contract.

81. Authority and reason both convince me, that *Martin*, into whose opinion the reporter recommends an inquiry[1], was wrong in his objection, if he meaned, as justice *Cokain* and the chief justice seem to have understood him, that no such action would lie for *non*fesance, even *though special damage had been stated*. His argument was, that the action before them *sounded in covenant* [*56] merely, and required a specialty to support it; but that, if the covenant had been changed into a *tort*, a good writ of trespass on the case might have been maintained: he gave, indeed, an example of *mis*fesance, but did not controvert the instances, which were given by the other judges.

82. It was not alledged in either of the cases just cited, that the defendant was to receive *pay* for the fesance of his work; but, since both defendants were described as *actually in trade*, it was not perhaps intended, that they were to work *for nothing*: I cannot however persuade myself, that there would have been any difference, had the promises been purely *gratuitous*, and had a special injury been caused by the breach of them. Suppose, for instance, that *Robert's* corn-fields are surrounded by a ditch or trench, in which the water from a certain spring used to have a free course, but which has of late been obstructed by soil and rubbish; and that, *Robert* informing his neighbour *Henry* of his intention speedily to clear the ditch, *Henry* offers and undertakes immediately to remove the obstruction and repair the banks *without re-*

[i] Yearb. 3. Hen. VI. 36. b. 37. a. *Stath*. Abr. tit. *Accions sur le cas*, pl. 20.[2]

[1] YB H. 3 Hen. VI f.36 pl. 33, at f.37: Quaere de l'Opinion de Martin.
[2] YB H. 3 Hen. VI f.36 pl. 33, at f.37; Stath. Abr., *Accions sur le Cas*, 20.

ward, he having business of the same kind to perform on his own grounds: if, in this case, *Henry* neglect to do the work undertaken, "and the water, not having its natural course, overflow the fields of *Robert* and spoil his corn," may not *Robert* maintain his action on the case? Most assuredly, and so in a thousand instances of proper bail-[*57]ments, that might be supposed; where a just reliance on the promise of the defendant prevented the plaintiff from employing another person, and was consequently the cause of the loss, which he sustained[k]; for it is, as it ought to be, a general rule, that, for every *damnum iniuriâ datum*, an action of some sort, which it is the province of the pleader to advise, may be maintained; and, although the *gratuitous* performance of an act be a *benefit* conferred, yet, according to the just maxim of PAULUS, *Adjuvari nos, non decipi, beneficio oportet*[l]: but the *special* damage, not the assumption, is the cause of *this* action; and, if *notice* be given by the mandatary, *before any damage incurred, and while another person may be employed*, that he cannot perform the work, no process of law can enforce the performance of it.

83. A case in *Brook*, made complete from the Year-book, to which he refers, *seems* directly in point; for, by chief justice FINEUX, *it had been adjudged*, that, "if a man assume to build a house for me by a certain day, and do not build it, *and I suffer damage by his nonfesance*, I shall have an action on the case, as well as if he had *done it amiss*:" but it is *possible*, that *Fineux* might suppose a consideration, though none be mentioned[m].

84. [*58] Actions on this contract are, indeed, very uncommon, for a reason not extremely flattering to human nature; because it is very uncommon to undertake any office of trouble *without compensation*; but, whether the case really happened, or the reward, which had actually been stipulated, was omitted in the declara-

[k] Yearb. 19. Hen. VI. 49.[1]
[l] D.13.6.17.3.
[m] Bro. Abr. *tit*. Action sur le Case, 72.[2]

[1] YB H. 19 Hen. VI f.49 pl. 5.
[2] Bro. Abr., *Accion sur le Case*, 72. Fitz. Abr., *Accion sur le Case*, 45; YB 21 Hen. VII f.41.

tion, the question, "whether a man was responsible for damage to certain goods occasioned by his negligence in performing a GRATUITOUS promise," came before the court, in which lord *Holt* presided, so lately as the second year of queen ANNE; and a point, which the first elements of the *Roman* law have so fully decided, that no court of judicature on the continent would suffer it to be debated, was thought in ENGLAND *to deserve*, what it certainly received, *very great consideration*[n].

85. The case was this: BERNARD had assumed *without pay* safely to remove several casks of brandy from one cellar, and lay them down *safely* in another, but managed them so negligently, that one of the casks was staved. After the general issue joined, and a verdict for the plaintiff COGGS, a motion was made in arrest of judgement on the irrelevancy of the declaration, in which it was neither alledged, that the defendant was to have *any recompense for his pains*, nor that he was a *common porter*: but the court were una-[*59]nimously of opinion, that the action lay; and, as it was thought a matter of great consequence, each of the judges delivered his opinion separately.

86. The chief justice, as it has before been intimated[o], pronounced a clear, methodical, elaborate argument; in which he distinguished bailments into *six* sorts, and gave a history of the principal authorities concerning each of them. This argument is justly represented by my learned friend, the annotator *on the First Institute*, as "a most masterly view of the whole subject of bailment[p];" and, if my little work be considered merely as a commentary on it, the

[n] Ld. Raym. 909-920. 1 Salk. 26. Com. 133. Farr. 13. 131. 528.[1]

[o] P. 35.

[p] Hargr. Co. Litt. 89. b. n. 3. The profession must lament the necessary suspension of this valuable work.[2]

[1] *Coggs* v. *Barnard* (1703) 2 Lord Raym. 909, 1 Salk. 26, 1 Com. 133, Holt 13, 131, 528. There are further reports at 2 Salk. 735, 3 Salk. 11, 268 and 3 Lord Raym. 163.

[2] Co. Litt. (13th edn., by Francis Hargrave, London, 1775), 89b, n.3. Only half of the edition was published at this time; as noted in the second and subsequent editions, it was completed by Charles Butler and published in 1788.

student may perhaps think, that my time and attention have not been unusefully bestowed.

87. For the decision of the principal case, it would have been sufficient, I imagine, to insist, that the point was *not new*, but had already been determined; that the writ in the REGISTER, called, in the strange dialect of our forefathers, *De pipâ vini cariandâ*[q], was not similar, but identical; for, had the reward been the *essence* of the action, it must have been inserted in the writ, and nothing would have been left for the declaration but the stating of the day, [*60] the year, and other circumstances; of which *Rastell* exhibits a complete example in a writ and declaration for *negligently and improvidently planting a quickset hedge*, which the defendant had promised to raise, *without any consideration alledged*; and issue was joined on a traverse of the negligence and improvidence[r]. How any answer could have been given to these authorities, I am at a loss even to conceive: but, although it is needless to prove the same thing twice, yet other authorities, equally unanswerable, were adduced by the court, and supported with reasons no less cogent; for *nothing*, said Mr. Justice *Powell* emphatically, *is law, that is not reason*[1]; a maxim, in theory excellent, but in practice dangerous, as many rules, true in the abstract, are false in the concrete; for, since the reason of *Titius* may, and frequently does, differ from the reason of *Septimius*, no man, who is not a lawyer, would ever know how to act, and no man, who is a lawyer, would in many instances know what to advise, unless courts were bound by *authority*, as firmly as the pagan deities were supposed to be bound by the decrees of fate.

88. Now the *reason* assigned by the learned judge for the cases in the *Register* and *Year-books*, which were the same with *Coggs* and *Bernard*, namely, "that the party's SPECIAL *assumpsit* and

[q] Reg. Orig. 110. a. see also 110. b. *De equo infirmo sanando*, and *De columbari reparando*.[2]

[r] Rast. Entr. 13. b.[3]

[1] *Coggs* v. *Barnard* (1703) 2 Lord Raym. 909, 911.

[2] *Registrum Omnium Brevium* (London, 1687), ff.110, 110v.

[3] W. Rastell, *Collection of Entrees* (London, 1596), f.13v.

undertaking obliged him *so* to do the thing, that the bailor came to no damage by his [*61] neglect[1]," seems to intimate, that the omission of the words *salvò et securè* would have made a difference in this case, as in that of a *deposit*; but I humbly contend, that those words are implied, by the nature of a contract which lies *in fesance*, agreeably to the distinction with which I began this article. As judgement, indeed, was to be given on the record merely, it was unnecessary, and might have been improper, to have extended the proposition beyond the point then before the court; but I cannot think, that the narrowness of the proposition in this instance affects the general doctrine, which I have presumed to lay down; and, in the strong case of the shepherd, *who had a flock to keep*, which he *suffered through negligence to be drowned*, neither a *reward* nor a *special* undertaking are stated[s]: that case, in the opinion of justice *Townsend*, depended upon the distinction between a bargain *executed* and *executory*; but I cannot doubt the relevancy of an action in the second case, as well as the first, *whenever actual damage is occasioned by the nonfesance*[t].

89. There seems little necessity after this, to mention the case of *Powtuary* and *Walton*, the *reason* of [*62] which applies directly to the present subject; and, though it may be objected that the defendant was stated as a *farrier*, and must be *presumed* to have acted *in his trade*, yet chief justice *Rolle* intimates no such presumption; but says expressly, that "an action on the case lies upon this matter, *without alledging any consideration*: for the *negligence* is the cause of action, and not the *assumpsit*[u]."

[s] Yearb. 2 Hen. VII. 11.[2]

[t] *Stath. Abr*. tit. *Accions sur le cas*, pl. 11. By justice *Paston*, "si un ferrour face covenant ove moy de ferrer mon chival, jeo die qe sil *ne ferra* mon chival, uncore jeo averai accion sur mon cas, qar en son default peraventure mon chival est perie."[3]

[u] 1 Ro. Abr. 10.[4]

[1] *Coggs* v. *Barnard* (1703) 2 Lord Raym. 909, 910.

[2] YB H. 2 Hen. VII f.11 pl. 9.

[3] Stath. Abr., *Accions sur le Cas*, 11, abridging YB 14 Hen. VI f.18 pl. 58.

[4] *Powtney* v. *Walton* (1597) Ro. Abr., *Action sur Case*, P.5.

90. A bailment without reward to *carry* from place to place is very different from a mandate to *perform a work*; and, there being nothing to take it out of the general rule, I cannot conceive that the bailee is responsible for *less* than *gross* neglect, unless there be a *special* acceptance: for instance, if *Stephen* desire *Philip* to carry a diamond-ring from *Bristol* to a person in *London*, and he put it *with bank-notes of his own* into a letter-case, out of which it is *stolen* at an inn, or seized by a robber on the road, *Philip* shall not be answerable for it; although a *very careful*, or perhaps a *commonly prudent*, man would have kept it in his purse at the inn, and have concealed it somewhere in the carriage; but, if he were to secrete *his own notes* with peculiar vigilance, and either leave the diamond in a open room, or wear it on his finger in the chaise, I think he would be bound, in case of a loss by stealth or robbery, to restore the value of it to *Stephen*: every thing, therefore, that has been [*63] expounded in the preceding article concerning *deposits*, may be applied exactly *to this sort* of bailment, which may be considered as a subdivision of the second species.

91. Since we have nothing in these cases analogous to the judgements of *infamy*, which were often pronounced at *Rome* and *Athens*, it is hardly necessary to add, what appears from the speech of CICERO for S. *Roscius* of *Ameria*, that "the ancient *Romans* considered a mandatary as *infamous*, if he broke his engagement, not only by actual *fraud*, but even by *more than ordinary negligence*[w]."

92. As to *exceptions* from the rule concerning the degree of neglect, for which a mandatary is responsible, almost all, that has been advanced before in the article of *deposits*, in regard to a special convention, a voluntary offer, and an interest accruing to both parties, or only to the bailee, may be applied to mandates: an un-

[w] "In privatis rebus, si quis rem *mandatam* non modo *malitiosiùs* gessisset, sui quaestûs aut commodi causâ, verùm etiam *negligentiùs*, eum majores summum admisisse dedecus existimabant: itaque *mandati* constitutum est judicium, non minùs turpe quàm *furti*." Pro S. Rosc. p. 116. *Glasg.*[1]

[1] Cicero, *Pro Sexto Roscio Amerino*, 38.11 (Edition cited: *M. Tullii Ciceronis Opera* (Glasgow, 1748-1749), 4.116-117).

dertaker of a work for the benefit of an absent person, and *without his knowledge*, is the *negotiorum gestor* of the civilians, and the obligation resulting from his implied contract has been incidentally mentioned in a preceding page.

93. [*64] III. On the third species of bailment, which is one of the most usual and most convenient in civil society, little remains to be observed; because our own, and the Roman, law are on this head perfectly coincident. I call it, after the *French* lawyers, *loan for use*, to distinguish it from their *loan for consumption*, or the MUTUUM of the *Romans*; by which is understood the lending of *money*, *wine*, *corn*, and other things, that may be valued by number, weight, or measure, and are to be restored only in equal value or quantity[x]: this latter contract, which, according to St. GERMAN, is most properly called a *loan*, does not belong to the present subject; but it may be right to remark, that, as the *specifick* things are not to be returned, the *absolute* property of them is transferred

[x] Doct. and Stud. dial. 2. ch. 38.[1] Bract. 99. a. b.[2] In Ld. Raym. 916.[3] where this passage from *Bracton* is cited by the chief justice, *mutuam* is printed for *commodatam*; but what then can be made of the words *ad* IPSAM *restituendam*? There is certainly some mistake in the passage, which must be very ancient, for the oldest MS. that I have seen, is conformable to *Tottel's* edition. I suspect the omission of a whole line after the word *precium*, where the manuscript has a full point; and possibly the sentence omitted may be thus supplied from *Justinian*, whom *Bracton* copied: "At is, qui *mutuum* accepit, obligatus remanet," si forte incendio, &c. *Inst.* 3.13.2.[4]

[1] St. German, *Doctor and Student*, 2.38 (91 S.S. 260).

[2] Bracton, *De Legibus et Consuetudinibus Angliae*, 99-99b (ed. Thorne, 2.284): Is autem cui res aliqua utenda datur, re obligatur quae commodata est. Sed magna differentia est inter mutuum et commodatum, quia is qui rem commodatam accepit ap ipsam restituendam tenetur vel eius pretium, si forte incendio, ruina, naufragio, aut latronum hostiumve incursu, consumpta fuerit vel deperdita, subtracta vel ablata.

[3] *Coggs* v. *Barnard* (1703) 2 Lord Raym. 909, 915-916.

[4] Inst. 3.13.2: Item is cui res aliqua utenda datur, id est commodatur, re obligatur et tenetur commodati actione. Sed is ab eo qui mutuum accepit longe distat: namque non ita res datur ut eius fiat, et ob id de ea re ipsa restituenda tenetur. Et is quidem qui mutuum accepit, si quolibet fortuito casu quod accepit amiserit, veluti incendio, ruina, naufragio aut latronum hostiumve incursu, nihilo minus obligatus permanet.

to the borrower, who must bear the loss of them, if they be destroyed by wreck, pillage, fire, or other inevitable misfortune. [*65] Very different is the nature of the bailment in question; for a horse, a chariot, a book, a greyhound, or a fowling-piece, which are lent for the use of the bailee, ought to be redelivered *specifically*; and the owner must abide the loss, if they perish through any accident, which a *very careful and vigilant man* could not have avoided. The negligence of the borrower, who alone receives benefit from the contract, is construed rigorously, and, although *slight*, makes him liable to indemnify the lender; nor will his incapacity to exert *more than ordinary* attention avail him on the ground of an *impossibility*, "which the law, says the rule, never demands;"[1] for that maxim relates merely to things *absolutely* impossible; and it was not only very *possible*, but very *expedient*, for him to have examined his own capacity of performing the undertaking, before he deluded his neighbour by engaging in it: if the lender, indeed, was not deceived, but perfectly knew the *quality*, as well as age, of the borrower, he must be supposed to have demanded no higher care, than that of which *such* a person was capable; as, if *Paul* lend a fine horse to a raw youth, he cannot exact the same degree of management and circumspection, which he would expect from a riding-master or an officer of dragoons[y].

94. From the rule, that a borrower is answerable for *slight* neglect, compared with the distinction [*66] before made between simple *theft* and *robbery*[z], it follows, that, if the borrowed goods be *stolen* out of his possession by any person whatever, he must pay the worth of them to the lender, unless he prove, that they were pur-

[y] *Dumoulin*, tract. *De eo quod interest*, n. 185.[2]
[z] See p. 44. and note [*o*].

[1] Above, 145 n.1.
[2] C. Dumoulin, *Tractatus de eo quod Interest*, s.185 (*Caroli Molinaei Opera Omnia* (Paris, 1681), 3.484), citing Baldus: si commodavi equum uni scholari, non requiram eam diligentiam, quam haberet expertus eques. Quoted by Pothier, *Traité du Prêt à Usage*, s.49.

loined notwithstanding his *extraordinary* care. The example, given by *Julian*, is the first and best that occurs: *Caius* borrows a silver ewer of *Titius*, and afterwards delivers it, that it may be safely restored, to a bearer of such approved fidelity and wariness, that no event could be less expected than its being stolen; if, after all, the bearer be met in the way by scoundrels, who contrive to *steal* it, *Caius* appears to be wholly blameless, and *Titius* has suffered *damnum sine iniuriâ*.[1] It seems hardly necessary to add, that the same care, which the bailee is bound to take of the *principal* thing bailed, must be extended to such *accessory* things, as belong to it, and were delivered with it: thus a man, who borrows a watch, is responsible for *slight* neglect of the chain and seals.

95. Although the laws of *Rome*, with which those of *England* in this respect agree, most expressly decide, that a borrower, using more than ordinary diligence, *shall not be chargeable, if there be a force which he cannot resist*[a], yet PUFENDORF employs much idle reasoning, which I am not idle enough to transcribe, in support of a new opinion; namely, "that the borrower ought [*67] to indemnify the lender, if the goods lent be destroyed by fire, shipwreck, or other inevitable accident, and *without his fault*, unless *his own* perish with them:"[2] for example, if *Paul* lend *William* a horse worth thirty guineas to ride from *Oxford* to *London*, and *William* be attacked on a heath in that road by highwaymen, who kill or seize the horse, he is obliged, according to *Pufendorf* and his annotator, to pay thirty guineas to *Paul*. The justice and good sense of the contrary decision are evinced beyond a doubt by M. POTHIER, who makes a distinction between those cases, where the loan was the *occasion* merely of damage to the lender, who might in the mean time have sustained a loss from other accidents, and

[a] D.44.7.1.4. Ld. Raym. 916.[3]

[1] D.13.6.20.
[2] S. Pufendorf, *De Jure Naturae et Gentium*, 5.4.6, with Barbeyrac's note 8.
[3] *Coggs* v. *Barnard* (1703) 2 Lord Raym. 909, 916.

those, where the loan was the sole efficient *cause* of his damage[b]; as if *Paul*, having *lent* his horse, should be forced in the interval by some pressing business to *hire* another for himself; in this case the borrower ought, indeed, to pay for the hired horse, unless the lender had voluntarily submitted to bear the inconvenience *caused* by the loan; for, in this sense and in this instance, *a benefit conferred should not be injurious to the benefactor*. As to a condition *presumed* to be imposed by the lender, that he would not abide by any loss *occasioned* by the lending, it seems the wildest and most unreasonable of presumptions: if *Paul* really intended to impose such a condition, he [*68] should have declared his mind; and I persuade myself, that *William* would have declined a favour so hardly obtained.

96. Had the borrower, indeed, been imprudent enough to leave the high road and pass through some thicket, where robbers might be supposed to lurk, or had he travelled in the dark at a very unseasonable hour, and had the horse, in either case, been taken from him or killed, he must have indemnified the owner; for *irresistible force* is no excuse, if a man put himself in the way of it by his own rashness. This is nearly the case, cited by *St. German* from the *Summa Rosella*, where a *loan* must be meaned, though the word *depositum* be erroneously used[c]; and it is there decided, that, if the borrower of a horse will imprudently ride by *a ruinous house in manifest danger of falling*, and part of it actually fall on the horse's head, and kill him, the lender is entitled to the price of him; but that, if the house were *in good condition* and *fell* by the violence of a sudden hurricane, the bailee shall be discharged. For the same, or a stronger, reason, if *William*, instead of coming to *London*, for which purpose the horse was lent, go towards *Bath*, or, having borrowed him for a week, keep him for a month, he

[b] Poth., *Prêt à Usage*, n. 55.[1] *Puf.* with *Barbeyrac's* notes, B. 5. C. 4. § 6.[2]
[c] *Doct.* and *Stud.* where before cited.[3]

[1] Pothier, *Traité du Prêt à Usage et du Précaire*, s.55.
[2] Pufendorf, *De Jure Naturae et Gentium*, 5.4.6, with Barbeyrac's notes.
[3] St. German, *Doctor and Student*, 2.38 (91 S.S. 259-260). Below, 186 n.q.

becomes responsible for any *accident*, that may befall the horse in his journey to *Bath*, or after the expiration of the week[d].

97. [*69] Thus, if *Charles*, in a case before put[e], wear the masked habit and jewels of *George* at the ball, for which they were borrowed, and be *robbed* of them in his return home at the usual time and by the usual way, he cannot be compelled to pay *George* the value of them; but it would be otherwise, if he were to go with the jewels from the theatre to a gaming-house, and were there to lose them by any casualty whatever. So, in the instances proposed by *Gaius* in the digest, if silver utensils be lent to a man for the purpose of entertaining a party of friends at supper *in the metropolis*, and he carry them *into the country*, there can be no doubt of his obligation to indemnify the lender, if the plate be lost by accident however irresistible.[1]

98. There are other cases, in which a borrower is chargeable for *inevitable mischance*, even when he has not, as he legally may, taken the whole risk upon himself by express agreement. For example, if the house of *Caius* be in flames, and he, being able to secure one thing only, save an urn of his own in preference to the silver ewer, which he had borrowed of *Titius*, he shall make the lender a compensation for the loss; especially if the ewer be the more valuable, and would consequently have been preferred, had he been owner of them both: even if his urn be the more precious, he must either leave it, and bring away the borrowed vessel, or pay *Titius* [*70] the value of that, which he has lost; unless the alarm was so sudden, and the fire so violent, that no deliberation or selection could be justly expected, and *Caius* had time only to snatch up the first utensil, that presented itself.

99. Since openness and honesty are the soul of contracts, and since "a suppression of truth is often as culpable as an express falsehood,"[2] I accede to the opinion of M. *Pothier*, that, if a sol-

[d] Ld. Raym. 915.[3]
[e] P. 50.

[1] D.44.7.1.4.
[2] *Cf.* Bracton, *De Legibus et Consuetudinibus Angliae*, f.414 (ed. Thorne, 4.287).
[3] *Coggs* v. *Barnard* (1703) 2 Lord Raym. 909, 915.

dier were to borrow a horse of his friend for a battle expected to be fought the next morning, and were *to conceal from him, that his own horse was as fit for the service*, and if the horse, so borrowed, were slain in the engagement, the lender ought to be indemnified; for probably the dissimulation of the borrower induced him to lend the horse; but, had the soldier openly and frankly acknowledged, *that he was unwilling to expose his own horse*, since, in case of a loss, he was unable to purchase another, and his friend, nevertheless, had generously lent him one, the lender would have run, as in other instances, the risk of the day.

100. If the bailee, to use the *Roman* expression, be IN MORA, that is, if *a legal demand* have been made by the bailor, he must answer for any casualty that happens *after the demand*; unless in cases, where it may be strongly presumed, that the same accident would have befallen the thing bailed, even if it had been restored at the proper time; or, unless the bailee have legally [*71] tendered the thing, and the bailor have put himself *in morâ* by refusing to accept it: this rule extends of course to every species of bailment.

101. "Whether, in case of a *valued loan*, or, where the goods lent are *estimated at a certain price*, the borrower must be considered as bound *in all events* to restore either the things lent or the value of them," is a question, upon which the civilians are as much divided, as they are upon the celebrated clause in the law *Contractus*: five or six commentators of high reputation enter the lists against as many of equal fame, and each side displays great ingenuity and address in this juridical tournament. *D'Avezan* supports the affirmative;[1] and *Pothier*, the negative;[2] but the second opinion seems the more reasonable. The word PERICULUM, used by *Ulpian*, is in itself equivocal: it means *hazard* in general, proceeding either from *accident* or from *neglect*; and in this latter sense it appears to have been taken by the *Roman* lawyer in the passage, which gave birth to the dispute. But, whatever be the true interpretation of that passage, I cannot satisfy myself, that, either

[1] D'Avezan, *Contractuum Liber Prior*, c.28, referred to by Pothier, *Traité du Prêt à Usage*, s.62.

[2] Pothier, *Traité du Prêt à Usage*, s.62.

in the *Customary Provinces* of FRANCE, or in ENGLAND, a borrower can be chargeable for all events *without his consent unequivocally given*: if *William*, indeed, had said to *Paul* alternatively, "I promise, on my return to *Oxford*, *either* to restore your horse *or* to pay you thirty guineas," he must *in all events* have performed [*72] one part of this disjunctive obligation[f]; but, if *Paul* had only said, "the horse, which I lend you for this journey, is fairly worth thirty guineas," no more could be implied from those words, than a design of preventing any future difficulty about the price, if the horse should be killed or injured through an omission of that *extraordinary* diligence, which the nature of the contract required.

102. Besides the *general* exception to the rule concerning the degrees of neglect, namely, *Si quid convenit vel plus vel minus*,[1] another is, where goods are lent for a use, in which the lender has *a common interest* with the borrower: in this case, as in other bailments *reciprocally* advantageous, the bailee can be responsible for no more than *ordinary* negligence; as, if *Stephen* and *Philip* invite some common friends to an entertainment prepared at their joint expense, for which purpose *Philip* lends a service of plate to his companion, who undertakes the whole management of the feast, *Stephen* is obliged only to take *ordinary* care of the plate;[2] but this, in truth, is rather the innominate contract *do ut facias*, than a proper loan.

103. Agreeably to this principle, it must be decided, that, if goods be lent for the *sole* advantage of the *lender*, the borrower is answerable for *gross* neglect only; as, if a passionate lover of [*73] musick were to lend his own instrument to a player in a concert, merely to augment his pleasure from the performance; but here again, the bailment is not so much a *loan*, as a *mandate*; and, if the musician were to play with all due skill and exertion, but were to break or hurt the instrument without any malice or very culpa-

[f] Palm. 551.[3]

[1] D.50.17.23.
[2] *Cf.* D.13.6.18.pr.
[3] *Williams* v. *Hide* (1628) Palmer 548, 551.

ble negligence, he would not be bound to indemnify the *amateur*, as he was not in want of the instrument, and had no particular desire to use it. If, indeed, a poor artist, having lost or spoiled his violin or flute, be much distressed by this loss, and a brother-musician obligingly, though *voluntarily*, offer to lend him his own, I cannot agree with DESPEISSES, a learned advocate of *Montpellier* and writer on *Roman* law, that the player may be less careful of it than any other borrower[1]: on the contrary, he is bound, in conscience at least, to raise his attention even to a higher degree; and his negligence ought to be construed with rigour.

104. By the law of MOSES, as it is commonly translated, a remarkable distinction was made between the loss of borrowed cattle or goods, happening in the *absence*, or the *presence*, of the OWNER; for, says the divine legislator, "if a man borrow aught of his neighbour, and it be hurt or die, *the owner thereof not being with it*, he shall surely make it good; but, if the *owner* thereof *be* with it, he shall *not* make it good[g]:" now it is by no means *certain*, [*74] that the original word signifies the *owner*, for it *may* signify the *possessor*, and the law *may* import, that the borrower ought not to lose sight, when he can possibly avoid it, of the thing borrowed; but, if it was intended, that the borrower should always answer for casualties, *except in the case*, which must rarely happen, of *the owner's presence*, this exception seems to prove, that no casualties were meaned, but such as *extraordinary* care might have prevented; for I cannot see, what difference could be made by the presence of the owner, if the force, productive of the injury, were wholly irresistible, or the accident inevitable.

105. An old *Athenian* law is preserved by *Demosthenes*, from which little can be gathered on account of its generality and the

[g] Exod. xxii. 14, 15.[2]

[1] A. Despeisses, *Traité des Contrats*, 1.7.4 (in *Oeuvres de M. Antoine D'Espeisses* (Lyons, 1750), 1.243); cited for a different point by Pothier, *Traité du Prêt à Usage*, s.52.
[2] Exodus 22. 14-15.

use of an ambiguous word[h]; it is understood by *Petit* as relating to guardians, mandataries, and commissioners; and it is cited by the orator in the case of a guardianship. The *Athenians* were, probably, satisfied with speaking very generally in their laws, and left their juries, for juries they certainly had, to decide favourably or severely, according to the circumstances of each particular case.

106. [*75] IV. As to the degree of diligence, which the law requires from a *pawnee*, I find myself again obliged to differ from Sir-*Edward Coke*, with whose opinion a similar liberty has before been taken in regard to a *depositary*; for that very learned man lays it down, that, "if goods be delivered to one as a *gage* or *pledge*, and they be *stolen*, he shall be discharged, because *he hath a property* in them; and, *therefore*, he ought to keep them *no otherwise than his own*[i]:" I deny the first proposition, the reason, and the conclusion.

107. Since the bailment, which is the subject of the present article, is beneficial to the *pawnee* by securing the payment of his debt, *and* to the *pawnor* by procuring him credit, the rule, which natural reason prescribes, and which the wisdom of nations has confirmed, makes it requisite for the person, to whom a gage or pledge is bailed, to take *ordinary* care of it; and he must consequently be responsible for *ordinary* neglect[k]. This is expressly holden by BRACTON; and, when I rely on his authority, I am perfectly aware, that he copied *Justinian* almost word for word, and

[h] *Περὶ ὧν καθυφῆκέ τις, ὁμοίως ὀφλισκάνειν, ὥσπερ ἂν αὐτὸς ἔχῃ.* Reiske's edition, 855. 3.[1] Here the verb καθυφιέναι, may imply *slight*, or *ordinary*, neglect; or even *fraud*, as *Petit* has rendered it.[2]

[i] 1 Inst. 89. a.[3] 4 Rep. 83. b.[4]

[k] Bract. 99. b.[5]

[1] Reiske, *Oratorum Graecorum*, 2.855. Demosthenes, *Against Aphobus*, 3.36: For as regards the purloining of funds at which you connived there is a law which expressly declares that you are responsible for them exactly as if you had them in your own possession.

[2] S. Petit, *Leges Atticae* (Leiden, 1742), 61, 643.

[3] Co. Litt. 89a.

[4] *Southcote* v. *Bennet* (1601) 4 Co. Rep. 83b.

[5] Bracton, *De Legibus et Consuetudinibus Angliae*, 99b (ed. Thorne, 2.284).

that lord *Holt*, who makes considerable use of his treatise, observes three or four times, "that he was an *old* author[l];" but, although he had been a civilian, yet he was also a [*76] great common-lawyer, and never, I believe, adopted the rules and expressions of the *Romans*, except when they coincided with the laws of *England* in his time: he is certainly the *best* of our juridical classicks; and, as to our *ancient* authors, if their doctrine be *not law*, it must be left to mere historians and antiquaries; but, if it remain unimpeached by any later decision, it is not only equally binding with the most recent law, but has the advantage of being matured and approved by the collected sagacity and experience of ages. The doctrine in question has the full assent of lord *Holt* himself; who declares it to be "*sufficient*, if the pawnee use *true*, and *ordinary*, diligence for restoring the goods, and that, so doing, he will be indemnified, and, notwithstanding the loss, shall resort to the pawnor for his debt[1]." Now it has been proved, that "a bailee cannot be considered as using *ordinary* diligence, who suffers the goods bailed to be taken by *stealth* out of his custody[m];" and it follows, that "a pawnee shall *not* be discharged, if the pawn be simply *stolen* from him;" but if he be forcibly *robbed* of it *without his fault*, his debt shall not be extinguished.

108. The passage in the *Roman* institutes, which *Bracton* has nearly transcribed, by no means convinced M. LE BRUN, that a *pawnee* and a *borrower* are not responsible for *one and the same* [*77] degree of negligence; and it is very certain, that *Ulpian*, speaking of the *Actio pignoratitia*, uses these remarkable words: "Venit in *hac* actione et *dolus* et *culpa* UT in *commodato*, venit et custodia; vis major non venit[2]." To solve this difficulty, *Noodt* has recourse to a conjectural emendation, and supposes UT to have been inadvertently written for AT[3]; but, if this was a mistake, it must have

[l] Ld. Raym. 915, 916, 919.[4]

[m] P. 44. note [*o*].

[1] *Coggs* v. *Barnard* (1703) 2 Lord Raym. 909, 917.
[2] D.13.7.13.1.
[3] G. Noodt, *Commentarium in … Libros XXVII Digestorum sive Pandectarum*, ad D.13.7 (= *Opera Omnia* (Leiden, 1724), 324).
[4] *Coggs* v. *Barnard* (1703) 2 Lord Raym. 909, 915, 916, 919.

been pretty ancient, for the *Greek* translators of this sentence use a particle of similitude, not an adversative: there seems, however, no occasion for so hazardous a mode of criticism. *Ulpian* has not said, "*talis* culpa *qualis* in commodato;" nor does the word UT imply an *exact* resemblance: he meaned, that a pawnee was answerable for *neglect*, and gave the first instance, that occurred, of another contract, in which the party was likewise answerable for *neglect*, but left the *sort* or *degree* of negligence to be determined by his *general* rule; conformably to which he himself expressly mentions PIGNUS among other contracts *reciprocally useful*, and distinguishes it from COMMODATUM, whence the borrower *solely* derives advantage[n].

109. It is rather less easy to answer the case in the book of *Assise*, which seems wholly subversive of my reasoning, and, if it stand unexplained, will break the harmony of my system; for there,[o] [*78] in an action of detinue for a hamper, which had been bailed by the plaintiff to the defendant, the bailee pleaded, "that it was delivered to him *in gage* for a certain sum of money; that he had put it among his other goods; and that all together had been *stolen* from him:" now, according to my doctrine, the plaintiff might have demurred to the plea; but he was *driven* to reply, "that he had *tendered* the money before the *stealing*, and that the creditor refused to accept it," on which fact issue was joined; and the reason, assigned by the chief justice, was, that, "if a man bail goods to me *to keep*, and I put them among my own, I shall not be charged, if they be *stolen*." To this case I answer: first, that, if the court really made no difference between a *pawnee* and a *depositary*, they were indubitably mistaken; for which assertion I have the authority of *Bracton*, lord *Holt*, and *St. German*, who ranks the taker of a *pledge* in the same class with a *hirer* of goods[p]; next, that in a much later case, in the reign of Hen. VI. where a

[n] Before, p. 16. [o] 29 Ass. pl. 28.[1] [p] Doct. and Stud. *dial*. 2. *ch*. 38.[2]

[1] YB 29 Lib. Ass. f.163 pl. 28.
[2] St. German, *Doctor and Student*, 2.38 (91 S.S. 261). *Cf.* Bracton, *De Legibus et Consuetudinibus Angliae*, 99b (ed. Thorne, 2.284); *Coggs* v. *Barnard* (1703) 2 Lord Raym. 909, 916-917.

hiring of custody seems to be meaned, the distinction between a *theft* and a *robbery* is taken agreeably to the *Roman* law[q]; and, lastly, that, although in the strict propriety of our *English* language, to *steal* is to take *clandestinely*, and to *rob* is to seize by *violence*, corresponding with the *Norman* verbs *embleer* and *robber*, yet those words are sometimes [*79] used inaccurately; and I always suspected, that the case in the book of *Assise* related to a *robbery*, or a taking *with force*; a suspicion confirmed beyond any doubt by the judicious *Brook*, who abridges this very case with the following title in the margin, "Que serra al perde, quant les biens sont *robbes*[r]:" and, in a modern work, where the old cases are referred to, it appears to have been settled, in conformity to them and to reason, "that if the pawn be laid up, and the pawnee be *robbed*, he shall not be answerable[s]:" but lord *Coke* seems to have used the word *stolen* in its proper sense, because he plainly compares a pawn with a deposit.

110. If, indeed, the thing pledged be taken *openly* and *violently* through the *fault* of the pledgee, he shall be responsible for it; and, after a *tender* and *refusal* of the money owed, which are equivalent to actual *payment*, *the whole property is instantly revested in the pledgor*, and he may consequently maintain an action of trover[t]: it is said in a most useful work, that by such tender and refusal the thing pawned "ceases to be a pledge and becomes a *deposit*[u];" but this must be an error of impression; for there can never be a *deposit* without the owner's consent, and a *depositary* would be chargeable only for [*80] *gross* negligence, whereas the

[q] Before, p. 44. note [*o*].
[r] Abr. *tit*. Bailment, pl. 7.[1]
[s] 2 Salk. 522.[2]
[t] 29 Ass. pl. 28.[3] Yelv. 179. *Ratcliff* and *Davis*.[4]
[u] Law of *Nisi Prius*, 72.[5]

[1] Bro. Abr., *Bailment*, 7.
[2] *Anon* (1693) 2 Salk. 522.
[3] YB 29 Lib. Ass. f.163 pl. 28.
[4] *Ratcliff* v. *Davis* (1610) Yelv. 178, 179.
[5] F. Buller, *An Introduction to the Law Relative to Trials at Nisi Prius* (3rd edn., London, 1781), 72.

pawnee, whose special property is determined by the wrongful detainer, becomes liable *in all possible events* to make good the thing lost, or to relinquish his debt[w].

111. The reason, given by *Coke* for his doctrine, namely, "because the pawnee has a *property* in the goods pledged," is applicable to every other sort of bailment, and proves nothing in regard to any *particular* species; for every bailee has a temporary *qualified* property in the things, of which possession is delivered to him by the bailor, and has, therefore, a possessory action or an appeal in his own name against any stranger, who may damage or purloin them[x]. By the *Roman* law, indeed, "even the possession of the depositary was holden to be that of the person depositing;"[1] but with us the general bailee has unquestionably a *limited* property in the goods intrusted to his care: he may not, however, *use* them on any account without the consent of the owner, either expressly given, if it can possibly be obtained, or at least strongly presumed; and this presumption varies, as the thing is likely to be better, or worse, or not at all affected, by usage; since, if *Caius* deposit a *setting-dog* with *Titius*, he can hardly be supposed unwilling, that the dog should be used for partridge-shooting, and thus be confirmed in [*81] those habits, which make him valuable; but, if *clothes* or *linen* be deposited by him, one can scarce imagine, that he would suffer them to be worn; and, on the other hand, it may justly be inferred, that he would gladly indulge *Titius* in the liberty of using the *books* of which he had the custody, since even moderate care would prevent them from being injured. In the same manner it has been holden, that the pawnee of goods, which will be *impaired* by usage, cannot use them; but it would be otherwise, I apprehend, if the things pawned actually *required* exercise and a continuance of habits, as sporting-dogs and horses: if they cannot be hurt by being worn, they may be used, but *at the*

[w] Ld. Raym. 917.[2]
[x] Yearb. 21 Hen. VII. 14. b. 15. a.[3]

[1] D.41.2.3.20.
[2] *Coggs* v. *Barnard* (1703) 2 Lord Raym. 909, 917.
[3] YB H.21 Hen. VII f.14 pl. 23, at f.15.

peril of the pledgee; as, if chains of gold, ear-rings, or bracelets, be left in pawn with a lady, and she wear them at a public place, and be *robbed* of them on her return, she must make them good: "if she keep them in a bag," says a learned and respectable writer, "and they are *stolen*, she shall not be charged[y];" but the bag could hardly be taken *privately and quietly* without her omission of *ordinary* diligence; and the manner, in which lord *Holt* puts the case, establishes my system, and confirms the answer just offered to the case from the Year-book; for, "if she keep the jewels," says he, "*locked up* in her cabinet, and her cabinet be *broken open*, and the jewels [*82] taken thence, she will not be answerable[z]." Again; it is said, that, where the pawnee is at any expense to maintain the thing given in pledge, as, if it be a horse or a cow, he may ride the horse moderately, and milk the cow regularly, by way of compensation for the charge[a]; and this doctrine must be equally applicable to a general bailee, who ought neither to be injured not benefited in any respect by the trust undertaken by him; but the *Roman* and *French* law, more agreeably to principle and analogy, permits indeed both the pawnee and the depositary to milk the cows delivered to them, but requires them to account with the respective owners for the value of the milk and calves, deducting the reasonable charges of their nourishment[b]. It follows from these remarks, that lord *Coke* has assigned an inadequate reason for the degree of diligence, which is demanded of a pawnee; and the true reason is, that the law requires nothing *extraordinary* of him.

[y] Law of *Nisi Prius*, 72.[1]
[z] Ld. Raym. 917.[2]
[a] Ow. 124.[3]
[b] Poth. *Dépôt*, n. 47.[4] *Nantissement*, n. 35.[5]

1 Buller, *Introduction to the Law Relative to Trials at Nisi Prius*, 72.
2 *Coggs* v. *Barnard* (1703) 2 Lord Raym. 909, 917.
3 *Mores* v. *Conham* (1609) Owen 123, 124.
4 Pothier, *Traité du Contrat de Dépôt*, s.47.
5 Pothier, *Traité du Contrat de Nantissement*, s.35.

112. But, if the receiver in pledge *were* the only bailee, who had a *special property* in the thing bailed, it could not be logically inferred, "that, *therefore*, he ought to keep it merely *as his own*:" for, even if *Caius* have an *absolute* undivided property in goods, jointly or in common with *Septimius*, he is bound by rational, as well as positive, law [*83] to take *more* care of them *than of his own*, unless he be in fact a prudent and thoughtful manager of his own concerns; since every man ought to use *ordinary* diligence in affairs, which interest *another* as well as himself: "*Aliena* negotia," says the emperor CONSTANTINE, "*exacto* officio geruntur[c]."

113. The conclusion, therefore, drawn by sir *Edward Coke*, is no less illogical than his premisses are weak; but here I must do M. *Le Brun* the justice to observe, that the argument, on which his whole system is founded, occurred likewise to the great oracle of *English* law; namely, that a person, who had a *property* in things committed to his charge, was only obliged to be *as careful of them as of his own* goods[1]; which may be very true, if the sentence be predicated of a man *ordinarily* careful of his own; and, if that was *Le Brun's* hypothesis, he has done little more than adopt the system of *Godefroi*, who exacts *ordinary* diligence from a *partner* and a *co-proprietor*, but requires a *higher* degree in eight of the ten preceding contracts[2].

114. Pledges for debt are of the highest antiquity: they were used in very early times by the roving *Arabs*, one of whom finely remarks, "that the life of man is no more than a *pledge* in the hands of Destiny[3];" and the salutary laws of MOSES, which forbade certain implements of husbandry and a widow's raiment to be

[c] C.4.35.21.

[1] Le Brun, *Essai sur la Prestation des Fautes*, limits this to situations of partnership and common ownership.

[2] Godefroy, *In Titulum Pandectarum De Diversis Regulis Iuris Antiqui Commentarius*, 126.

[3] "The Poem of Amru", in *The Moallakat; or Seven Arabian Poems which were suspended on the Temple at Mecca*, verse 23 (Jones, *Works*, 10.[9] (pagination defective)).

given [*84] in pawn[1], deserve to be imitated as well as admired. The distinction between *pledging*, where possession is transferred to the creditor, and *hypothecation*, where it remains with the debtor, was originally *Attick*; but scarce any part of the *Athenian* laws on this subject can be gleaned from the ancient orators, except what relates to bottomry in five speeches of *Demosthenes*.

115. I cannot end this article, without mentioning a singular case from a curious manuscript preserved at *Cambridge*, which contains a collection of queries in *Turkish*, together with the decisions or concise answers of the MUFTI at *Constantinople*: it is commonly imagined, that the *Turks* have a translation in their own language of the *Greek* code, from which they have supplied the defects of their *Tartarian* and *Arabian* jurisprudence[d]; but I have not met with any such translation, although I admit the conjecture to be highly probable, and am persuaded, that their numerous treatises on *Mahomedan* law are worthy on many accounts of an attentive examination. The case was this: "*Zaid* had left with *Amru* divers goods in pledge for a certain sum of money, and some *ruffians*, having entered the house of *Amru*, took away his own goods together with those pawned by *Zaid*." Now we must necessarily suppose, that the creditor had by *his own fault* given occasion to this robbery; otherwise we may boldly pronounce, [*85] that the *Turks* are wholly unacquainted with the imperial laws of *Byzantium*, and that their own rules are totally repugnant to natural justice; for the party proceeds to ask, "whether, *since the debt became extinct by the loss of the pledge*, and since the goods pawned exceeded in value the amount of the debt, *Zaid* could legally demand the balance of *Amru*;" to which question the great law-officer of the *Othman* court answered with

[d] *Duck* de Auth. Jur. Civ. Rom. I. 2. 6.[2]

[1] Deuteronomy 24. 6; 24. 14.
[2] A. Duck, *De Usu et Authoritate Juris Civilis Romanorum* (London, 1679), 25.

the brevity usual on such occasions, OLMAZ, *It cannot be*[e]. This custom, we must confess, of proposing cases both of law and conscience under *feigned* names to the supreme judge, whose answers are considered as solemn *decrees*, is admirably calculated to prevent partiality and to save the charges of litigation.

116. V. The last species of bailment is by no means the least important of the five, whether we consider the infinite convenience and daily use of the contract itself, or the variety of its branches, each of which shall now be succinctly, but accurately, examined.

117. 1. *Locatio*, or *locatio-conductio*, REI, is a contract, by which the hirer gains a transient qualified property in the *thing* hired, and the owner acquires an absolute property in the stipend, or price, of the hiring; so that, in truth, it bears a [*86] strong resemblance to the contract of *emptio-venditio*, or SALE[1]; and, since it is advantageous to *both* contracting parties, the harmonious consent of nations will be interrupted, and one object of this essay defeated, if the laws of *England* shall be found, on a fair inquiry, to demand of the hirer a *more than ordinary* degree of diligence. In the most recent publication, that I have read on any legal subject, it is expressly said, "that the hirer is to take *all imaginable* care of the goods delivered for hire[f]:" the words *all imaginable*, if the principles before established be just, are too strong for practice even in the strict case of *borrowing*; but, if we take them in the mildest sense, they must imply an *extraordinary* degree of care; and this doctrine, I presume, is founded on that of lord *Holt* in the case of *Coggs and Bernard*, where the great judge lays it down, "that, if goods are let out for a *reward*, the *hirer* is bound to the

[e] Publ. Lib. Cambr. MSS. Dd. 4. 3.[2] See Wotton, LL. *Hywel Dda*. lib. 2. cap. 2. § 29. *note* x.[3] It may *possibly* be the usage in *Turky* to *stipulate* "ut amissio pignoris liberet debitorem," as in C. 4. 24. 6.

[f] Law of *Nisi Prius*, 3d edition corrected, 72.[4]

[1] Inst. 3.24.pr.

[2] Cambridge University Library, MS Dd 4.3 ff.6v-7.

[3] W. Wotton, *Cyfreithjeu Hywel Dda Ac Eraill, seu Leges Wallicae Ecclesiasticae et Civiles Hoeli Boni* (London, 1730), 103 (= 2.4.29), note x.

[4] Buller, *Introduction to the Law Relative to Trials at Nisi Prius*, 72.

UTMOST diligence, such as the MOST *diligent father of a family* uses[g]." It may seem bold to controvert so respectable an opinion; but, without insisting on the palpable injustice of making a *borrower* and a *hirer* answerable for precisely the *same* degree of neglect, and without urging, that the point was not then before the court, I will engage to show, by tracing the doctrine up to its real source, that the *dictum* of the chief justice was entirely [*87] grounded on a grammatical mistake in the translation of a single *Latin* word.

118. In the first place, it is indubitable, that his lordship relied *solely* on the authority of *Bracton*; whose words he cites at large, and immediately subjoins, "*whence it appears, &c.*" now the words "talis ab eo desideratur custodia, qualem DILIGENTISSIMUS *paterfamilias* suis rebus adhibet," on which the whole question depends, are copied exactly from *Justinian*[h], who informs us in the *proeme* to his Institutes, that his decisions in that work were extracted *principally from the Commentaries of* GAIUS; and the epithet *diligentissimus* is in fact used by this ancient lawyer[i], *and by him alone*, on the subject of hiring: but *Gaius* is remarked for writing with energy, and for being fond of using *superlatives*, where all other writers are satisfied with *positives*[k]; so that his forcible manner of expressing himself, in this instance as in some others, misled the compilers employed by the Emperor, whose words *Theophilus* rendered more than literally, and *Bracton* transcribed; and thus an epithet, which ought to have been translated

[g] Ld. Raym. 916.[1]
[h] Bract. 62. b.[2] Justin. Inst. 3.25.5.[3] where *Theophilus* has ὁ σφόδρα ἐπιμελέςατος.[4]
[i] D. 19. 2. 25. 7.
[k] Le Brun, p. 93.[5]

[1] *Coggs* v. *Barnard* (1703) 2 Lord Raym. 909, 916.
[2] Bracton, *De Legibus et Consuetudinibus Angliae*, 62b (ed. Thorne, 2.184).
[3] Inst. 3.24.5.
[4] Theophilus, *Paraphrasis*, 3.24.5 (ed. E. C. Ferrini, Berlin 1897), 359: ὁ σφόδρα ἐπεμελέστατος.
[5] Le Brun, *Essai sur la Prestation des Fautes*, 93.

ordinarily diligent, has been supposed to mean *extremely* careful. By rectifying this mistake, we restore the broken harmony of the *pandects* with the *institutes*, which, together with the *code*, [*88] form *one connected work*[l], and, when properly understood, explain and illustrate each other; nor is it necessary, I conceive, to adopt the interpretation of M. DE FERRIERE, who imagines, that both *Justinian* and *Gaius* are speaking only of cases, which *from their nature* demand *extraordinary* care[m].

119. There is no authority then against the rule, which requires of a *hirer* the same degree of diligence, that *all prudent men*, that is, *the generality of mankind*, use in keeping their own goods; and the just distinction between *borrowing* and *hiring*, which the *Jewish* lawgiver emphatically makes, by saying, "if it be an hired thing, it came for its hire[n]," remains established by the concurrent wisdom of nations in all ages.

120. If *Caius* therefore hire a horse, he is bound to ride it as moderately and treat it as carefully, as any man of *common discretion* would ride and treat *his own* horse; and if, through his negligence, as by leaving the door of his stable open at night, the horse be *stolen*, he must answer for it; but not if he be *robbed* of it by highwaymen, unless by his imprudence he gave occasion to the robbery, as by travelling at unusual hours, or by taking an unusual road: if, indeed, he hire a carriage and any number of horses, and the [*89] owner send with them his postilion or coachman, *Caius* is discharged from all attention to the horses, and remains obliged only to take ordinary care of the glasses and inside of the carriage, while he sits in it.

121. Since the negligence of a servant, *acting under his master's directions express or implied*, is the negligence of the master, it

[l] Burr. 426.[1]
[m] *Inst*. vol. V. p. 138.[2]
[n] Exod. xxii. 15.[3]

[1] *Windham* v. *Chetwynd* (1757) 1 Burr. 414, 426.
[2] C. de Ferrière, ed., *Nouvelle Traduction des Institutes de L'Empereur Justinien* (Paris, 1770), 138-139, ad Inst. 3.25.5.
[3] Exodus 22. 15.

follows, that, if the *servant* of *Caius* injure or kill the horse by riding it immoderately, or, by leaving the stable-door open, suffer thieves to steal it, *Caius* must make the owner a compensation for his loss[o]; and it is just the same, if he take a ready-furnished lodging, and his guests, or servants, while they act under the authority given by him, damage the furniture by the omission of ordinary care. At *Rome* the law was not quite so rigid; for POMPONIUS, whose opinion on this point was generally adopted, made the master liable, only *when he was culpably negligent in admitting careless guests or servants*, whose bad qualities he ought to have known[p]: but this distinction must have been perplexing enough in practice; and the rule, which, by making the head of a family answerable indiscriminately for the faults of those, whom he receives or employs, compels him to keep a vigilant eye on all his domesticks, is not only more simple, but more conducive to the publick security, although it may be rather harsh [*90] in some particular instances[q]. It may here be observed, that this is the only contract, to which the *French*, from whom our word *bailment* was borrowed, apply a word of the same origin; for the letting of a house or chamber for hire is by them called *bail à loyer*, and the letter for hire, *bailleur*, that is, *bailor*, both derived from the old verb *bailler*, to deliver; and, though the contracts, which are the subject of this essay, be generally confined to *moveable* things, yet it will not be improper to add, that, if *immoveable* property, as an orchard, a garden, or a farm, be letten by parol, with no other stipulation than for the price or rent, the lessee is bound to use the same diligence in preserving the trees, plants, or implements, that *every prudent person* would use, if the orchard, garden, or farm, were his own.

[o] Salk. 282.[1] Ld. Raym. 916.[2]
[p] D.19.2.11.[3]
[q] Poth. *Louage*, n. 193.[4]

[1] *Middleton* v. *Fowler* (1698) 1 Salk. 282.
[2] *Coggs* v. *Barnard* (1703) 2 Lord Raym. 909, 916.
[3] D.19.2.11.pr.
[4] Pothier, *Traité du Contrat de Louage*, s.193.

122. 2. *Locatio* OPERIS, which is properly subdivisible into two branches, namely, *faciendi*, and *mercium vehendarum*, has a most extensive influence in civil life; but the principles, by which the obligations of the contracting parties may be ascertained, are no less obvious and rational, than the objects of the contract are often vast and important[r].

123. [*91] If *Titius* deliver silk or velvet to a tailor for a suit of clothes, or a gem to a jeweller to be set or engraved, or timber to a carpenter for the rafters of his house, the tailor, the engraver, and the builder, are not only obliged to perform their several undertakings in a workmanly manner[s]: but, *since they are entitled to a reward*, either by express bargain or by implication, they must also take *ordinary* care of the things respectively bailed to them: and thus, if a horse be delivered either to an agisting farmer for the purpose of depasturing in his meadows, or to an hostler to be dressed and fed in his stable, the bailees are answerable for the loss of the horse, if it be occasioned by the *ordinary* neglect of themselves or their servants. It has, indeed, been adjudged, that, if the horse of a guest be sent *to pasture* by *the owner's desire*, the innholder is not, *as such*, responsible for the loss of [*92] him by

[r] It may be useful to mention a nicety of the *Latin* langage in the application of the verbs *locare* and *conducere*: the employer, who gives the reward, is *locator operis*, but *conductor operarum*; while the party employed, who receives the pay, is *locator operarum*, but *conductor operis*. HEINECC. in *Pand.* par. 3. § 320.[1] So, in *Horace*,

"Tu secanda marmora
Locas"[2] –

which the stonehewer or mason *conduxit*.

[s] 1 Ventr. 268.[3] erroneously printed 1 *Vern.* 268. in all the editions of *Bl. Comm.* II. 452. The innumerable multitude of inaccurate or idle references, in our best reports and law-tracts, is the bane of the student and of the practiser.

[1] J. G. Heineccius, *Elementa Iuris Civilis Secundum Ordinem Pandectarum*, 3.320 (in *Opera ad Universam Jurisprudentiam* (Geneva, 1744), 5.330).

[2] Horace, *Odes*, 2.18, 17-18.

[3] *Best* v. *Yates* (1675) 1 Ventr. 268.

theft or accident[t]; and, in the case of *Mosley* and *Fosset*, an action against an agister for keeping a horse *so negligently that it was stolen*, is said to have been held maintainable *only* by reason of a *special* assumption[u]; but the case is differently reported by *Rolle*, who mentions no such reason; and, according to him, chief justice *Popham* advanced generally, in conformity to the principles before established, that, "if a man, to whom horses are bailed for agistment, *leave open the gates of his field*, in consequence of which neglect they stray and are *stolen*, the owner has an action against him[1]:" it is the same, if the innkeeper send his guest's horse to a meadow *of his own accord*, for he is bound to keep safely all such things as his guests deposit *within his inn*, and shall not discharge himself by his own act from that obligation; and, even when he turns out the horse *by order of the owner*, and receives pay for his grass and care, he is chargeable, surely, for *ordinary* negligence, as *a bailee for hire*, though not *as an innkeeper* by the general custom of the realm. It may be worth while to investigate the reasons of this *general custom*, which in truth means no more than *common law*, concerning innholders[w].

124. Although a stipend or reward in *money* be the essence of the contract called *locatio*, yet the [*93] same responsibility for neglect is justly demanded in any of the *innominate* contracts, or, whenever a valuable consideration of any kind is given or stipulated. This is the case, where the contract *do ut des* is formed by a *reciprocal bailment for use*, as if *Robert* permit *Henry* to use his *pleasure-boat* for a day, *in consideration* that *Henry* will give him the use of his *chariot* for the same time; and so in ten thousand in-

[t] 8. Rep. 32. *Calye's* case.[2]
[u] Mo. 543. 1 Ro. Abr. 4.[3]
[w] Reg. Orig. 105. a.[4] Noy, Max. ch. 43.[5]

[1] Ro. Abr., 1.4 (*Action sur Case*, F 5).
[2] *Calye's Case* (1584) 8 Co. Rep. 32.
[3] *Mosley* v. *Fosset* (1594) Moo. 543; Ro Abr, 1.4 (*Action sur Case*, F 3, 5).
[4] *Registrum Omnium Brevium* (London, 1687), 105.
[5] W. Noy, *A Treatise of the Principall Grounds and Maxims of the Laws of this Nation* (London, 1677), 93.

stances, that might be imagined, of *double bailments*: this too is the case, if the *absolute* property of one thing be given as an equivalent for the *temporary* or limited property of another, as if *Charles* gives *George* a brace of pointers for the use of his *hunter* during the season. The same rule is applicable to the contract *facio ut facias*, where two persons agree to perform *reciprocal works*; as if a mason and a carpenter have each *respectively* undertaken to build an edifice, and they mutually agree, that the first shall finish all the masonry, and the second all the wood-work, in their respective buildings; but, if a goldsmith make a bargain with an architect to give him a quantity of wrought plate for building his house, this is the contract *do ut facias*, or *facio ut des*; and, in all these cases, the bailees must answer for the omission of *ordinary* diligence in preserving the things, with which they are intrusted: so, when *Jacob* undertook the care of *Laban's* flocks and herds for no less a reward than his younger daughter, whom [*94] he loved so passionately, that *seven years were in his eyes like a few days*[1], he was bound to be just as vigilant, as if he had been paid in shekels of silver.

125. Now the obligation is precisely the same, as we have already hinted[x], when a man takes upon himself the custody of goods *in consequence and consideration of another gainful contract*; and, though an innholder be not paid in *money* for securing the traveller's trunk, yet the guest *facit ut faciat*, and alights at the inn, not solely for his own refreshment, but also that his goods may be safe: independently of this reasoning, the custody of the goods may be considered as *accessary* to the principal contract, and the money paid for the apartments as extending to the care of the box or portmanteau; in which light *Gaius* and, as great a man as he, lord *Holt*, seem to view the obligation; for they agree, "that, although a bargeman and a master of a ship receive their fare for the passage of travellers, and an innkeeper his pay for the accommodation and entertainment of them, but have no pecuniary reward for the *mere custody* of the goods belonging to the pas-

[x] P. 49, 50.

[1] Genesis 29. 15-30, at 20.

sengers or guests, yet they are obliged to take *ordinary* care of those goods; as a fuller and a mender are paid for their *skill only*, yet are answerable, *ex locato*, for *ordinary* neglect, if the clothes be lost or damaged[y]."

126. [*95] In whatever point of view we consider this bailment, no more is *regularly* demanded of the bailee than the care, which *every prudent man* takes of his own property; but it has long been holden, that an *innkeeper* is bound to restitution, if the trunks or parcels of his guests, committed to him either personally or through one of his agents, be damaged *in his inn*, or *stolen out of it*, by *any person whatever*[z]; nor shall he discharge himself from this responsibility by a refusal to take any care of the goods, *because there are suspected persons in the house, for whose conduct he cannot be answerable*[a]: it is otherwise, indeed, if he refuse admission to a traveller, because he really has no room for him, and the traveller, nevertheless, insist upon entering, and place his baggage in a chamber without the keeper's consent[b].

127. Add to this, that, if he fail to provide honest *servants* and honest *inmates*, according to the confidence reposed in him by the publick, his negligence in that respect is highly culpable, and he ought to answer *civilly* for their acts, even if they should *rob* the guests, who sleep in his chambers[c]. Rigorous as this law may seem, and hard as it may actually be in one or two particular instances, it is founded on the great princi-[*96]ple of publick utility, to which all private considerations ought to yield; for travellers, who must be numerous in a rich and commercial country, are

[y] D.4.9.5. and 12 Mod. 487.[1]
[z] Yearb. 10 Hen. VII. 26.[2] 2 Cro. 189.[3]
[a] Mo. 78.[4]
[b] Dy. 158. b. 1 And. 29.[5]
[c] 1 Bl. Comm. 430.[6]

[1] *Lane* v. *Cotton* (1701) 12 Mod. 472, 487.
[2] YB T. 10 Hen. VII f.25 pl. 3, at f.26.
[3] *Gelley* v. *Clerk* (1607) Cro. Jac. 188, 189.
[4] *Anon* (1565) Moo. 78.
[5] *White's Case* (1558) Dyer 158b, 1 And. 29 (sub nom. *Bird* v. *Bird*).
[6] Blackstone, *Commentaries*, 1.430 (1.418 in the first edition).

obliged to rely almost implicitly on the good faith of innholders, whose education and morals are usually none of the best, and who might have frequent opportunities of associating with ruffians or pilferers, while the injured guest could seldom or never obtain legal proof of such combinations, or even of their *negligence*, if no actual fraud had been committed by them. Hence the Praetor declared, according to POMPONIUS, *his desire of securing the publick from the dishonesty of such men*, and by his *edict* gave an action against them, if the goods of travellers or passengers were lost or hurt by any means, except *damno fatali*, or by *inevitable accident*[1]; and *Ulpian* intimates, that even this severity could not restrain them from knavish practices or suspicious neglect[d].

128. In all such cases, however, it is competent for the innholder to repel the *presumption* of his knavery or default, by *proving* that he took *ordinary* care, or that the *force*, which occasioned the loss or damage, was truly *irresistible*.

129. When a private man demands and receives a compensation for the *bare custody* of goods in his warehouse or store-room, this is *not* properly a *deposit*, but a *hiring of care and attention*: it may be called *locatio custodiae*, and might have [97] been made a distinct branch of this last sort of bailment, if it had not seemed useless to multiply subdivisions; and the bailee may still be denominated *locator operae*, since the *vigilance and care*, which he *lets out* for pay, are in truth a mental *operation*. Whatever be his appellation, either in *English* or *Latin*, he is clearly responsible, like other interested bailees, for *ordinary* negligence; and, although St. *German* seems to make no difference in this respect between *a keeper of goods for hire* and *a simple depositary*, yet he uses the word DEFAULT, like the CULPA of the *Romans*, as a generical term, and leaves the *degree* of it to be ascertained by the rules of law[e].

[d] D.4.9.1. and 3.[2]
[e] *Doct.* and *Stud.* where before cited.[3]

[1] D.4.9.3.1.
[2] D.4.9.1.1; D.4.9.3.1.
[3] St. German, *Doctor and Student*, 2.38 (91 S.S. 260-261).

130. In the sentence immediately following, he makes a very material distinction between the two contracts; for, "if a man, says he, have *a certain recompense* for the keeping of goods, and promise, at the time of the delivery, *to redeliver them safe at his peril*, then he shall be charged with *all chances*, that may befall; but, if he make *that* promise, and *have nothing* for keeping them, he is bound to *no casualties*, but such as are wilful, and happen *by his own default*:" now the word PERIL, like *periculum*, from which it is derived, is in itself ambiguous, and sometimes denotes the *risk* of *inevitable mischance*, sometimes the *danger* [*98] arising from *a want of due circumspection*; and *the stronger sense* of the word *was taken* in the first case *against him, who uttered it*; but, in the second, where the construction is favourable, the *milder* sense was justly preferred[f]. Thus, when a person, who, if he were wholly *uninterested*, would be a *mandatary*, undertakes for a *reward* to perform *any work*, he must be considered as bound still more strongly, *to use a degree of diligence adequate to the performance of it*: his obligation must be rigorously construed, and he would, perhaps, be answerable for *slight* neglect, where no more could be required of a *mandatary* than *ordinary* exertions. This is the case of commissioners, factors, and bailiffs, when their undertaking *lies in fesance*, and not simply in *custody*: hence, as peculiar care is demanded in removing and raising a fine column of granate or porphyry, without injuring the shaft or the capital, *Gaius* seems to exact *more than ordinary* diligence from the undertaker of such a work for a stipulated compensation[g]. Lord *Coke* considers a factor in the light of a *servant*, and thence deduces his obligation; but, with great submission, his *reward* is the true reason, and *the nature of the business* is the just measure, of his duty[h]; which cannot, however, extend to a responsibility for

[f] See before, p. 45.
[g] D.19.2.7.[1]
[h] 4. Rep. 84.[2] Ld. Raym. 918.[3]

[1] D.19.2.25.7.
[2] *Southcote* v. *Bennet* (1601) 4 Co. Rep. 83b, 84.
[3] *Coggs* v. *Barnard* (1703) 2 Lord Raym. 909, 918.

mere accident [*99] or *open robbery*[i]; and, even in the case of *theft*, a factor has been holden excused, when he showed, "that he had *laid up* the goods of his principal in a warehouse, out of which they were *stolen* by certain malefactors to him unknown[k].

131. Where *skill* is required, as well as *care*, in performing the work undertaken, the bailee for *hire* must be supposed to have engaged himself for *a due application of the necessary art*: it is his own fault, if he undertake a work above his strength; and all, that has before been advanced on this head concerning a *mandatary*, may be applied with much greater force to a *conductor operis faciendi*[l]. I conceive, however, that, where the bailor has not been deluded by any but himself, and voluntarily employs in one art a man, who openly exercises another, his folly has no claim to indulgence; and that, unless the bailee make false pretensions, or a *special* undertaking, no more can fairly be demanded of him than the best of his ability[m]. The case, which SADI relates with elegance and humour in his *Gulistan* or *Rose-garden*, and which *Pufendorf* cites with approbation[n], is not inapplicable to the present subject, and may serve as a [*100] specimen of *Mahomedan law*, which is not so different from ours, as we are taught to imagine: 'A man, who had a disorder in his eyes, called on a *farrier* for a remedy; and he applied to them a medicine commonly used for *his* patients: the man lost his sight, and brought an action for damages; but the judge said, "No action lies, for, if the complainant had not himself been an *ass*, he would never have employed a *farrier*;" and *Sadi* proceeds to intimate, that, "if a person will employ a common *mat-maker* to weave or

[i] 1 Inst. 89. a.[1]

[k] 1 Vent. 121. *Vere* and *Smith*.[2]

[l] *Spondet*, say the *Roman* lawyers, *peritiam artis*.[3]

[m] P. 54.

[n] De Jure Nat. et Gent. lib. 5. cap. 5. § 3.[4]

[1] Co. Litt. 89a.

[2] *Vere* v. *Smith* (1671) 1 Ventr. 121.

[3] Pothier, *Traité du Contrat de Louage*, s.425.

[4] Pufendorf, *De Jure Naturae et Gentium*, 5.4.3.

embroider *a fine carpet*, he must impute the bad workmanship to his own folly[o].'"

132. In regard to the distinction before-mentioned between the *non*fesance and the *mis*fesance of a workman[p], it is *indisputably* clear, that an action lies in *both* cases for a reparation in damages, whenever the work was undertaken for a *reward*, either actually paid, *expressly* stipulated, or, in the case of a *common* trader, strongly *implied*; of which BLACKSTONE gives [*101] the following instance: "If a *builder* promises, undertakes, or assumes to *Caius*, that he will build and cover his house within a time limited, and fails to do it, *Caius* has an action on the case against the builder for this breach of his express promise, and shall recover a pecuniary satisfaction for the injury sustained by such delay[q]." The learned author meaned, I presume, a *common* builder, or supposed a *consideration* to be given; and for this reason I forbore to cite his doctrine as in point on the subject of an action for the *non*performance of a *mandatary*[r].

133. Before we leave this article, it seems proper to remark, that every bailee for *pay*, whether *conductor*[1] *rei* or *conductor operis*, must be supposed to know, that the goods and chattels of his bailor are in *many* cases *distrainable* for rent, if his landlord, who might otherwise be shamelessly defrauded, find them on the premisses[s]; and, as they cannot be distrained and sold without his *or*-

[o] Rosar. Polit. cap. 7.[2] There are numberless tracts in *Arabick*, *Persian*, and *Turkish*, on every branch of jurisprudence; from the best of which it would not be difficult to extract a complete system, and to compare it with our own; nor would it be less easy, to explain in *Persian* or *Arabick* such parts of our *English* law, as either coincide with that of the *Asiaticks*, or are manifestly preferable to it.

[p] P. 54, &c.

[q] 3 Comm. 157.[3]

[r] P. 56. 57. 61.

[s] Burr. 1498. &c.[4]

[1] Text: *locator*; corrected to *conductor* by corrigendum, and in second and subsequent editions.

[2] M. Sadi, *Rosarium Politicum* (trans. G. Gentius, Amsterdam, 1687), 215-216.

[3] Blackstone, *Commentaries*, 3.157.

[4] *Francis* v. *Wyatt* (1764) 3 Burr. 1498.

dinary default *at least*, the owner has a remedy over against him, and must receive a compensation for his loss[t]: even if a *depositary* were to remove or conceal *his own* goods, and those of his depositor were to be seized for rent-arrere, he would unquestionably be bound to make re-[*102]stitution; but there is no obligation in the bailee to *suggest wise precautions against inevitable accident*; and he cannot, therefore, be obliged *to advise insurance from fire*; much less *to insure* the things bailed without an authority from the bailor.

134. It may be right also to mention, that the distinction, before taken in regard to loans[u], between an obligation to restore the *specifick* things, and a power or necessity of returning *others equal in value*, holds good likewise in the contracts of *hiring* and *depositing*: in the first case, it is a regular *bailment*; in the second, it becomes a *debt*. Thus, according to ALFENUS in his famous law, on which the judicious *Bynkershoek* has learnedly commented, "if an ingot of silver be delivered to a silver-smith to make an urn, the *whole* property is transferred, and the employer is only a *creditor* of metal equally valuable, which the workman engages to *pay* in a certain shape[w]:" the smith may consequently apply it to his own use; but, if it perish, even by unavoidable mischance or irresistible violence, he, as owner of it, must abide the loss, and the creditor must have his urn in due time. It would be otherwise, no doubt, if the *same* silver, on account of its peculiar fineness, or any uncommon metal, according to the whim of the owner, were agreed [*103] to be *specifically* redelivered in the form of a cup or standish.

135. 3. *Locatio operis* MERCIUM VEHENDARUM is a contract, which admits of many varieties in *form*, but of none, as it seems *at length* to be settled, in the *substantial* obligations of the bailee.

[t] 3. Bl. Comm. 8.[1]
[u] P. 64, 65.
[w] D.19.2.31. Bynk *Obs. Jur. Rom.* lib. VIII.[2]

[1] Blackstone, *Commentaries*, 3.8.
[2] C. van Bynkershoek, *Observationum Juris Romani* 8.1-8.8 (Leiden 1733, 2.422-467, esp. at 445-449).

136. A *carrier for hire* ought, by the rule, to be responsible only for *ordinary* neglect; and, in the time of HENRY VIII., it appears to have been generally holden, "that a *common* carrier was chargeable, in case of a loss by *robbery*, only when he had travelled by *ways dangerous for robbing*, or driven by *night*, or at any *inconvenient hour*[x]:" but, in the commercial reign of ELIZABETH, it was resolved, upon the same broad principles of policy and convenience, that have been mentioned in the case of *innholders*, "that, if a *common carrier* be *robbed* of the goods delivered to him, he shall answer for the value of them[y]."

137. Now the *reward* or *hire*, which is considered by *Sir Edward Coke* as the reason of this decision, and on which the principal stress is often laid in our own times, makes the carrier liable, indeed, for the omission of *ordinary* care, but cannot extend to *irresistible force*; and, though some other bailees have a *recompense*, as *factors* and *workmen* [*104] *for pay*, yet, even in *Woodliefe's* case, the chief justice admitted, that *robbery* was a good plea for a *factor*, though it was a bad one for a *carrier*: the true ground of that resolution is the *publick employment* exercised by the carrier, and the danger of his combining with *robbers* to the infinite injury of commerce and extreme inconvenience of society[z].

138. The modern rule concerning a *common* carrier is, that "nothing will excuse him, except *the act of* GOD, or of *the King's enemies*[a];" but a momentary attention to the principles must convince us, that this exception is in truth part of the rule itself, and that the responsibility for a loss by *robbers* is only an exception to it: a

[x] Doct. and Stud. where often before cited.[1]
[y] 1 Inst. 89. a.[2] Mo. 462. 1 Ro. Abr. 2. *Woodliefe* and *Curties*.[3]
[z] Ld. Raym. 917.[4] 12. Mod. 487.[5]
[a] Law of *Nisi Prius*, 70, 71.[6]

[1] St. German, *Doctor and Student*, 2.38 (91 S.S. 261).
[2] Co. Litt. 89a.
[3] *Woodlife* v. *Curties* (1597) Moo. 462; Ro. Abr., *Action sur Case*, C.4.
[4] *Coggs* v. *Barnard* (1703) 2 Lord Raym. 909, 917-918.
[5] *Lane* v. *Cotton* (1701) 12 Mod. 472, 487.
[6] Buller, *An Introduction to the Law Relative to Trials at Nisi Prius*, 70, 71.

carrier is *regularly* answerable for neglect, but not, *regularly*, for damage occasioned by the attacks of *ruffians*, any more than for *hostile* violence, or unavoidable *misfortune*; but the great maxims of policy and good government make it necessary to *except* from this rule the case of *robbery*, lest confederacies should be formed between carriers and desperate villains with little or no chance of detection.

139. Although the *Act of God*, which the ancients too called *Θεῶ βίαν* and *Vim divinam*, be an expression, which long habit has rendered familiar to us, yet perhaps, on that very account, it might be more proper, as well as more decent, [*105] to substitute in its place *inevitable accident*: religion and reason, which can never be at variance without certain injury to one of them, assure us, that "not a gust of wind blows, nor a flash of lightning gleams, without the knowledge and guidance of a superintending mind;" but this doctrine loses its dignity and sublimity by a technical application of it, which may in some instances border even upon profaneness; and law, which is merely a practical science, cannot use terms too popular and perspicuous.

140. In a recent case of an action against a carrier, it was holden to be no excuse, "that the ship was tight, when the goods were placed on board, but that a rat, by gnawing out the oakum, had made a small hole, through which the water had gushed[b];" but the true reason of this decision is not mentioned by the reporter: it was in fact *at least ordinary* negligence, to let a rat do such mischief in the vessel; and the *Roman* law has, on this principle, decided, that, "si fullo vestimenta polienda acceperit, eaque *mures roserint*, ex locato tenetur, quia *debuit ab hac re cavere*[c]."

141. Whatever doubt there may be, among civilians and common-lawyers, in regard to *a casket, the contents of which are concealed from the* [*106] DEPOSITARY[d], it seems to be generally un-

[b] 1 Wils. part 1. 281. *Dale* and *Hall.*[1]
[c] D.19.2.13.6.
[d] Before, p. 37, 38, 39.

[1] *Dale* v. *Hall* (1750) 1 Wils. 281.

derstood, that *a common carrier is* answerable for the loss of a box or parcel, be he ever so *ignorant of its contents*, or be those contents ever so valuable, *unless* he make a *special* acceptance[d]: but *gross fraud and imposition* by the bailor will deprive him of his action, and if there be proof, that the parties were apprized of each other's intentions, although there was no personal communication, the bailee may be considered as a *special* acceptor: this was adjudged in a very modern case particularly circumstanced, in which the former cases in *Ventris*, *Alleyne*, and *Carthew*, are examined with liberality and wisdom; but, in all of them, too great stress is laid on the *reward*, and too little on the important motives of *publick utility*, which alone distinguish a *carrier* from other *bailees for hire*[e].

142. Though no substantial difference is assignable between carriage by *land* and carriage by *water*, or, in other words, between a *waggon* and a *barge*, yet it soon became necessary for the courts to declare, as they did in the reign of JAMES I., that a *common hoyman*, like a common *waggoner*, is responsible for goods committed to his [*107] custody, even if he be *robbed* of them[f]; but the reason said to have been given for this judgement, namely, because *he had his hire*, is not the true one; since, as we have before suggested, the *recompense* could only make him liable for *temerity* and *imprudence*, as if a bargemaster were rashly to shoot a bridge, *when the bent of the weather is tempestuous*; but not for a *mere casualty*, as if a hoy in good condition, shooting a bridge *at a proper time*, were driven against a pier by a sudden breeze,

[d] 1 Stra. 145. *Titchburn* and *White.*[1]
[e] Burr. 2298. *Gibbon* and *Paynton.*[2] See 1 Vent. 238.[3] All. 93.[4] Carth. 485.[5]
[f] Hob. *ca.* 30. 2 Cro. 330. *Rich* and *Kneeland.*[6] "The *first* case of the kind, said lord *Holt*, to be found in our books." 12 Mod. 480.[7]

[1] *Titchburne* v. *White* (1718) 1 Stra. 145.
[2] *Gibbon* v. *Paynton* (1769) 4 Burr. 2298.
[3] *Morse* v. *Slue* (1672) 1 Ventr. 238.
[4] *Kenrig* v. *Eggleston* (1648) Aleyn 93.
[5] *Tyly* v. *Morrice* (1699) Carth. 485.
[6] *Rich* v. *Kneeland* (1613) Hob. 17, Cro. Jac 330.
[7] *Lane* v. *Cotton* (1701) 12 Mod. 472, 480.

and overset by the violence of the shock[h]; nor, by parity of reason, for any other force too great to be resisted[i]: the *publick* employment of the *hoyman*, and that *distrust*, which an ancient writer justly calls the *sinew of wisdom*[1], are the real grounds of the law's rigour in making such a person responsible for a loss by *robbery*.

143. All, that has just been advanced concerning a *land*-carrier, may, therefore, be applied to a *bargemaster* or *boatman*; but, in case of a tempest, it may sometimes happen, that the law of *jetson* and *average* may occasion a difference. [*108] *Barcroft's* case, as it is cited by chief justice *Rolle*, has some appearance of hardship: "a box of *jewels* had been delivered to a ferryman, *who knew not what it contained*, and, a sudden storm arising in the passage, he threw the box into the sea; yet it was resolved, *that he should answer for it*[k]:" now I cannot help suspecting, that there was proof in this case of *culpable negligence*, and probably the casket was both *small* and *light* enough, to have been kept longer on board than other goods; for, in the case of *Gravesend* barge[2], cited on the bench by lord *Coke*, it appears, that the pack, which was thrown overboard in a tempest, and for which the bargeman was holden *not answerable*, was of great value *and great weight*; although this last circumstance be omitted by *Rolle*, who says only, that the master of the vessel had *no information of its contents*[l].

[h] 1 Stra. 128. *Amies* and *Stevens*.[3]

[i] Palm. 548. W. Jo. 159.[4] See the doctrine of *inevitable accident* most learnedly discussed in *Desid. Heraldi* Animadv. in *Salmasii* Observ. in Jus *Att.* et *Rom.* cap. xv.[5]

[k] All. 93.[6]

[l] 2 Bulstr. 280. 2. Ro. Abr. 567.[7]

[1] Quintus Cicero, *Commentariolum Petitionis*, 39 (ed. G. Laser, Darmstadt, 2001, 80).

[2] *Mouse's Case* (1608) 12 Co. Rep. 63.

[3] *Amies* v. *Stevens* (1719) 1 Stra. 128.

[4] *Williams* v. *Hide* (1628) Palmer 548, Jones W. 179.

[5] Desiderius Heraldus, *Observationes ad Ius Atticum et Romanum* (Paris, 1650), 70-80.

[6] *Barcroft's Case*, cited in *Kenrig* v. *Eggleston* (1648) Aleyn 93.

[7] *Bird* v. *Astcock* (1614) 2 Bulst. 280; Ro. Abr., *Trespas*, K.2.

144. The subtilty of the human mind, in finding distinctions, has no bounds; and it was imagined by some, that, whatever might be the obligation of a *barge*-master, there was no reason to be equally rigorous in regard to the master of a *ship*; who, if he carry goods for *profit*, must indubitably answer for the *ordinary neglect* of himself or his mariners, but ought not, they said, to be chargeable for the violence of *robbers*: it was, however, otherwise decided in the great case of [*109] *Mors* and *Slew*, where "eleven persons armed came on board the ship *in the river*, under pretence of *impressing seamen*, and forcibly took the chests, which the defendant had engaged to carry;" and, though the master was entirely blameless, yet Sir *Matthew Hale* and his brethren, having heard both civilians and common-lawyers, and, among them, Mr. HOLT for the plaintiff, determined, on the principles just before established, that the bailor ought to recover[m]. This case was frequently mentioned afterwards by lord *Holt*, who said, that "the declaration was drawn by the greatest pleader in *England* of his time[n]."

145. Still farther: since neither the *element*, on which goods are carried, nor the *magnitude* and *form* of the carriage, make any difference in the responsibility of the bailee, one would hardly have conceived, that a diversity could have been taken between a *letter* and any other thing. Our *common* law, indeed, was acquainted with no such diversity; and a *private* post-master was precisely in the situation of another carrier; but the statute of CHARLES II. having established a *general* post-office, and taken away the liberty of sending letters by a *private* post[o], it was thought, that an alteration was made in the obligation of the post-master *general*; and, in the [*110] case of *Lane* and *Cotton*, three judges deter-

[m] 1 Ventr. 190. 238. Raym. 220.[1]
[n] Ld. Raym. 920.[2]
[o] 12 Cha. II. ch. 35. See the subsequent statutes.[3]

[1] *Mors* v. *Slue* (1672) 1 Ventr. 190, 1 Ventr. 238, T. Raym. 220.
[2] *Coggs* v. *Barnard* (1703) 2 Lord Raym. 909, 920.
[3] Stat. 12 Car. II c.35 (1660); Stat. 9 Anne c.11 (10) (1710); Stat. 4 Geo. II c.33 (1730); Stat. 22 Geo. II c.25 (1748); Stat. 5 Geo. III c.25 (1765).

mined, against the fixed and well-supported opinion of chief justice HOLT, "that the post-master was *not* answerable for the loss of a letter with exchequer-bills in it[p]:" now this case was a case of *ordinary* neglect, for the bills were *stolen* out of the plaintiff's letter *in the defendant's office*[q]; and, as the master has a great *salary* for the discharge of his trust; as he ought clearly to answer for the acts of his clerks and agents; as the statute, professedly enacted for *safety* as well as *dispatch*, could not have been intended to deprive the subject of any benefit, which he before enjoyed; for these reasons, and for many others, I believe that *Cicero* would have said, what he wrote on a similar occasion [*111] to *Trebatius*, "Ego tamen SCAEVOLAE assentior[r]." It would, perhaps, have been different *under the statute*, if the post had been *robbed*, either by day or by *night*, when there is a necessity of travelling, but even that question would have been disputable; and here I may conclude this division of my essay, with observing, in the plain but emphatical language of St. GERMAN, "that all the *former* diversities be granted by secondary conclusions derived upon the law of reason, *without any statute made in that behalf*; and, per-

[p] Carth. 487. 12 Mod. 482.[1]
[q] In addition to the authorities, before cited, p. 44. n. [*o*], for the distinction between a loss by *stealth* and by *robbery*, see *Dumoulin*, tract. *De eo quod interest*, n. 184.[2] and ROSELLA CASUUM, 28.b. This last is the book, which *St. German* improperly calls *Summa Rosella*, and by misquoting which he misled me in the passage concerning *the fall of a house*, p.68. The words of the author, *Trovamala*, are these: "Domus tua *minabatur ruinam*; domus corruit, et interficit equum tibi *commodatum*; certè non potest dici casus fortuitus; quia *diligentissimus* reparâsset domum, vel ibi non habitâsset; si autem domus *non* minabatur ruinam, sed *impetu tempestatis* validae corruit, non est tibi imputandum."[3]
[r] Epist. ad Fam. VII. 22.[4]

[1] *Lane* v. *Cotton* (1701) Carth. 487, 12 Mod. 472, 482.
[2] C. Dumoulin, *Tractatus de eo quod Interest*, s.184 (*Caroli Molinaei Opera Omnia* (Paris, 1681), 3.484).
[3] B. Trovamala, *Summa Roselle*, 28v, *sub tit. Casus Fortuitus* (Strasbourg, 1516) (text reads *interfecit* rather than Jones's *interficit*).
[4] Cicero, *Epistulae ad Familiares*, VII.22 (ed. D. R. Shackleton-Bailey (Cambridge, 1977), Letter 331).

adventure, laws and the conclusions therein be the more plain and the more open; for *if any statute were made therein*, I thnk verily, more doubts and questions would arise *upon the statute*, than doth now, when they be only argued and judged after the *common* law[s]."

146. Before I finish the *historical* part of my essay, in which I undertook to demonstrate, "that a perfect harmony subsisted on this interesting branch of jurisprudence in the codes of nations *most eminent for legal wisdom*[t]," I cannot forbear adding a few remarks on the institutions of those nations, who are generally called *barbarous*, and who seem in many instances to have deserved that epithet: although [*112] traces of sound reasoning and solid judgement appear in most of their ordinances.

147. By the ancient laws of the WISIGOTHS, which are indeed rather obscure, the "keeper of a horse or an ox for *hire*, as well as a *hirer for use*, was obliged, if the animal *perished*, to return another of equal worth:" the law of the *Baiuvarians* on this head is nearly in the same words; and the rule is adopted with little alteration in the capitularies of *Charlemagne* and *Lewis the Pious*[u], where the *Mosaick* law before cited concerning a *borrower* may also be found[w]. In all these codes a *depositary* of gold, silver, or valuable trinkets, is made chargeable, if they are destroyed by *fire*, and *his own* goods perish *not* with them; a circumstance, which some other legislators have considered as *conclusive* evi-

[s] Doct. and Stud. *dial*. 2. *chap*. 38. last sentence.[1]
[t] P. 11.
[u] Lindenbrog, LL. *Wisigoth*. lib. 5. tit. 5. § 1, 2, 3.[2] and LL. *Baiuvar*. tit. 14. § 1, 2, 3, 4.[3] *Capitul*. lib. 5. § 204.[4]
[w] *Capitul*. lib. 6. § 22.[5] Exod. xxii. 14, 15.[6]

[1] St. German, Doctor and Student 2.38 (91 S.S. 261).
[2] F. Lindenbrog, *Codex Legum Antiquarum* (Frankfurt, 1713), 107-108. K. Zeumer, ed., *Leges Visigothorum* (M.G.H. Legum vol. 1, Hanover, 1902), 227-228.
[3] Lindenbrog, *Codex Legum Antiquarum*, 427-428. E. Schwind, ed., *Lex Baiwariorum* (M.G.H. Legum, vol. 5.2, Hanover, 1926), 421-424 (here numbered 15.1-4).
[4] Lindenbrog, *Codex Legum Antiquarum*, 963.
[5] Lindenbrog, *Codex Legum Antiquarum*, 985.
[6] Exodus 22.14, 15.

dence of gross neglect or fraud: thus, by the old *British* tract, called the book of CYNAWG, a person, who had been *robbed* of a deposit, was allowed to clear himself by making oath, with compurgators, that he had no concern in the robbery, *unless he had saved his own goods*; and it was the same, I believe, among the *Britons* in the case of a loss by *fire*, which happened without the fault of the bailee; although HOWEL *the Good* seems to [*113] have been rigorous in this case, for the sake of publick security[x]. There was one regulation in the *northern* code, which I have not seen in that of any other nation: if precious things were deposited and *stolen*, time was given to search for the thief, and, if he could not be found within the time limited, a *moiety* of the value was to be paid by the depositary to the owner, "ut damnum ex medio uterque sustineret[y]."

148. Now I can scarce persuade myself, that the phrase used in these laws, *si id perierit*, extends to a perishing by *inevitable accident*; nor can I think, that the old *Gothick* law, cited by *Stiernhook*, fully proves his assertion, that, "a depositary was responsible for *irresistible force*[1];" but I observe, that the military lawgivers of the north, who entertained very high notions of good faith and honour, were more strict than the *Romans* in the duties, by which depositaries and other trustees were bound: an exact conformity could hardly be expected between the ordinances of polished states, and those of a people, who could suffer disputes concerning bailments to be decided by *combat*; for it was the Em-

[x] LL. *Hywel Dda*, lib. 3. cap. 4. § 22. and lib. 3. cap. 3. § 40.[2] See also *Stiernh*. De Jur. Sveon. p. 256, 257.[3]

[y] LL. *Wisigoth*. lib. 5. tit. 5. § 3.[4]

[1] J. O. Stiernhöök, *De Jure Sveonum et Gothorum* (Stockholm 1672), 256: Sed in deposito (inlagdz fáá nostro jure) etiam vis major.

[2] Wotton, *Cyfreithjeu Hywel Dda Ac Eraill, seu Leges Wallicae Ecclesiasticae et Civiles Hoeli Boni*, 228, 216. *Ancient Laws and Customs of Wales* (London, 1841), 126 (= Venodotian Code, 3.3.21: Whoever shall take a thing under his care as a deposit, or promise to keep it secure, let him pay for it, although burned, as before); *ibid*, 509 (= "Anomalous" Laws, 9.7.5).

[3] Stiernhöök, *De Jure Sveonum et Gothorum*, 256, 257.

[4] Lindenbrog, *Codex Legum Antiquarum*, 107. Zeumer, *Leges Visigothorum*, 228.

peror *Frederick* II., who [*114] abolished the trial by battle in cases of contested deposits, and substituted a more rational mode of proof[z].

149. I purposely reserved to the last the mention of the HINDU, or *Indian*, code, which the learning and industry of my much-esteemed friend Mr. *Halhed* has made accessible to *Europeans*[1], and the PERSIAN translation of which I have had the pleasure of seeing: these laws, which must *in all times* be a singular object of curiosity, are *now* of infinite importance; since the happiness of millions, whom a series of amazing events has subjected to a *British* power, depends on a strict observance of them.

150. It is pleasing to remark the similarity, or rather identity, of those conclusions, which pure unbiassed reason in all ages and nations seldom fails to draw, in such juridical inquiries as are not fettered and manacled by *positive* institution; and, although the rules of the *Pundits* concerning *succession* to *property*, the *punishment* of *offences*, and the *ceremonies* of *religion*, are widely different from ours, yet, in the great system of *contracts* and the common intercourse between man and man, the POOTEE of the *Indians* and the DIGEST of the *Romans* are by no means dissimilar[a].

151. [*115] Thus, it is ordained by the sages of *Hindustán*, that "a depositor shall carefully inquire into the character of his intended depositary; who, if he undertake to keep the goods, shall preserve them with *care* and *attention*; but shall not be bound to restore the value of them, if they be *spoiled by unforeseen accident*, or

[z] LL. *Longobard.* lib. 2. tit. 55. § 35.[2] *Constit. Neapol.* lib. 2. tit. 34.[3]

[a] "Haec omnia, says GROTIUS, *Romanis* quidem congruunt legibus, sed non ex illis primitùs, sed ex *aequitate naturali*, veniunt: quare eadem apud alias quoque gentes reperire est." De Jure *Belli* ac *Pacis*, lib. 2. cap. 12. § 13.[4]

[1] N. Halhed, *A Code of Gentoo Laws* (London, 1776).

[2] Lindenbrog, *Codex Legum Antiquarum*, 663. A. Boretius, ed., *Liber Legis Langobardorum Papiensis* (M.G.H. Legum (folio series), vol. 4, Hanover, 1868), 574.

[3] Lindenbrog, *Codex Legum Antiquarum*, 779-780. James M. Powell, ed., *The Liber Augustalis* (Syracuse, New York, 1971), 93.

[4] Grotius, *De Jure Belli ac Pacis*, 2.12.13.2.

burned, or *stolen*; UNLESS he *conceal* any part of them, that has been saved, or unless *his own effects be secured*, or unless the accident happen after his *refusal* to redeliver the goods on a demand made by the depositor, or while the depositary, against the nature of the trust, presumes to *make use* of them:" in other words, "the bailee is made answerable for *fraud*, or for *such negligence* as approaches to it[b]."

152. So, a *borrower* is declared to be chargeable even for *casualty* or *violence*, if he fail to return the thing after the completion of the business, for which he borrowed it; but not, if it be *accidentally* lost or *forcibly* seized, *before* the expiration of the time, or the conclusion of the affair, for which it was lent[c]: in another place, it is provided, that, if a *pledge* be damaged or lost by *unforeseen accident*, the creditor shall never-[*116]theless recover his debt with interest, but the debtor shall not be entitled to the value of his pawn[d]; and that, if the pledgee *use* the thing pledged, he shall pay the value of it to the pledgor in case of its loss or damage, whilst he uses it[e].

153. In the same manner, if a person *hire* a thing *for use*, or if any *metal* be delivered to a *workman*, for the purpose of making vessels or ornaments, the bailees are holden to be discharged, if the thing bailed be destroyed or spoiled by *natural* misfortune or the injustice of the *ruling power*, UNLESS it be kept *after the time* limited for the return of the goods, or the performance of the work[f].

154. All these provisions are consonant to the principles established in this essay; and I cannot help thinking, that a clear and

[b] *Gentoo* Laws, chap. IV. See before, p. 47.[1]
[c] Same chapter.[2] See before, p. 68.
[d] Chap. I. Sect. I. Before, *p*. 84, 85.[3]
[e] Chap. I. Sect. II.[4] Before, p. 81.
[f] Chap. IV. and Chap. X. Before, p. 88, 91.

[1] Halhed, *Code of Gentoo Laws*, 119-122 (paraphrased).
[2] Halhed, *Code of Gentoo Laws*, 121.
[3] Halhed, *Code of Gentoo Laws*, 9.
[4] Halhed, *Code of Gentoo Laws*, 10.

concise treatise, written in the *Persian* or *Arabian* language, on the law of *Contracts*, and evincing the general conformity between the *Asiatick* and *European* systems, would contribute, as much as any regulation whatever, to bring our *English* law into good odour among those, whose fate it is to be under our dominion, and whose happiness ought to be a serious and continual object of our care.

155. Thus I have proved, agreeably to my undertaking, that *the plain elements of natural law*, [*117] on the subject of BAILMENTS, *which have been traced by a short analysis*, are recognised and confirmed by the wisdom of nations[g]; and I hasten to the third, or *synthetical*, part of my work, in which, from the nature of it, most of the *definitions* and *rules*, already given, must be repeated with little variation in *form*, and none in *substance*: it was at first my design, to subjoin, with a few alterations, the *Synopsis* of DELRIO;[1] but finding, that, as *Bynkershoek* expresses himself with an honest pride, *I had leisure sometimes to write, but never to copy*,[2] and thinking it unjust to embellish any production of mine with the inventions of another, I changed my plan; and shall barely recapitulate the doctrine expounded in the preceding pages, observing the method, which logicians call *Synthesis*, and in which all sciences ought to be explained.

156. I. To begin then with *definitions*: 1. BAILMENT *is a delivery of goods in trust, on a contract expressed or implied, that the trust shall be duly executed, and the goods redelivered, as soon as the time or use, for which they were bailed, shall have elapsed or be performed.*

157. 2. DEPOSIT *is a bailment* of goods *to be kept for the bailor without a recompense.*

158. 3. MANDATE is a *bailment* of goods, *without reward*, to be *carried from place to place*, or *to have some act performed about them*.

[g] Before, p. 4 and 11.

[1] Del Rio, *Exercitatio ad L. Contractus 23 de Diversis Regulis Iuris Antiqui*, 292.
[2] Perhaps C. van Bynkershoek, *Quaestionum Juris Publici Libri Duo* (Leiden, 1737, reprinted Oxford, 1930), *Ad Lectorem*.

159. [*118] 4. LENDING FOR USE is a *bailment* of *a thing* for a certain time *to be used* by the borrower *without paying for it.*

160. 5. PLEDGING is a *bailment* of goods by a debtor to his creditor *to be kept till the debt be discharged.*

161. 6. LETTING TO HIRE is 1. a *bailment* of A THING *to be used* by the hirer *for a compensation in money*; or, 2. a *letting out* OF WORK and LABOUR to be *done*, or CARE and ATTENTION to be *bestowed*, by the bailee *on the goods bailed*, and that for *a pecuniary recompense*; or, 3. of CARE and PAINS in *carrying the things delivered from one place to another for a stipulated or implied reward.*

162. 7. INNOMINATE BAILMENTS are those, where the *compensation* for the *use* of a thing, or for *labour* and *attention*, is *not pecuniary*, but either 1. the *reciprocal use* or the *gift* of some *other* thing; or, 2. *work* and *pains*, *reciprocally* undertaken; or, 3. the *use* or *gift* of another thing in consideration of *care* and *labour*, and conversely.

163. 8. ORDINARY *neglect* is the *omission* of that *care*, which *every man of common prudence, and capable of governing a family*, takes of *his own* concerns.

164. 9. GROSS *neglect* is the *want* of that care, which *every man of common sense, how inattentive soever*, takes of *his own* property.

165. 10. SLIGHT neglect is the *omission* of that *diligence*, which *very circumspect and thoughtful* [*119] *persons* use in securing *their own* goods and chattels.

166. 11. A NAKED CONTRACT is a contract made without *consideration* or *recompense*.

167. II. The *rules*, which may be considered as *axioms* flowing from natural reason, good morals, and sound policy, are these:

168. 1. A bailee, who derives *no benefit* from his undertaking, is responsible only for GROSS neglect.

169. 2. A bailee, who *alone* receives *benefit* from the bailment, is responsible for SLIGHT neglect.

170. 3. When the bailment is *beneficial* to *both* parties, the bailee must answer for ORDINARY neglect.

171. 4. A SPECIAL AGREEMENT of any bailee to answer for *more or less*, is in general valid.

172. 5. ALL bailees are answerable for actual FRAUD, even *though the contrary be stipulated.*

173. 6. NO bailee shall be charged for a loss by *inevitable* ACCIDENT or *irresistible* FORCE, except by *special agreement.*

174. 7. ROBBERY by *force* is considered as *irresistible*; but a loss by *private* STEALTH is *presumptive* evidence of *ordinary* neglect.

175. 8. GROSS neglect is *a violation of good faith.*

176. 9. NO ACTION lies to compel performance of a *naked contract.*

177. 10. A reparation may be obtained by suit for every DAMAGE occasioned by an INJURY.

178. [*120] 11. The negligence of a SERVANT, acting *by his master's express or implied order*, is the negligence of the MASTER.

179. III. From these *rules* the following *propositions* are evidently deducible:

180. 1. A DEPOSITARY is responsible only for GROSS neglect; or, in other words, for *a violation of good faith.*

181. 2. A DEPOSITARY, whose character is known to his depositor, shall not answer for *mere neglect*, if he take *no better care of his own* goods, and *they also* be spoiled or destroyed.

182. 3. A MANDATARY *to carry* is responsible only for GROSS neglect, or *a breach of good faith.*

183. 4. A MANDATARY *to perform a work* is bound to use *a degree of diligence adequate to the performance of it.*

184. 5. A man cannot be compelled by ACTION to perform his promise of engaging in a DEPOSIT or a MANDATE.

185. 6. A reparation may be obtained by suit for DAMAGE occasioned by the *nonperformance* of a promise to become a DEPOSITARY or a MANDATARY.

186. 7. A BORROWER FOR USE is responsible for SLIGHT negligence.

187. 8. A PAWNEE is answerable for ORDINARY neglect.

188. 9. The HIRER of a THING is answerable for ORDINARY neglect.

189. [*121] 10. A WORKMAN for HIRE must answer for ORDINARY neglect of the goods bailed, and apply a *degree* of SKILL *equal to his undertaking.*

190. 11. A LETTER TO HIRE of his CARE and ATTENTION is responsible for ORDINARY negligence.

191. 12. A CARRIER for HIRE, by *land* or by *water*, is answerable for ORDINARY neglect.

192. IV. To these *rules* and *propositions* there are some *exceptions*:

193. 1. A man, who *spontaneously* and *officiously* engages to *keep*, or to *carry*, the goods of another, though *without reward*, must answer for SLIGHT neglect.

194. 2. If a man, through *strong persuasion* and with *reluctance*, undertake the execution of a MANDATE, no more can be required of him than *a fair exertion of his ability*.

195. 3. ALL bailees become responsible for losses by CASUALTY or VIOLENCE, *after* their *refusal* to return the things bailed on a LAWFUL DEMAND.

196. 4. A BORROWER and a HIRER are answerable in ALL EVENTS, if they *keep* the things borrowed or hired *after the stipulated time*, or *use* them *differently* from their agreement.

197. 5. A DEPOSITARY and a PAWNEE are answerable in ALL EVENTS, if they *use* the things deposited or pawned.

198. 6. An INNKEEPER is chargeable for the goods of his guest *within his inn*, if the guest be *robbed* by the *servants* or *inmates* of the keeper.

199. [*122] 7. A COMMON CARRIER, by *land* or by *water*, must indemnify the owner of the goods carried, if he be ROBBED of them.

200. V. It is *no* exception, but a *corollary*, from the *rules*, that "every bailee is responsible for a loss by ACCIDENT or FORCE, however *inevitable* or *irresistible*, if it be *occasioned* by that *degree of negligence*, for which the nature of his contract makes him generally answerable;" and I may here conclude my discussion of this important title in jurisprudence with a general and obvious *remark*; that "*all* the preceding rules and propositions may be diversified to *infinity* by the *circumstances* of every particular case;" on which circumstances it is on the *continent* the province of a *judge* appointed by the sovereign, and in ENGLAND, to our constant honour and happiness, of a *jury* freely chosen by the

parties, *finally* to decide: thus, when a painted *cartoon*, pasted on canvas, had been *deposited*, and the bailee kept it so near a damp wall, that it peeled and was much injured, the question "whether the depositary had been guilty of GROSS neglect," was properly left to the jury, and, on a verdict for the plaintiff with pretty large damages, the court refused to grant a new trial[h]; but it was the judge, who determined, that the defendant was by *law* responsible for *gross* negligence *only*; and, if it had been proved, that the bailee had kept *his own* pictures *of the same* [*123] *sort* in the same place and manner, and that *they too* had been spoiled, a new trial would, I conceive, have been granted; and so, if no more than SLIGHT neglect had been committed, and the jury had, nevertheless, taken upon themselves to decide against law, that a bailee *without reward* was responsible for it.

201. Should the *method* used in this little tract be approved, I may possibly not want inclination, if I do not want leisure, to discuss in the same form *every* branch of *English* law, *civil* and *criminal*, *private* and *publick*; after which it will be easy to separate and mould into distinct works, the three principal divisions, or the *analytical*, the *historical*, and the *synthetical*. parts.

202. The great system of jurisprudence, like that of the Universe, consists of many subordinate systems, all of which are connected by nice links and beautiful dependencies; and each of them, as I have fully persuaded myself, is reducible to a few plain *elements*, either the wise *maxims* of national policy and general convenience, or the *positive* rules of our forefathers, which are seldom deficient in wisdom or utility: if LAW *be* a *science*, and really deserve so sublime a name, it must be founded on principle, and claim an exalted rank in the empire of *reason*; but, if it be *merely* an unconnected series of decrees and ordinances, its use may remain, though its dignity be lessened, and He will become the greatest lawyer, who has the strongest habitual, or arti-[*124]ficial, *memory*. In practice, law certainly employs *two* of the mental faculties; *reason*, in the primary investigation and de-

[h] 2 Stra. 1099. *Mytton* and *Cock*.[1]

[1] *Mytton* v. *Cock* (1739) 2 Stra. 1099.

cision of points *entirely new*; and *memory*, in transmitting to us the reason of sage and learned men, to which our own ought invariably to yield, if not from a becoming modesty, at least from a just attention to that object, for which all laws are framed, and all societies instituted, THE GOOD OF MANKIND.

ADVERTISEMENT.

[*129] AFTER I had finished the preceding tract, to the satisfaction of several friends, but not to my own, I was informed, that the learned CHRISTIAN THOMASIUS had published a dissertation on the same subject with the following title: *De Usu Practico Doctrinae difficillimae Juris Romani de Culparum Praestatione in Contractibus*; HALAE, MDCCV[1]. The fame of this author, and the high applause, which the very sensible *Bynkershoek* bestows on him,[2] impressed me with a most favourable idea of his work, and with a strong desire to procure it; but, to my extreme disappointment, I cannot find it in any library, publick or private, in the Metropolis or in either of our Universities: I have sent for it, however, to *Germany*, and, when I receive it, shall take a sincere pleasure in correcting such [*130] errors, as it may enable me to detect in my essay, or in confirming the system, which I have adopted, by so respectable authority.

[1] C. Thomasius, resp. C. G. Kreß, *De Usu Practico Doctrinae Difficillimae Juris Romani de Culparum Praestatione in Contractibus* (Halle, 1705, reprinted 1731 and 1774).
[2] Bynkershoek, *Quaestionum Juris Publici Libri Duo*, 1.2.

BIBLIOGRAPHY

Ackroyd, P.: *Dressing Up* (London: Thames and Hudson, 1979).

Anderson, M. R.: 'Islamic Law and the Colonial Encounter in British India', in D. Arnold and P. Robb, eds., *Institutions and Ideologies: A SOAS South Asia Reader* (London: Curzon Press, 1993), 165.

Anon.: 'A Barrister's First Speech' (1837) 14 *Legal Observer* 456.

'Biographical List of Living English Poets' (1792) 62 *Gentleman's Magazine* 505.

'Law School at Cambridge' (1833) 36 (59) *North American Review* 395.

Laws Concerning Travelling (London, 1718).

Liber Placitandi (London, 1671).

'The Life and Writings of Sir William Jones' (1830) 2 *United States Law Intelligencer and Review* 1, 37, 77, 157.

Obituary of Jones (1795) 65 *Gentleman's Magazine* 347.

Obituary of Jones (1795) 21 *Analytical Review* 246, note.

Obituary of Jones (1797) 31 *European Magazine* 40.

Review of Jones's *Essay on the Law of Bailments*: (1781) *New Annual Register*, 216.

Review of Jones's *Poeseos Asiaticos Commentariorum Libri Sex.* (1774) 44 *Gentleman's Magazine* 579.

Review of Story's *Commentaries on the Law of Bailments*: (1832) 7 *American Jurist* 128.

Review of Story's *Commentaries on the Law of Bailments*: (1839) 4 *Monthly Law Magazine* 84, 208, 288; (1840) 7 *Monthly Law Magazine* 267; (1840) 8 *Monthly Law Magazine* 69, 151, 229; (1840) 9 *Monthly Law Magazine* 61, 134, 195; (1841) 10 *Monthly Law Magazine* 193.

Arangio-Ruiz, V.: *Responsabilità Contrattuale in Diritto Romano* (Naples: Jovene, 1933).

Arberry, A. J.: *Asiatic Jones* (London: Longmans, 1946).

Arnold, D. and Robb, P., eds.: *Institutions and Ideologies: A SOAS South Asia Reader* (London: Curzon Press, 1993).

Aston, R.: *Placita Latine Rediviva* (London, 1661).

Ayliffe, John: *A New Pandect of the Roman Civil Law* (London, 1734).

The Law of Pledges, or Pawns, as it was in Use among the Romans, and as it is now practiced in most Foreign Nations (London, 1732).

Banerjee, A. C.: *English Law in India* (New Delhi, Abhinav Publications, 1984).

Baker, J. H.: *Oxford History of the Laws of England, Volume 6* (Oxford: Oxford University Press, 2003).

Baker, J. H. and Milsom, S. F. C.: *Sources of English Legal History* (London: Butterworths, 1986).

Barton, J. L.: 'Legal Studies', in L. S. Sutherland and L. G. Mitchell, eds., *The History of the University of Oxford, Volume V, The Eighteenth Century* (Oxford: Oxford University Press, 1986).

Barton, J. L., ed., *Towards a General Law of Contract* (Berlin: Dunker and Humblot, 1990).

Beale, J. H.: 'Southcott *v.* Bennett' (1899) 13 *Harvard Law Review* 43.

Bever, Thomas: *A Discourse on the Study of Jurisprudence and the Civil Law* (Oxford, 1766).

Bingen, J., Coupez, A., and Mawet, F., eds., *Recherches de Linguistique: Hommages à Maurice Leroy* (Brussels: Université de Bruxelles, 1980).

Biondi, B., ed., *Conferenze Romanistiche* (Milan: Giuffrè, 1960).

Birks, P.: 'Negligence in the Eighteenth Century Common Law', in E. J. H. Schrage, ed., *Negligence: The Comparative Legal History of the Law of Torts* (Berlin: Dunker and Humblot, 2001), 173.

Blackstone, Sir William: *Commentaries on the Law of England* (London, 1765).

Bocer, H.: *Commentarii in Celebrem L Contractus 23 D De Regulis Iuris* (Speyer, 1587).

Bordwell, P.: 'Property in Chattels' (1916) 29 *Harvard Law Review* 731.

Boretius, A., ed.: *Liber Legis Langobardorum Papiensis* (M.G.H. Legum (folio series), vol. 4; Hanover, 1868).

Bourguignon, Henry J.: *Sir William Scott, Lord Stowell* (Cambridge: Cambridge University Press, 1987).

Bracton, H.: *De Legibus et Consuetudinibus Anglie* (London, 1569); G. Woodbine, ed., and S E Thorne, trans., *Bracton, On the Laws and Customs of England* (Cambridge Mass.: Belknap Press, 1968).

Breckenridge, C. A. and van der Veer, P., eds.: *Orientalism and the Post-colonial Predicament* (Philadelphia: University of Pennsylvania Press, 1993).

Brettschneider, G. and Lehmann, C., eds.: *Wege zur Universalienforschung* (Tübingen: Narr, 1980).

Britton (ed. F. M. Nichols, Oxford, 1865).

Browne, W.: *Formulae Bene Placitandi* (London, 1674).

Brownlow, R.: *Latine Redivivus* (London, 1693).

Declarations and Pleadings in English (London, 1659).

Buckland, W. W.: 'The Duty to Take Care' (1935) 51 *Law Quarterly Review* 637

Buller, F.: *An Introduction to the Law Relative to Trials at Nisi Prius* (3rd edn., London, 1781).

Burrows, A. and Rodger, Lord, eds., *Mapping the Law: Essays in Memory of Peter Birks* (Oxford: Oxford University Press, 2006).

Cannon, Garland: 'The Literary Place of Sir William Jones (1746-94)' (1960) 11 *Journal of the Asiatic Society* (4th series) 47.

The Letters of Sir William Jones (Cambridge: Cambridge University Press, 1970).

Sir William Jones: a Bibliography of Primary and Secondary Sources (Amsterdam: Benjamins, 1979).

The Life and Mind of Oriental Jones (Cambridge: Cambridge University Press, 1990).

Cannon, G. and Brine, K. R., eds.: *Objects of Enquiry* (New York: New York University Press, 1995).

Christian, E.: *A Syllabus; or, the Heads of Lectures Publicly Delivered in the University of Cambridge* (London, 1797).

Cicero, Marcus Tullius: *M. Tullii Ciceronis Opera* (Glasgow, 1748-1749).

Epistulae ad Familiares (ed. D. R. Shackleton-Bailey; Cambridge: Cambridge University Press, 1977).

Cicero, Quintus: *Commentariolum Petitionis* (ed. G. Laser, Darmstadt: Wissenschaftliche Buchgesellschaft, 2001).

Cinus Campanus, H.: *Ad Utilissimam l. Contractus ff. De Regulis Iuris* (Paris, 1574).

Clarke, J. J.: *Oriental Enlightenment* (London: Routledge, 1997).

Clift, H.: *A New Book of Declarations* (London, 1703).

Codex Theodosiani Libri XVI (Paris, 1586).

Cohn, Bernard S.: 'Law and the Colonial State in India', in J. Starr and J. F. Collier, eds., *History and Power in the Study of Law* (Ithaca: Cornell University Press, 1989), 131.

Coke, Sir Edward: *Commentary on Littleton* (13th edn., by Francis Hargrave, London, 1775; completed by Charles Butler, London, 1788).

Second Institute (London, 1642).

Colebrooke, Henry: *A Digest of Hindu Law on Contracts and Successions, with a Commentary* (Calcutta, 1797-8).

Treatise on Obligations and Contracts (London, 1818).

Coquillette, D.: *The Civilian Writers of Doctors' Commons, London* (Berlin: Dunker and Humblot, 1988).

Cruise, W.: *Essay on the Nature and Operation of Fines* (London, 1783).

Essay on the Nature and Operation of Fines and Recoveries (London, 1786).

Cujas, J.: *Opera* (Prato, 1838).

Curry, W.: *The Commentaries of Sir William Blackstone ... Carefully Abridged* (London, 1796).

D'Avezan, J.: *Contractuum Liber Prior*, in *Novus Thesaurus Juris Civilis et Canonici* (The Hague, 1752), 4.49-64.

Davies, Anna Morpurgo: *Nineteenth-Century Linguistics* (= G. Lepschy, ed., *History of Linguistics*, vol. IV) (London: Longman, 1998).

Davis, Donald R., Jr.: 'Intermediate Realms of Law: Corporate Groups and Rulers in Medieval India' (2005) 48 *Journal of the Economic and Social History of the Orient* 92.

'A Realist View of Hindu Law' (2006) 19 *Ratio Juris* 287.

de Beer, E. S., ed., *The Correspondence of John Locke* (Oxford: Clarendon Press, 1976).

de Ferrière, C., ed.: *Nouvelle Traduction des Institutes de L'Empereur Justinien* (Paris, 1770).

Del Rio, M. A.: *Repetitio L. Transigere C. de Transactionibus. Eiusdem Exercitatio ad L. Contractus 23 de Diversis Regulis Iuris Antiqui Totam Culpae Praestandae Materiae Comprehendens* (Lyons, 1606).

Derrett, J. D. M.: *Religion, Law and the State in India* (Oxford: Oxford University Press, 1999).

Despeisses, A.: *Oeuvres de M. Antoine D'Espeisses* (Lyons, 1750).

Domat, J.: *Les Loix Civiles dans leur Ordre Naturel* (Paris, 1689).

Donellus, H.: *Opera* (Florence, 1842).

Drew, John: *India and the Romantic Imagination* (Delhi: Oxford University Press, 1987).

Duck, A.: *De Usu et Authoritate Juris Civilis Romanorum* (London, 1679), 25.

Dufour, A.: 'Pufendorfs Ausstrahlung im französischen und im anglo-amerikanischen Kulturraum', in K. Å. Modéer, ed., *Samuel von Pufendorf 1632-1982* (Stockholm: Nordiska Bokhandolen, 1986), 96.

Duman, Daniel: *The Judicial Bench in England 1727-1875* (London: Royal Historical Society, 1982).

Eden, R.: *Jurisprudentia Philologica* (Oxford, 1744).

Ensinck, J. and Gaeffke, P., eds.: *India Maior: Congratulatory Volume Presented to J. Gonda* (Leiden: Brill, 1972).

Faber, A.: *De Erroribus Pragmaticorum et Interpretum Iuris* (Lyons, 1658).

Faber, P.: *Ad Titulum de Diversis Regulis Iuris Antiqui Commentarium* (Paris, 1585).

Ferguson, Robert A.: 'The Emulation of Sir William Jones in the Early Republic' (1979) 52 *New England Quarterly* 3.

Finch, H.: *Law, or a Discourse Thereof* (London, 1627).

Finnis, J. M.: 'Blackstone's Theoretical Intentions' (1967) 12 *Natural Law Forum* 163.

Fleta (ed. H. G. Richardson and G. O. Sayles, Selden Society vol. 72; London, 1953).

Fletcher, E. G. M.: *The Carrier's Liability* (London: Stevens, 1932).

Fonblanque, J.: *Treatise of Equity* (Dublin, 1795).

Fortescue, J.: *De Laudibus Legum Angliae*, with notes by John Selden (London, 1727); *De Laudibus Legum Anglie* (ed. S. B. Chrimes, Cambridge: Cambridge University Press, 1942).

Franklin, Michael J.: *Sir William Jones* (Cardiff: University of Wales Press, 1995).

'Accessing India: Orientalism, Anti-'Indianism' and the Rhetoric of Jones and Burke', in T. Fulford and P. J. Kitson, eds., *Romanticism and Colonialism* (Cambridge: Cambridge University Press, 1998), 48.

Fulford, T. and Kitson, P. J., eds.: *Romanticism and Colonialism* (Cambridge: Cambridge University Press, 1998).

Gilbert, J.: *The Law of Evidence, by Lord Chief Baron Gilbert, Enlarged by Capel Lofft* (Dublin, 1795).

Giphanius, H.: *Commentarii in Titulum Digestorum de Diversis Regulis Iuris Antiqui* (Frankfurt, 1606).

Glanvill: *The Treatise on the Laws and Customs of the Realm of England Commonly Called Glanvill* (ed. G. D. G. Hall, London: Nelson, 1965).

Godefroy, D.: *Corpus Iuris Civilis cum Notis Dionisii Gothofredi* (Frankfurt, 1663).

Godefroy, J.: *In Titulum Pandectarum De Diversis Regulis Iuris Antiqui Commentarius* (Geneva, 1652).

Gordley, J.: *The Philosophical Origins of Modern Contract Doctrine* (Oxford: Oxford University Press, 1991).

Gravina, J. V.: *Origines Iuris Civilis* (Leipzig, 1708).

Grotius, Hugo: *De Jure Belli ac Pacis* (Paris, 1625).

Of the Law of Warre and Peace (London, 1654).

Gundling, N.: *Ius Naturae et Gentium* (3rd edn., Halle, 1736).

Haakonssen, Knud: 'Divine/Natural Law Theories in Ethics', in Daniel Garber and Michael Ayers, eds., *The Cambridge History of Seventeenth-Century Philosophy* (Cambridge: Cambridge University Press, 1998).

Natural Law and Moral Philosophy (Cambridge: Cambridge University Press, 1996).

Haakonssen, Knud, ed., *Grotius, Pufendorf and Modern Natural Law* (Aldershot: Dartmouth, 1999).

Hacker, P.: 'Dharma in Hinduism', trans. D. Davis Jr., (2006) 34 *Journal of Indian Philosophy* 479.

Halbfass, Wilhelm: *India and Europe: An Essay in Understanding* (New York: State University of New York Press, 1988).

Hale, Matthew.: *Historia Placitorum Coronae* (London, 1736).

Halhed, Nathaniel Brassey: *A Code of Gentoo Laws* (London, 1776).

A Grammar of the Bengal Language (Hoogly, 1778).

Hallifax, S.: *An Analysis of the Roman Civil Law* (London, 1774).

Harmenopulus, Constantine: *Manuale Legum sive Hexabiblos* (ed. G. Heimbach, Leipzig, 1841).

Hausmaninger, H.: '*Diligentia Quam in Suis*: A Standard of Contractual Liability from Ancient Roman to Modern Soviet Law' (1985) 18 *Cornell International Law Journal* 179.

Hawkins, Laetitia-Matilda: *Memoirs, Anecdotes, Facts and Opinions* (London, 1824).

Heimbach, G. E., ed.: *Basilicorum Libri LX* (Leipzig, 1833).

Heineccius, J. G.: *Opera Omnia* (Geneva, 1747).

Heineccius, J. G.: *A Methodical System of Universal Law: or, the Laws of Nature and Nations deduced from Certain Principles, and applied to Proper Cases* (trans. G. Turnbull, London, 1763).

Helmholz, R. and Zimmermann, R., eds.: *Itinera Fiduciae* (Berlin: Dunker and Humblot, 1998).

Heraldus, Desiderius: *Observationes ad Ius Atticum et Romanum* (Paris, 1650).

Herne, J.: *The Pleader* (London, 1657).

Hicks, S. C. and Ramsay, C.: 'Law, Order and the Bankruptcy Commissions of Early Nineteenth Century England' (1987) 55 *Tijdschrift voor Rechtsgeschiedenis* 123.

Hochstrasser, T.: *Natural Law Theories in the Early Enlightenment* (Cambridge: Cambridge University Press, 2000).

Hoffmann, H.-J.: *Die Abstufung der Fahrlässigkeit in der Rechtsgeschichte* (Berlin: De Gruyter, 1968).

Holmes, O. W.: *The Common Law* (ed. M. DeWolfe Howe, London: Macmillan, 1968).

Hont, I. and Ignatieff, M., eds., *Wealth and Virtue: The Shaping of Political Economy in the Scottish Enlightenment* (Cambridge: Cambridge University Press, 1983).

Hoüard, D, *Anciennes Loix des François Conservées dans les Coutumes Angloises* (Rouen, 1766).

Howell, T. B.: *A Complete Collection of State Trials* (London, 1814).

Hutchinson, J.: *A Catalogue of Notable Middle Templars* (London, 1902).

Ibbetson, David J.: 'Consideration and the Theory of Contract in Sixteenth Century Common Law', in J. Barton, ed., *Towards a General law of Contract* (Berlin: Dunker and Humblot, 1990).

'Absolute Liability in Contract: the Antecedents of *Paradine* v. *Jayne*', in F. D. Rose, ed., *Consensus ad Idem* (London: Sweet and Maxwell, 1996), 1.

'Sir William Jones as a Comparative Lawyer', in A. Murray, ed., *Sir William Jones, 1746-94: A Commemoration* (Oxford: Oxford University Press, 1998), 19.

A Historical Introduction to the Law of Obligations (Oxford: Oxford University Press, 1999).

'Sir William Jones', in T. G. Watkin, ed., *Legal Wales: Its Past, Its Future* (Welsh Legal History Society, vol.1; Cardiff, 2001), 41.

'Natural Law and Common Law' (2001) 5 *Edinburgh Law Review* 4.

'The Tort of Negligence in the Common Law in the Nineteenth and Twentieth Centuries', in E. J. H. Schrage, ed., *Negligence: The Comparative Legal History of the Law of Torts* (Berlin: Dunker and Humblot, 2001), 229.

'Sir William Jones and the Nature of Law', in A. Burrows and Lord Rodger, eds., *Mapping the Law: Essays in Memory of Peter Birks* (Oxford: Oxford University Press, 2006), 619.

John of Salisbury, *Polycraticus* (ed. C. J. Nederman, Cambridge: Cambridge University Press, 1990).

Jones, Alan: 'Sir William Jones as an Arabist', in A. Murray, ed., *Sir William Jones, 1746-94: A Commemoration* (Oxford: Oxford University Press, 1998), 69.

Jones, N. G.: 'Uses, Trusts, and a Path to Privity' [1997] *Cambridge Law Journal* 175.

Jones, W., Sr.,: 'Of Logarithms' (1771) 61 *Philosophical Transactions of the Royal Society* 455.

'Properties of the Conic Sections; deduced by a Compendious Method' (1773) 63 *Philosophical Transactions of the Royal Society* 340.

Jones, Sir William: *The Works of Sir William Jones* (London, 1807).

An Oration Intended to have been Spoken in the Theatre at Oxford IX July MDCCLXXIII, printed with *An Inquiry into the Legal Mode of Suppressing Riots* (2nd edn., London, 1782), 61-75.

Kantorowicz, H.: *Bractonian Problems* (Glasgow: Jackson, 1941).

Kaufmann, H.: 'Causa Debendi und Causa Petendi bei Glanvill' (1961) 17 *Traditio* 107.

Kaul, R. K.: *Studies in William Jones: An Interpretation of Oriental Literature* (Shimla: Indian Institute of Advanced Study, 1995).

Kelly, J. M.: *A Short History of Western Legal Theory* (Oxford: Oxford University Press, 1992).

Kejariwal, P.: *The Asiatic Society of Bengal and the Discovery of India's Past* (New Delhi: Oxford University Press, 1988).

Kent, James: *Commentaries on American Law* (New York, 1826-30).

Kepler, J. S.: 'The Operating Potential of London Marine Insurance in the 1570's' (1975) 17 *Business History* 44.

Krieger, L.: *The Politics of Discretion* (Chicago: University of Chicago Press, 1965).

Lariviere, Richard W.: 'Dharmaśāstra, Custom, 'Real Law' and 'Apocryphal' Smṛtis' (2004) 32 *Journal of Indian Philosophy* 611.

Le Brun, D.: *Essai sur la Prestation des Fautes* (Paris, 1764).

Le Conte (Contius), A.: *Ad L. Contractus de Diversis Regulis Iuris Antiqui Dictatae Praelectiones* (Bourges, 1574).

Leibniz, G.: *Nova Methodus Discendae Docendaeque Iurisprudentiae* (Leipzig, 1748).

Lemmings, D., ed.: *The British and their Laws in the Eighteenth Century* (Woodbridge: Boydell Press, 2005).

Levy, L. W.: *Origins of the Bill of Rights* (New Haven: Yale University Press, 1999).

Lieberman, David: *The Province of Legislation Determined* (Cambridge: Cambridge University Press, 1989).

Lindenbrog, F.: *Codex Legum Antiquarum* (Frankfurt, 1713).

Lingat, R.: *The Classical Law of India* (trans. J. D. M. Derrett; Berkeley: University of California Press, 1973).

Lobban, M.: *The Common Law and English Jurisprudence, 1760-1850* (Oxford: Clarendon Press, 1991).

'Custom, Nature, and Authority: the Roots of English Legal Positivism', in D. Lemmings, ed., *The British and their Laws in the Eighteenth Century* (Woodbridge: Boydell Press, 2005), 27.

Locke, John: 'Some Thoughts Concerning Reading and Study for a Gentleman', in *A Collection of Several Pieces by Mr John Locke* (London, 1720).

Lyall, C. J., ed.: *The Mufaddalīyāt* (Oxford: Oxford University Press, 1918).

Mackintosh, James: *Discourse on the Study of the Law of Nature and Nations* (Dublin, 1799).

MacCormack, G.: 'Custodia and Culpa' (1972) 89 *Zeitschrift der Savigny-Stiftung für Rechtsgeschichte (Romanistische Abteilung)* 149.
Maclean, I.: *Interpretation and Meaning in the Renaissance* (Cambridge: Cambridge University Press, 1992).
Macnair, M.: 'The Conceptual Basis of Trusts in the Later 17th and Early 18th Centuries', in R. Helmholz and R. Zimmermann, eds., *Itinera Fiduciae* (Berlin: Dunker and Humblot, 1998).
Maimonides, M.: *Doctor Perplexorum* (trans. Johannes Buxtorfius, Basle, 1629).
Maitland, F. W. *Bracton and Azo* (Selden Society vol. 8; London, 1894).
Majeed, J.: *Ungoverned Imaginings: James Mill's The History of British India and Orientalism* (Oxford: Oxford University Press, 1992).
Malynes, G.: *Consuetudo vel Lex Mercatoria* (London, 1622).
Marriner, S.: 'English Bankruptcy Records and Statistics before 1850' (1980) 33 *Economic History Review* 351, 361-365.
Marvin, John: *Legal Bibliography* (Philadelphia, 1847).
Mayrhofer, M.: 'Sanskrit und die Sprachen Alteuropas' (*Nachrichten von der Akademie der Wissenschaften in Göttingen, Philologisch-Historische Klasse*, Göttingen 1983, no. 5).
Milsom, S. F. C.: *Historical Foundations of the Common Law* (2nd edn., London: Butterworth, 1981).
'The Nature of Blackstone's Achievement' (2001) 1 *Oxford Journal of Legal Studies* 1.
The Mirror of Justices (ed. W. J. Whitaker, Selden Society vol. 7; London, 1893).
Modéer, K. Å., ed.: *Samuel von Pufendorf 1632-1982* (Stockholm: Nordiska Bokhandolen, 1986).
Molinaeus, Carolus: *Caroli Molinaei Opera Omnia* (Paris, 1681).
Monéger, J., Sourioux, J.-L., and Terrasson de Fougères, A.: *Robert-Joseph Pothier; d'Hier à Aujourd'hui* (Paris: Economica, 2001).
Moore, J. and Silverthorne, M.: 'Gershom Carmichael and the Natural Jurisprudence Tradition in Eighteenth-Century Scotland', in I. Hont and M. Ignatieff, eds., *Wealth and Virtue: The Shaping of Political Economy in the Scottish Enlightenment* (Cambridge: Cambridge University Press, 1983).
Morgan, Victor: *A History of the University of Cambridge, Volume II, 1546-1750* (Cambridge: Cambridge University Press, 2004).

Mukherjee, S. N.: *Sir William Jones: A Study in Eighteenth-Century British Attitudes to India* (London: Cambridge University Press, 1987).

Muller, J.-C.: 'Early Stages of Language Comparison from Sassetti to Sir William Jones (1786)' (1986) 31 *Kratylos* 1.

Murr, S.: *L'Inde Philosophique entre Bossuet et Voltaire, vol. 2, L'Indologie du Père Coeurdoux: Stratégies, Apologétique et Scientificité* (Publications de l'Ecole Francaise d'Extreme-Orient, vol. 146(2), Paris, 1987).

Murray, A., ed.: *Sir William Jones, 1746-94: A Commemoration* (Oxford: Oxford University Press, 1998).

Newton, Isaac, *Analysis Per Quantitatum Series, Fluxiones, ac Differentias* (London, 1711).

Niranjana, Tejaswini: *Siting Translation: History, Post-Structuralism, and the Colonial Context* (Berkeley: University of California Press, 1992).

Noodt, G.: *Opera Omnia* (Leiden, 1724).

Nörr, D.: 'Die Entwicklung des Utilitätsgedankens im Römischen Haftungsrecht' (1956) 73 *Zeitschrift der Savigny Stiftung für Rechtsgeschichte (Romanistische Abteilung)* 68.

Noy, W.: *A Treatise of the Principall Grounds and Maxims of the Laws of this Nation* (London, 1677).

Oldham, J.: *The Mansfield Manuscripts* (Chapel Hill: University of North Carolina Press, 1992).

'The Survival of Sir William Jones in American Jurisprudence', in G. Cannon and K. R. Brine, eds., *Objects of Enquiry* (New York: New York University Press, 1995).

Olivelle, P.: *Manu's Code of Law* (Oxford: Oxford University Press, 2005).

Paley, William: *Principles of Moral and Political Philosophy* (London, 1785).

Palmer, N. E.: *Bailment* (2nd edn., London: Sweet and Maxwell, 1991).

Paton, G. W. *Bailment in the Common Law* (London: Stevens, 1952).

Petit, S.: *Leges Atticae* (Leiden, 1742).

Politianus, Angelus: *Angeli Politiani Opera* (Lyons, 1528).

Pollock, F. and Maitland, F. W.: *History of English Law* (2nd edn., reissued, Cambridge: Cambridge University Press, 1968).

Pothier, Robert-Joseph: *Oeuvres de R.-J. Pothier* (Brussels, 1831).

Powell, James M., ed.: *The Liber Augustalis* (Syracuse, New York: Syracuse University Press, 1971).

Prichard, M. J.: *Scott v. Shepherd (1773) and the Emergence of the Tort of Negligence* (London: Selden Society, 1976).

Pufendorf, Samuel.: *Elementorum Jurisprudentiae Universalis Libri Duo* (The Hague, 1660) (reprint, with translation by W. A. Oldfather, Oxford, 1931).

De Jure Naturae et Gentium (Lund, 1672).

De Officio Hominis et Civis (Lund, 1673).

On the Whole Duty of Man according to the Law of Nature (trans. A. Tooke, London, 1691),

On the Law of Nature and Nations (trans. Basil Kennet, London, 1703).

Pugh, R. B.: *Imprisonment in Medieval England* (Cambridge: Cambridge University Press, 1968).

Rastell, W.: *Collection of Entrees* (London, 1596).

Registrum Omnium Brevium (London, 1687).

Reiske, J. J.: *Oratorum Graecorum* (Leipzig, 1770).

Reuss, J. D.: *Das Gelehrte England* (Berlin, 1804).

Ribeiro, A.: *Dress in Eighteenth-Century Europe* (New Haven: Yale University Press, 2002).

Riccobono, S.: *Fontes Iuris Romani Anteiustiniani* (Florence: Barbèra, 1968).

Rittershusius, C.: *Commentarius Novus Pulcherrimus et Utilissimus: in Celeberrimam Legem XXIII Contractus Digesti De Regulis Juris Antiqui* (Strasbourg, 1616).

Robins, R. H.: 'The Life and Work of Sir William Jones' (1987) 85 *Transactions of the Philological Society* 1.

Robinson, R. B.: 'The Two Institutes of Thomas Wood: A Study in Eighteenth Century Legal Scholarship' (1991) 35 *American Journal of Legal History* 432.

Robinson, T.: *Book of Special Entries* (London, 1684).

Rocher, L.: 'Schools of Hindu Law', in J. Ensinck and P. Gaeffke, eds., *India Maior: Congratulatory Volume Presented to J. Gonda* (Leiden: Brill, 1972), 166.

Rocher, L., ed.: *Jīmūtavāna's Dāyabhāga: the Hindu Law of Inheritance in Bengal* (Oxford: Oxford University Press, 2002).

Rocher, Rosane: *Orientalism, Poetry, and the Millennium: The Checkered Life of Nathaniel Brassey Halhed, 1751-1830* (Delhi: Motilal Banarsidass, 1983).

'Nathaniel Brassey Halhed, Sir William Jones and Comparative Indo-European Linguistics', in J. Bingen, A. Coupez and F. Mawet, eds., *Recherches de Linguistique: Hommages à Maurice Leroy* (Brussels: Université de Bruzelles, 1980), 173.

'British Orientalism in the Eighteenth Century: The Dialectics of Knowledge and Government', in C. A. Breckenridge and P. van der Veer, eds., *Orientalism and the Postcolonial Predicament* (Philadelphia: University of Pennsylvania Press, 1993), 215.

'Weaving Knowledge: Sir William Jones and Indian Pandits', in G. Cannon and K. R. Brine, eds., *Objects of Enquiry* (New York: New York University Press, 1995), 57.

Rodenberg, C. and Pauls, V.: *Die Anfänge der Christian-Albrechts Universität Keil* (Neumünster: Karl Wachholtz Verlag, 1955).

Röd, W.: *Geometrischer Geist und Naturrecht* (*Bayerische Akademie der Wissenschaften, Phil.-Hist. Klasse Abhandlungen*, N.F. 70) (Munich, 1970).

Rogers, J. E. Thorold: *A History of Agriculture and Prices in England* (Oxford: Clarendon Press, 1866-1902).

Roscoe, Henry: *Lives of Eminent British Lawyers* (London, 1830).

Rose, F. D. ed.: *Consensus ad Idem* (London: Sweet and Maxwell, 1996).

Rudden, B.: 'Pothier et la *Common Law*', in J. Monéger, J.-L. Sourioux, and A. Terrasson de Fougères, *Robert-Joseph Pothier; d'Hier à Aujourd'hui* (Paris, 2001), 91.

Rutherforth, Thomas: *Institutes of Natural Law* (London, 1754-6).

Sadi, M.: *Rosarium Politicum* (trans. G. Gentius, Amsterdam, 1687).

Said, Edward: *Orientalism* (London: Penguin, 1995).

St. German, C.: *Doctor and Student*, 2.38 (ed. T. F. T. Plucknett and J. L. Barton, Selden Society vol. 91; London, 1974).

Sastry, L.S.R. Krishna: *Sir William Jones: Interpreter of India to the West* (Visakhapatnam, 1998).

Saunders, David: 'The Natural Jurisprudence of Jean Barbeyrac: Translation as an Art of Political Adjustment' (2003) 36 *Eighteenth Century Studies* 473.

Sharpe, Jenny: 'The Violence of Light in the Land of Desire; Or, How William Jones Discovered India' (1993) 20 *boundary 2* 26.

Schrage, E. J. H., ed.: *Negligence: The Comparative Legal History of the Law of Torts* (Berlin: Dunker and Humblot, 2001).

Schröder, J., ed.: *Entwicklung der Methodenlehre in Rechtswissenschaft und Philosophie vom 16. bis zum 18. Jahrhundert* (Stuttgart: F. Steiner, 1998).

Schwab, R.: *The Oriental Renaissance: Europe's Rediscovery of India and the East, 1680-1880* (trans. G. Patterson-Black and V. Reinking (New York: Columbia University Press, 1984).

Schwind, E., ed.: *Lex Baiwariorum* (M.G.H. Legum, vol. 5.2, Hanover, 1926).

Searby, Peter: *A History of the University of Cambridge, Volume III, 1750-1870* (Cambridge: Cambridge University Press, 1997).

Sharp, Granville: *The Ancient Common Law Right of Associating with the Vicinage*, in *Tracts, Concerning the Ancient and Only True Means of National Defence by a Free Militia* (London, 1781).

Sheppard, W.: *Actions upon the Case for Deeds* (London, 1675).

Simmonds, N. E.: *The Decline of Juridical Reason* (Manchester: Manchester University Press, 1984).

'Reason, History and Privilege: Blackstone's Debt to Natural Law' (1988) 105 *Zeitschrift der Savigny Stiftung für Rechtsgeschichte (Germanistische Abteilung)* 200.

Simpson, A. W. B.: 'Innovation in Nineteenth Century Contract Law' (1975) 91 *Law Quarterly Review* 247.

'The Rise and Fall of the Legal Treatise: Legal Principles and the Forms of Legal Literature' (1981) 49 *University of Chicago Law Review* 626

Biographical Dictionary of the Common Law (London: Butterworths, 1984).

Smith, J. W.: *A Selection of Leading Cases on Various Branches of the Law* (London, 1837).

Starr, J. and Collier, J. F., eds.: *History and Power in the Study of Law* (Ithaca: Cornell University Press, 1989).

Stein, Peter: 'Systematisation of Private Law in the Sixteenth and Seventeenth Centuries', in J. Schröder, ed., *Entwicklung der Methodenle hre in Rechtswissenschaft und Philosophie vom 16. bis zum 18. Jahrhundert* (Stuttgart: F. Steiner, 1998).

The Teaching of Roman Law in England around 1200 (Selden Society Supplementary Series, vol. 8; London, 1990).

Stiernhöök, J. O.: *De Jure Sveonum et Gothorum* (Stockholm 1672).

Stoljar, S.: 'The Early History of Bailment' (1957) 1 *American Journal of Legal History* 1.

Story, Joseph: *Commentaries on the Law of Bailments; with Illustrations from the Civil and the Foreign Law* (Cambridge, Mass., 1832; English reprint, London, 1839).

Story, W. W.: *Life and Letters of Joseph Story* (London, 1851).

Strange, Sir Thomas: *Elements of Hindu Law, Referable to British Judicature in India* (London, 1825).

Sutherland, L. S. and Mitchell, L. G., eds., *The History of the University of Oxford, Volume V, The Eighteenth Century* (Oxford: Oxford University Press, 1986).

Swain, W.: 'The Changing Nature of the Doctrine of Consideration, 1750-1850' (2005) 26 *Journal of Legal History* 47.

Szemerényi, O.: 'About Unrewriting the History of Linguistics', in G. Brettschneider and C. Lehmann, eds., *Wege zur Universalienforschung* (Tübingen: Narr, 1980).

Taurelli, L. and Taurelli, F. *Digestorum seu Pandectarum Libri Quinquaginta ex Florentinis Pandectis Re Praesentati* (Florence, 1553).

Taylor, J.: *Elements of the Civil Law* (Cambridge, 1755).

Teltscher, Kate: *India Inscribed: European and British Writing on India 1600-1800* (New Delhi: Oxford University Press, 1995).

Theophilus, *Paraphrasis* (ed. E. C. Ferrini, Berlin, 1897).

Thieme, H.: *Das Naturrecht und die Europäische Privatrechtsgeschichte* (Basel, 1954).

Thomasius, C.: *Larva Legis Aquiliae* (Halle, 1703) (ed. M. Hewett and R. Zimmermann, Oxford: Hart, 2000).

Thomasius, C. resp. C. G. Kreß: *De Usu Practico Doctrinae Difficillimae Juris Romani de Culparum Praestatione in Contractibus* (Halle, 1705).

Touchet, John: Review of *Essay on the Law of Bailments* (1782) 66(1) *Monthly Review* 298.

Trautmann, Thomas R.: *Aryans and British India* (Berkeley: University of California Press, 1997).
Trovamala, B.: *Summa Roselle* (Strasbourg, 1516).
Turnbull, G.: 'A Supplement concerning the Duties of Subjects and Magistrates', in J. G. Heineccius, *A Methodical System of Universal Law: or, the Laws of Nature and Nations deduced from Certain Principles, and applied to Proper Cases* (trans. G. Turnbull, London, 1763).
Vacarius: *The Liber Pauperum of Vacarius* (ed. F. de Zulueta, Selden Society vol. 44; London 1927).
van Bynkershoek, C.: *Observationum Juris Romani* (Leiden, 1733).
Quaestionum Juris Publici Libri Duo (Leiden, 1737, reprinted Oxford, 1930).
van Caenegem, R.: *Royal Writs from the Conquest to Glanvill* (Selden Society vol. 71; London, 1952).
Vesey-Fitzgerald, S. G.: 'Sir William Jones the Jurist' (1946) 11 *Bulletin of the School of Oriental and African Studies* 807.
Vidian, A.: *The Exact Pleader* (London 1684).
Vinnius, A.: *In Quatuor Libros Institutionum Imperialium Commentarius* (Amsterdam, 1703).
Voci, P.: ''Diligentia', 'Custodia', 'Culpa'. I Dati Fondamentali' (1990) 56 *Studia et Documenta Historiae et Iuris* 29.
Wallace, J. B.: 'Remarks upon the Law of Bailment' (1837) 16 *American Jurist and Law Magazine* 253.
Weigel, E.: *Synopsis Jurisprudentiae Mnemoneutica* (Jena, 1669).
Arithmetische Beschreibung der Moralweisheit (Jena, 1674).
Wezler, Albrecht: 'Dharma in the Veda and the Dharmaśāstras' (2004) 32 *Journal of Indian Philosophy* 629.
Wharton, F.: *A Treatise on the Law of Negligence* (Philadelphia, 1874).
Wieacker, F.: *A History of Private Law in Europe* (trans. T Weir, Oxford: Oxford University Press, 1995).
Winch, H.: *Le Beau-Pledeur* (London 1680).
Wolff, C.: *Jus Naturae Methodo Scientifica Pertractatum* (Frankfurt, 1740-48).
Wood, Thomas: *New Institute of the Imperial or Civil Law* (London, 1704).
Woods, J. A.: 'The City of London and Impressment 1776-1777' (1956) 8 *Proceedings of the Leeds Philosophical and Literary Society* 111.

Wotton, W.: *Cyfreithjeu Hywel Dda Ac Eraill, seu Leges Wallicae Ecclesiasticae et Civiles Hoeli Boni* (London, 1730).

Yolton, John W. and Yolton, Jean S., eds.: John Locke, *Some Thoughts Concerning Education* (1693) (Oxford: Oxford University Press, 1989).

Zasius, U.: *Opera Omnia* (Lyons, 1550).

Zeumer, K., ed.: *Leges Visigothorum* (M.G.H. Legum vol. 1, Hanover, 1902).

Zimmermann, R. *The Law of Obligations: Roman Foundations of the Civilian Tradition* (Cape Town: Juta, 1990).

INDEX

n yma ar gael i chi hyd y dyddiad
... isod, oni bai fod darllenydd